D0976276

Lloyd

Blossoms and Bayonets:
A Story of Love, Faith and Courage
under Japanese Occupation

Here's to blossoms ... of all kinds!

by

Jana McBurney-Lin
and Hi-Dong Chai

최희동 ☺

Jana McBurney-Lin

REDWOOD PUBLISHING

This is a work of fiction. While the war events are historically accurate, the characters are either a product of the authors' imaginations or are used fictitiously, and any resemblance to actual persons, living or dead, is entirely coincidental.

Please note: language evolves and changes over time. The use of the word *Jap* in this story is not meant to malign or offend, but to evoke a certain period in our history.

Grateful acknowledgement is made to the following:
Dana and Chuck Eaton for our book jacket design
Robert Alan Kato for the photograph of Jana McBurney-Lin

ISBN 978-0-9884940-1-5

My deepest gratitude to Uncle Chai for opening his storybag to me,
To my critique group—Cyndy Furze, Becky Levine, Beth Proudfoot and
Terri Thayer—for their endless support when I couldn't put that bag down,
And to my family: you are precious.—JM

To my loving family: Phyllis, David and Julie,
And to Jana, who made this novel a reality.—HC

Our thanks to Redwood Publishing for their belief in this story,
and to Dana and Chuck Eaton for our lovely cover.

Glossary

Aigo: oh, dear/oh, God.
Bahduk: chess
Bakayaro: idiot
Bento: lunch
Cheemar: Korean woman's dress
Eebul: mattress
Fourth year in high school: sophomore
Ggul-mul: honey water
Gomushin: woman's rubber shoes
Ike: Go!
Kimchee: spicy pickled cabbage
Manghal Jarshik: bastard
Mangne: youngest son
Oy: Hey!
Uhmony: mother
Yubo: Dear

Japan has done her utmost to prevent this war, but in self-preservation and for self-existence, we could not help declaring war, considering the past attitude and actions of the United States.
—**Premier Hideki Tojo over Tokyo Radio, 1941**

Monday, February 23, 1942—Seoul, Korea

He-Seung

"Lunch is postponed today." Watanabe *Sensei* peeked outside our classroom and down the hall. Despite the cold, he took out his handkerchief and wiped sweat from his forehead. He turned back to our class. "For reasons you'll soon appreciate."

"I doubt it," I muttered. I sat in the back of our class, kicking my feet from side to side. I pictured myself dribbling my red soccer ball from foot to foot just like my buddy Gong-Tae had shown me earlier. I couldn't wait to practice for real. I leaned back, whispering to Gong-Tae. "You'd think *Sensei* was waiting for permission from the Emperor to dismiss us. Although why the Emperor would bother with the likes of him—"

"Haven't you had enough for one day?" Gong-Tae nudged my arm, his eyes on Watanabe *Sensei*.

This morning, *Sensei* had slapped me on the head for doodling a picture of Korea on my language paper. He'd kicked me in the shin for mispronouncing my Jap name, "Hiroshi." During Social Studies, when I'd asked how he really knew the Japs were in control of the thirteen countries they'd invaded, he'd punched me. Gong-Tae said that at the rate I was going Watanabe *Sensei* would strangle me by the end of the day.

I sighed loudly, at the same time scratching one of my sores. I had tiny sores all over, a rash from birth. Mother insisted I use her homemade salve—a mixture of baby He-Dong's high protein piss with rice. Sometimes the piss-paste worked. But most of the time, like now, I itched.

"You're just making it worse," Gong-Tae whispered.

"Thank you, Mother dear." I wasn't sure if he was talking about my sores or my bad start with that fool of a *Sensei*. Probably both. I leaned down and scratched at my calf, muttering, "This is a total waste of our time."

The mouse of a class monitor who sat in the front row let out a squeak.

"Uh-oh." Gong-Tae sucked in a deep breath.

I sat up, expecting to see Watanabe *Sensei* in front of me, his bully fist aimed at my face. But he stood by the door, bowing so low I thought he would dust the floor with his flat nose. A soldier in a tight brown uniform and long brown shiny boots posed at the doorway, one hand on his black sword.

Forty chairs scraped the floor as everyone stood. I pushed myself up. My friend Jim from California had never bowed to anyone before living in Korea—not even to his own father. Jim had always pretended he was just stretching.

I reached for my feet while the rest of the class gave a perfect bow. Then I flopped back down in my seat. The rest of the class sat down as quietly as if the army man had assigned them to a secret mission.

"Class, this is Officer Matsumoto." Watanabe *Sensei* stood erect, then bowed again and again as he ushered the man to the front of the room. "He has some special…some important news for us."

Was Officer Shiny Boots going to give us a severed limb-by-limb description of the Japs most recent victory over the English colony of Singapore? Would he show us how he had conquered the Brits with his pretty black sword?

"This is a special moment in history." Shiny Boots scrutinized each one of us with his dark, cold eyes. "We've annihilated the Americans at Pearl Harbor. We've humiliated the British in Singapore and Malaya. We are poised to take our rightful position as Ruler of the World."

Rightful position? The only rightful position the Japs had was to take their interfering butts back to Japan. Quit telling us what flowers to plant, what religion to believe in, what air to breathe. I let out a disgusted sigh.

Officer Shiny Boots put his hands behind his back. "His Majesty, Emperor Hirohito has just informed the Imperial Youth Corps that we can allow fifth- and sixth-year boys to participate in our noble effort to bring peace to the world."

"Wrong class," I muttered.

Gong-Tae kicked the legs of my chair.

Officer Shiny Boots looked in our direction. "His Majesty has also generously invited fourth-year students to share the glory, as long as they're sixteen years of age."

My birthday wasn't until August, but several of the boys around me sat up taller. As if actually proud. Tough boy Kang-Dae who had pushed me in the shoulder one too many times and now knew better, that suck-up Duck-Young, the tennis boy Sung-In. They were all old enough. So was— I felt a tightening around my chest—so was my buddy, Gong-Tae.

But it would be ridiculous for him to join the Youth Corps. His lovely girlfriend Myung-Hae was here. Soccer was here. Life was here.

Gong-Tae's knees bounced up and down, intermittently kicking my chair. I felt his tension like a heat wave on my back. Or perhaps that was my own tension.

"Isn't it wonderful?" Watanabe *Sensei* nodded so vigorously I thought his shiny ball of a head would fall off his neck. "The Emperor is including Korea in this noble effort."

"Including Korea?" I snorted, perhaps a bit too loud. Officer Shiny Boots directed his attentions to the back row. I put my head down, whispering, "He makes it sound like a party invitation."

Gong-Tae stabbed the end of his pencil in my back.

"A little to the left." I wiggled against the back of my chair, pointing to my left shoulder blade. "Harder."

Officer Shiny Boots looked directly at me, his eyes hard. "For those of you unfortunately too young to participate in this grand creation of our new world, don't despair. You, too, can help."

I expected Officer Shiny Boots to encourage us to tell our friends to leave their schooling and pick up the sword. I gave a quick shake of my head mostly for Gong-Tae's benefit. I wouldn't let him fall under the spell of this noble nonsense, even if they promised him the world, even if they promised him a rice field full of soccer balls.

"If you have older unmarried sisters," the Officer raised his eyebrows. "Tell us. We need women for our factories. The Imperial Government not only pays well, but will reward your loyalty and your family's with extra food rations." He looked around the room, expecting a raise of hands.

I was tempted. I didn't have sisters anymore, but I had lots of questions. If the Japs were so victorious, why did they need participation from the high schools? Korean high schools, at that?

"All of you honorable men interested in sharing the glory of the Imperial Army, come to the Principal's office during your lunch period." He gave a curt nod to Watanabe *Sensei* and headed out the door. We all stood and bowed. Watanabe *Sensei* followed Shiny Boots out the door, bowing up and down, as though his nose had gotten hooked onto the Officer's backside.

The older boys—Kang-Dae, Duck-Young, Sung-In—did not look at one another. They did not talk. But I could see in the set of their faces that they were heading to the Principal as soon as Watanabe *Sensei* came back to dismiss us. I felt sick to my stomach.

"This is terrible." Gong-Tae's voice squeaked as he sank back into his chair. "What am I going to do?"

"Just what you planned all along." I flopped down in my seat and turned to face him. "Teach me how to dribble with both feet, so I can impress Myung-Hae."

Gong-Tae's eyes widened. "She's mine."

"Well, she won't be if you're busy with Officer Shiny Boots."

He punched me in the shoulder, the only person in the class who I allowed to do so. Because he was my friend.

"I wonder what Han-Joo's going to do." Gong-Tae's legs bounced up and down again.

"Probably not a lot." I gave Gong-Tae a look. Han-Joo was also old enough to join the Imperial party, but he'd stepped on a nail at the last soccer game. He'd been home ever since. "Besides, he can't go anywhere. He's our best forward."

"What about me?" Gong-Tae protested. "Myung-Hae said she'd never seen anyone as fast as me."

I laughed. That was more like it. In a falsetto voice I repeated, "Myung-Hae said—"

"Shut up." Gong-Tae kicked the back of my chair so hard the legs skid out from beneath me. I grabbed onto his desk, stopping myself from falling to the floor. The sound of the desk scraping across the wooden floor filled the room. And obviously the hall.

"Hiroshi-san!" Watanabe *Sensei* came back into the class. His nostrils flared. He bounded over to my desk, reached out and cuffed my right ear, grunting with the effort. "What's all this noise?"

My ear throbbed. My insides boiled. *Sensei* had wasted half our lunch time with this Japanese Youth Corps nonsense, and now he was beating up on me, again. I wanted to pummel his flat face into the ground. I looked up, wrinkling my nose at his foul tobacco breath.

I felt a tug on my shirt from behind. Gong-Tae. With great effort I bowed my head to *Sensei*, mumbling, "I was so impressed by the esteemed Officer's visit, I lost my balance."

"This is good news." *Sensei's* small black eyes bored holes into the top of my head for several long moments. He gave my arm a shove before he returned to the front of the class. There he leaned down and made a note on a piece of paper.

"What have you done?" Gong-Tae moaned.

I rubbed the back of my ear. "He's an idiot."

But I wondered. Did Watanabe *Sensei* with his pencil have enough influence to nominate younger students to the Emperor's honorable party? How much time would pass before the Japanese God decided all fourth-year students were old enough? And what about spoiled babies like my 8-year-old brother, He-Dong? Now I wanted to be dismissed more than anything, not to learn how to dribble the soccer ball better, but to tell Father it was time. Time to re-join the resistance.

*As the 1930s gave way to the 1940s, the people of the United States
thought little of the Empire of Japan. Americans worried about their
economy, which had wallowed on the brink of collapse for a decade, and
wished to stay out of the world's problems...Roosevelt endeavored to curb
Japan's expansion by a series of economic and diplomatic measures
backed up by the U.S. military—the smallest and least-equipped force of
any industrialized nation in the world.*
—**Hugh Ambrose, Historian**

Monday, February 23, 1942—same day

Baby He-Dong

I sat in my second-grade class, wondering when our new teacher Ito
Sensei would announce Class Monitor for the year. Last year, my *sensei*
had smiled at me, walking toward me with her hands folded in front of her.
She had told us first thing.

Ito *Sensei* was different. She didn't look much older than my eldest
brother He-Chul. She wasn't even as tall as my second brother, He-Seung.
But she talked fast, held her cane all the time, and frowned at the slightest
noises.

The boy next to me made lots of noises. He fidgeted and tapped his
pencil on the side of his desk. He was new this year.

I'd seen him reading during lunch time. I wondered if I'd see him soon
at church. Father always said the smartest boys went to church.

Surely this new boy wanted to be the revered leader of the class, too,
and that caused all his anxiety. But there was only one position, awarded at
the beginning of the year to the smartest, most helpful, most obedient of
the sixty-four boys in our class. Last year, I was top in my grade, but then
maybe this boy had better marks from another school.

"It's hard to wait for the announcement," I whispered.

"The brain can only hold so much information," he whispered back.
"And my brain is overflowing. Besides, I don't understand her Japanese."

So maybe he didn't have such good marks. I would be it. I would be the
new Class Monitor. I couldn't wait to tell Mother and Father. Lately they'd
been worrying about what people said about them and the church. They
would be proud to say I was leader of the class.

"She's talking about how, during winter break, the Japanese occupied
British Hong Kong and Singapore." I leaned over to explain in Korean. "In
celebration of the victory, Emperor Hirohito has sent us each a red rubber
ball. This will make the twelfth. No, the thirt—"

"Yoshimitsu?" Ito Sensei stood near my desk. "What is all this talk? In Korean, no less. Stand up and move to the front of the class. Now."

I moved to the front, smiling, knowing that when I got to her desk she would say, "Class, stand and bow to your new Class Monitor."

She followed behind me, tapping her cane. That made me feel strange. When I reached the front, I turned to the class, my head bowed in humility.

Sensei whacked my wrists. "Hold your hands up."

What? Why was this punishment happening? What had I done?

My whole body burned with shame as I held my arms out in front of me. I felt tears welling in my eyes and quickly glanced out the window. Just beyond the school wall was the path that led home. I only had to walk ten minutes to our house, twenty-five in the autumn time when I stopped to pick persimmons along the way. I could imagine the soapy smell of Mother, could see her pushing her hair out of her eyes, squinting as she threaded a needle. I wanted to be at home, sitting and looking through one of my brother's comic books about the strongman *Jangsah* while Mother sat nearby and sewed.

Every other student I'd seen holding their arms out in front of them for three minutes as punishment never made it, and ended up getting a caning. I would not suffer the double humiliation. I was used to sitting still in church for hours. I could do this. I started counting. I had only gotten to seven seconds when my arms started wobbling.

"Put-your arms back up." Ito *Sensei's* voice came from my right where she stood beneath the picture of the Emperor of Japan, a man who was younger than my father.

I raised my arms in front of me. Higher. Ten seconds. Eleven. Twelve.

"I heard you were a smart boy." Ito *Sensei* tapped her long bamboo stick on her hand, as though ready at any moment to reach out and whip my hands. "But you can't obey the Emperor. You can't obey your teacher. You can't do anything. You can't even hold your skinny little arms up."

That wasn't true. All last year, people had expected me to lead them, just like my real name suggested. He-Dong: *Brightness in the East*. Father said some families had even joined All Holiness Church hoping their children would be like me. I opened my mouth to explain this. I imagined Mother nodding at me in encouragement. Sixteen seconds. Seventeen. My arms floated down.

"Keep those arms up." Ito *Sensei* flicked her bamboo stick at my arm. The tip stung my skin like a red hot coal from our kitchen brazier.

I clenched my lips together and raised my hands, my eyesight blurring. Father always said that our behavior reflected on his character, on the character of All Holiness Church, on the name of the good Lord. My punishment was certainly not something God would be proud of. Twenty-two, twenty-three, twenty-four.

"You will never speak Korean in school again." Ito Sensei turned her attention to the entire class.

I waited for one of my classmates to raise his hand, confused. Korean was the language we were born to speak. Ever since I could remember, we'd also learned Japanese. But, it had never been wrong to speak our own language. Besides, all I'd done was translate into Korean what Ito *Sensei* had said about Japan's victories. Thirty-four seconds. My arms trembled.

"Do you understand?" She tapped the cane on her wooden desk.

"*Hai*," our entire class of seven- to nine-year-old boys said in Japanese. Yes.

"Now that His Imperial Majesty is assuming a larger leadership role in the world, there is no need to learn or speak anything but Japanese. For anything. Do you understand?"

"*Hai*," the boys said, including Mr. I-Can't-Understand-What-The-*Sensei*-Is-Saying.

I did not respond, though. Did this rule apply only to us students or everyone? If it was everyone, what would Father do? Would he have to preach his sermons in Japanese? He would never do that. My classmates shuffled in their seats, trying not to exchange looks.

"Say it louder." Ito *Sensei* turned to watch me speak. "In unison."

"*Hai*."

Ito *Sensei* smiled and nodded as though enjoying a radio concert. Then she walked over to the blackboard and wrote what looked like hen scratches.

Was this what my brother He-Seung had meant when he said the Japanese were tightening control over us? I always thought control was a good thing. A strong thing. Father had said it was important to be in control of your emotions and your actions. In fact, yesterday when he found He-Seung playing soccer on the Lord's holy day, he'd shouted all day long about self-control. I decided, as my arms quivered, I didn't like Ito *Sensei's* kind of control.

My outstretched arms trembled as if I were holding two giant sacks of rice out in front of me. I had lost count of where I was in this three minutes of agony, as my mind worried about Father. But, surely, I must be finished soon. I swayed, losing my balance, and bumped against Ito *Sensei*'s desk. My arms fell to my sides for one wonderful moment of relief.

I shut my eyes tight, certain I'd feel the burning sensation of her cane against the back of my calves, on my disobedient arms. Instead, I heard a bark of laughter.

"What are you snickering about, Taiji-*san*?" Ito *Sensei* cracked her cane on the side of a desk.

I opened my eyes. Ito *Sensei* had moved away from the board, not noticing my disobedience. I quickly put my arms back up, as she pointed her cane at that bully Kee-Wok. Taiji was his Japanese name. We all had Japanese names now. Another new rule. Mine was Yoshimitsu, meaning something silly like 'shining good luck.' Besides, Yo-shi-mi-tsu was such a mouthful of sounds, I hated to say it.

"Is there something funny about the Japanese alphabet?" Ito *Sensei* leaned over Kee-Wok.

"I'm sorry, Ito *Sensei*." Kee-Wok pulled his mouth into a frown as he glanced up at me. "I just thought of something funny, that's all."

He'd been laughing at the old class monitor stumbling like the neighbor who drank too much. I hoped he wouldn't say anything. I didn't want to be punished further.

Ito *Sensei* frowned. Kee-Wok smiled back.

He was one of the older boys. He reminded me of the Japanese flag pole—tall, skinny, tough as iron. He stole homework and called it his own. He pushed classmates out of his way as if they were just leaves in the wind. He took the best food from their lunchboxes. He gave orders like a lieutenant, and my classmates obeyed him like sergeants.

He'd never bothered me before, though. I had always been Class Monitor.

Ito *Sensei* moved closer. She was waiting.

Kee-Wok glanced up at me again. "I was just thinking about a boy who dared his little brother to touch a bunch of chili peppers, then touch his eyes. The little brother took the stupid dare, and those chili peppers made his eyes burn. The fool rubbed harder and harder to try to get the burn to go away, each time making the pain worse."

I held my breath. What was he up to?

Ito *Sensei* tapped her cane across her palm. Certainly she'd heard this story before, although the Japanese didn't eat spicy foods like we did. "What bearing does this story have on our Japanese language lesson?"

Kee-Wok nodded in my direction. "Yoshimitsu-*san* looks as if he ate a thousand chili peppers."

Ito *Sensei* rested her stick on top of Kee-Wok's wooden desk as she turned to look at me. Sweat ran down my forehead. My eyes stung. My arms shuddered as if they were limbs from the cherry tree in our backyard, shaking in a winter storm. I watched them flail up and down, helpless.

"Go sit down." She waved her cane at me, then marched to the board at the front of the room. "You've wasted enough of our lesson time."

I dropped my arms and bowed to Ito *Sensei*. My arms pulsed with pain, my fingertips throbbed. I must have held my arms up at least two and a half minutes. Maybe I'd held them up so long I'd broken my shoulders. I hurried back to my seat.

"It's such a shame when a smart boy behaves so poorly." Ito *Sensei* said. "We need a true model of citizenship to lead our boys. That is why I've decided to delegate Nobuyuki as your new class leader."

His real name was Bon-Hwa. He wasn't that smart or such a big model of whatever she said. He-Seung would call him a tofu brain. I felt my lips tremble as we all stood and bowed to him.

Last year I'd been excited about this wonderful new activity called school. A lot of boys didn't get to come, because they had to help their parents sell fish or vegetables at the open-air market. Father, as the esteemed pastor of All Holiness Church, was able to send me and my brothers to school. Nothing was more important than education, he said. Every day last year I thanked God I was so lucky. Today, though, I found I couldn't even focus on the words coming out of Ito *Sensei's* mouth.

Mother said to pay attention as there was a lesson to be learned from everything. But after Ito *Sensei* hit me with her bamboo cane and named Bon-Hwa the new Class Monitor, my brain stopped learning. All day she had us repeat sounds, like *ah-ee-oo-eh-oo*, *sa-shi-su-se-so* and *ta-tchi-tsu-tse-tso*. I moved my mouth making these animal sounds, like an ox chewing cud, but meanwhile my brain saw me, the ex-Classroom Monitor, standing in front of the entire world holding his arms out. I kept seeing Ito *Sensei* swinging her cane at me. *You can't do anything, can you*? I kept seeing her write Bon-Hwa's name, "Nobuyuki," under the title Class Monitor on the blackboard. What shame I had brought on myself, my family, God.

When the school bell finally rang at the end of the day, we all stood and bowed to Ito *Sensei*. I picked up my rucksack and my new red rubber ball. I followed my classmates in a single-file line out to the courtyard.

Some people raced outside the yard to get in line to buy candy from the candy cart. Some went off to play soccer or catch. Kee-Wok and his lieutenants headed for the outside wall. He had saved me from thirty seconds or less of further punishment. I should have gone to thank him. But all I wanted to do was disappear.

I dragged myself across the schoolyard and over the electric trolley tracks. I passed the public bath where Mother made us go once a month. I passed a row of recently-planted cherry blossom trees, their branches heavy with green buds. With each step I took, I apologized. Sorry. God. Sorry. Father. Sorry. Mother. Sorry. God. But the steel tracks looked cold, the bath house looked dark and angry, the bare branches of the trees pointed at me like a thousand canes.

Too soon I was standing on our porch. Unlike other people's homes which were made of thatched roofing and straw, we lived in a two-story brick house with a large front porch. Reverend Thomas and his family had left us their American-style house two years ago when they moved back to California.

Father used one of the rooms on the second story of the house as his extra parish office, so we often had callers. Mother always had friends visiting to get her advice on this or that, or to have her hem a dress. I hoped Father and Mother both had visitors. Then I wouldn't have to say anything about school and not being named Class Monitor. At least not right away.

My head throbbed. I leaned against the door, listening. I heard my ragged breath and the tunes of Mother singing off-key, "*My gracious redeemer. My savior art thou.*" I didn't hear any other voices, but perhaps the visitor was listening. I knocked at the door.

The humming stopped. Mother's light footsteps shuffled closer and she opened the door. Her long black hair was pulled back into a ball at the back of her head. Her measuring string was draped across her shoulders. She held a bunch of pink cloth in her hands.

"You're home." She smiled.

Her happy face and her soft voice made my throat feel funny. I glanced over to the shoe rack inside the door. I only spotted Mother's worn white rubber *gomushin*. "No visitors?"

"It's just you and me."

God was disappointed. He didn't fill the house with visitors, and let me slink upstairs. He was going to sit and listen to me tell Mother every shameful word. I went inside and flopped down at the entrance, dropping my book bag. I reached down to untie my shoes. My breath came in short gasps.

"He-Dong?" Mother gave her watching-me look as she led me from the entrance into the living room, her warm fingers gripping my hand. We had a big living room, cold water that came from a spout, electricity, a western toilet, even a bathtub which we never used except to hold an extra supply of water. She seated me on our heated *ondol* floor. Pipes from the stove in the kitchen ran beneath the flooring, keeping it warm during the winter. "What is it?"

My whole day had been filled with shame. I had been scolded by the teacher. I'd lost my position as Class Monitor. I couldn't even hold my arms out long enough without the whole class laughing at me.

"I spoke Korean in class." I let out a sob. I could still see myself standing in front of the classroom, my arms wobbling out in front of me. "And Ito *Sensei* punished me. She didn't name me Class Monitor."

Mother's jaw tightened. "Oh."

"Mother, I'm sorry." No longer would she thank God for giving me intelligence. "I didn't mean to bring shame on—"

"Sh..sh..sh." She wiped the tears from my cheeks with the back of her hand. Her fingers felt like a warm stone, solid and reassuring. "It's hard to know what's right and what's wrong these days."

"But how can the Japanese expect us never to speak Korean? It's like—It's like—It's like telling us not to breathe." I sat on my trembling hands.

"Just listen more carefully to your teacher." She picked at a thread hanging loose from my pants. "The teacher knows what is—what is best."

"And what about Father?" I stood up. "Will he have to give sermons in Japanese? How will he do such a —"

"Sh..sh..sh." Mother looked to the window as she did a lot these days, as if someone was watching. "God will show us the way. Besides, if you study hard and learn enough Japanese, you can be Father's translator."

I enjoyed the warm feeling that came from her words. "Do you think so?"

I imagined myself standing next to Father in front of the church. He leaned down to tell me the next line in his sermon and I shouted out the Japanese in as loud and serious a voice as I could. At the end of the service, as Father and I left the sanctuary, every member of the congregation bowed deep at the waist. I felt so important.

"I know so." Mother's eyes shone bright. "Do your best. Stand tall."

It felt good that Mother believed in me. Even if my teacher didn't. But what would Father say? I could already see his eyes bulging with anger, his mouth turned in a frown. As if just by thinking of him, I thought I heard a key in the door. But Mother didn't jump up to meet him. To remove his shoes. To offer him some tea after a long day working with his followers. Certainly I was still imagining things.

"Go wash your hands and face." She brushed at a patch of dirt on my shirt. "I'll get you a cup of *ggul-mul*."

Ggul-mul. Water with honey and ginger. That was special. For the first moment since all that horrible stuff at school, I felt relief. "But what about—"

"Your father?" Mother looked down in her lap where she kneaded her hands together as though pressing dough for noodles. "He has many things on his mind these days."

I'd heard them whispering late into the night in the living room. Something about the church. Lately, the Japanese didn't like Father's church.

Mother looked up, her eyes sparkling. She rubbed the right side of her head with her forefingers. "This issue Father doesn't need to know."

"What issue?" He-Seung stepped into the living room. His high school uniform hung open, unbuttoned at the top collar, a fashion Mother often scolded him for. A fashion certainly God was not pleased with. He tapped his stocking foot up and down on the *ondol* floor. I scooted closer to Mother.

"You're home early." Mother stood to greet him, putting herself as a barrier between us. "I didn't hear you come in."

I had. I'd thought it was just my imagination. Oh, why couldn't it have been?

"What issue doesn't Father need to know?" he asked again.

"I was just about to get He-Dong some *ggul-mul*." Mother clasped her hands together. "Would you like a cup?"

"Let me see." He laughed a short, deep laugh, cocking his head to the side. His pocketknife dangled from his belt loop. "Baby brother got into a fight?" He grabbed onto the knife and flipped it around and around in his thick palm. "Naah. Can't see that." His voice was eager, his eyes wide as if he could see through me back to my classroom, back to the teacher whipping me with her cane.

"He-Dong made an error in judgment." Mother picked at the front of her white *cheemar*.

"Error?" I could see him ready to get out the cane and hand it to Father. Or perhaps as older brother, he would come over and slap me. "What *error in judgment* did the spoiled Bean-curd boy make?"

Mother frowned at his words. "He was punished for speaking Korean in class."

He-Seung emitted air from his lips, as though spitting a bone to the floor. He gripped tight to his knife. Then he shook his head. "Those Jap bastards!"

"He-Seung." Mother stood up and waved her hands up and down, as if shooing his dirty words away. She looked out the window.

"Why don't they go back to their own damn country?" he yelled, stuffing his knife in his pocket so hard I heard a rip. He left the room, banging his way up the steps. The entire house shook.

Mother looked to the window. She covered her mouth with her hand. Her cheeks were now pale, her eyes wide and glassy.

"Mother?"

"Never mind." Mother stood, looking up toward the steps. She shook her head. "Let me get you some *ggul-mul*."

The whole way home I'd prayed that Mother wouldn't be disappointed, that she wouldn't need to tell Father of my bad behavior at school. That God wouldn't be angry. I had forgotten to pray about He-Seung, though, and look what happened. He was worse than an angry winter cloud. Raining, thundering, soaking everyone to the bone. Making our home feel cold, dark, miserable. I flopped face down on our warm ondol floor, closed my eyes, and prayed some more.

*Japan is expanding, and what country in its expansion
has ever failed to be trying to its neighbors?
Ask the American Indians or the Mexicans
how excruciatingly trying the young United States
used to be once upon a time.*
—**Foreign Minister Yosuke Matsuoka, 1940s**

Monday, February 23, 1942—same day

He-Seung

I slammed my bedroom door. Dumped my schoolbag on the desk near my window. My heart beat so hard I couldn't breathe. My head hurt.

Let me get you some ggul-mul. I could still hear Mother's voice, still see He-Dong whimpering beside her. I hoped I hadn't crossed the thick line of Mother's tolerance with my anger, but her hand-holding and honey talk would just turn He-Dong into a worse baby than he already was. Besides, this false sweetness was just avoiding the real issue—the Japs.

I tore off my school jacket and threw it on the floor. The black cloth, the brass buttons, the high collar all cried out Japanese military. *Manghal jarshik.*

Bastards.

If Mother had asked for my opinion about He-Dong's snivels, I would have told her I wasn't surprised he was bullied by his teacher. He was, after all, a minister's son. The Japs didn't like anyone who held influence over people's thoughts—especially religious people.

The Japs reminded me of obnoxious relatives who invited themselves over and never left. First knocking politely at the door and acting interested in our life, then using our things as their own, then forgetting altogether that our house was not theirs, treating us like slaves and expecting us to feel grateful. These uninvited guests had already been living in Korea thirty-two years and had promised to leave when we attained *national strength*—whatever that meant.

He-Dong had better be prepared for a lot more bullying. I would have told Mother that if she had asked. But she didn't expect too many smart thoughts from my head. My older brother, He-Chul, was the intelligent one, off studying on a fancy scholarship in Manchuria. Or *Manchukuo* as the Japanese now called it.

Hell, Mother gave more credit to baby He-Dong than to me. He-Dong who was like a blade of grass—a whisper would knock him to the ground. He-Dong who needed a glass of *Ggul-mul* to make him feel better. Honey water. As if that would make any difference.

From my window, I spotted the bobbing heads of long black hair beyond our compound wall. The girls from Eehwa High School. I rushed over to my desk next to the window where I had a good view of the side yard, our compound walls, the road. Father said it wasn't right to look at girls. I wondered why, as my whole body got warm all over when I caught sight of their silky long hair, small budding peaches and rounded hips.

I rarely saw girls except on Sunday when they came to church. Or if they came to the house with their mothers for a dress fitting. Or now when I could watch them sashay by.

I bent down and grabbed my stupid Japanese uniform jacket. I draped the irritating clothing over my shoulders, casually, to hide my sores. It wasn't as if anyone could see me, but it made me feel less exposed. Then I rifled through my school rucksack and pulled out the Japanese history reader. I sat at my desk, holding the small book up, pretending to read about Japan's "New Order in East Asia." In other words, their plans for gobbling up Asia and then the world. When I guessed the silky black heads had reached the opening in the compound wall, I forced my neck to turn. A casual glance out the window.

Damn. It was only some short stick of a girl and Dr. Lee's youngest daughter, Purple Face. I'd fooled around too long downstairs with He-Dong and his nonsense. Surely I'd missed seeing Myung-Hae walk home.

Dr. Lee had only two children. Both girls. While some people in the neighborhood whispered that Dr. Lee must not be very good at his profession—he couldn't even get his wife to have a boy—Mother trusted him with all of our sicknesses. The baby-piss ointment was his idea. In turn, Mother was asked to do all their sewing.

Myung-Hae was his older daughter, the beautiful one. She was the one who could force thoughts of soccer from Gong-Tae's brain. She was the one who would keep Gong-Tae's butt in school rather than off imperializing the world for Hirohito.

I pressed my face against the window hoping for even the smallest glimpse of the lovely girl. She couldn't be too far ahead of her ugly sister, Purple Face. My head knocked against the window pane, and both of the girls glanced up, laughing.

I looked quickly away, although why should I care? Purple Face was my age, but she was a sight. She had a hideous purple birthmark on the right side of her face. She'd never find a husband.

I hazarded another quick look. Purple Face had her arm linked to the flat-chested girl. Her other hand danced in the air as she talked. Had Shiny Boots visited their school to espouse the wonders of building weapons for the Japs? Were these ugly ducks actually dreaming of the day they were old enough to contribute to the war effort by joining the factories? I scowled at them and turned away.

Outside my bedroom door, a creaking sounded. Mother? My mouth was dry—from my anger with the Japs, disgust with stupid He-Dong. I'd be happy for just a glass of water. Her footsteps sounded heavy. Disappointed, perhaps. Still, we needed to call a bastard a bastard, not hide behind sewing and happy thoughts.

My door opened fast. Father. Thank goodness. Normally he didn't come to talk with me. Perhaps he'd heard rumors of the military visiting the schools. I couldn't wait to tell him about the Army officers invading our classroom in search of volunteers.

He wore a three-piece suit, his tie a perfect knot at his neck. He had high cheekbones, dark thick hair with patches of grey at his sideburns. Those patches had gotten bigger since Jim and his family had left Korea. Since the Japs had started hovering over the church. He had a vein at his right temple which pulsed when he was angry. It was pulsing now.

Perhaps his rush to get to my room had nothing to do with the military. I stood and bowed, my uniform jacket sliding to the floor.

"Come to my office." He pushed the door open wide. "Now."

There was only one reason to go to Father's office. I needed punishment. Not for the first time I wished Father's office was on the other side of the city or even downstairs near the women's quarters, so he had time to walk off the heat on his face. But before I even had time to breathe, he'd opened the door to his office. He walked straight to the closet for his whipping cane. My calves itched.

"Father, please." My voice was edged with a whine I wouldn't want even those ugly girls from Eehwa High to hear.

I moved to my punishment spot at the side of his desk. I would stand facing the desk, while he caned me five times. I would have to count with him, then bow to him. I held onto the edge of the desk. The cold musty smell of the room made me shiver.

"You weren't listening in church yesterday, were you?" He held so tight to the cane, his hand trembled.

Church yesterday? Not my disrespectful behavior at school? Not my calling the Japs names?

His black leather Bible stared at me from the center of his desk. A stubby candle sat next to the Bible, the wax having dribbled down the sides and hardened. "Of course I listened."

"Tell me." He swatted the side of the desk so hard the bamboo cracked. "What you remember."

I opened my mouth. The group of girls sitting in the pews behind me had smelled like flowers. There weren't as many followers as last week—

in fact every Sunday Father drew a smaller and smaller crowd. The rash on my legs itched. Mr. Kang stood by the door on the lookout for Japs. A swarm of flies buzzed nearby. None of these memories would please Father. I closed my mouth.

He pointed the split bamboo cane at my face. "If you had been listening, really listening, then I wouldn't return home to hear you've been badmouthing the Japanese."

"Yes, Father."

"The Spirit Himself bears witness that we are children of God." His voice was deep and strong as though he stood before a packed congregation.

Had he said this yesterday? Still, even if we were all *children of God*, some kids—the Japs for example—were devils who needed more than a Bible verse to teach them how to behave.

"For Heaven's sake." He paced back and forth next to the desk with the cane behind his back. "What if the neighbors heard you? Or a passerby?"

I could already hear him saying that the neighbors would be appalled. That they didn't appreciate our Christian ways as it was, and felt threatened with us around. I could already hear him saying how my yelling just wasn't right. Everything was right and wrong, according to Father. *It's not right to play soccer on the Lord's day. It's not right to look at girls. It's not right to call people Japs.* But I seemed to be the only one Father judged. Was it right for the Japs to invade our country? Was it right for them to kick out Reverend Thomas and Jim? Was it right to take away our names, our trees, our language? Why didn't Father see all of these things, too? "They came to our school today."

"Who?" Father snapped.

"The Japs—"

"Pssshhht." He thwacked my calf with the cane.

My calf burned as I stood erect. Tears sprung to my eyes. "God's child—" I started over. "Military officials."

"What for?" He lowered his voice, glancing at the door.

"They want—need— volunteers."

Father's whipping cane dropped to the floor, and he didn't reach to retrieve it. "You?"

I remembered Watanabe *Sensei* staring at me, then making a notation in his ledger. "They're starting with the fifth- and sixth-year students, only taking some of the fourth-years, as long as they're sixteen."

"The older students." Father let out a deep sigh. "Let us thank the Lord your brother is off in Manchuria—Manchukuo—safe." He paused as though offering up a prayer of thanks.

"He-Chul is safe." I swallowed. "But what about—in five months, I'll be sixteen."

"Be anxious for nothing." He put his hands together. *"But in everything by prayer and supplication, with thanksgiving, let your requests be made known to God."*

"But, Father." We prayed all the time, not just for hours each Sunday at church, but before meals, when guests came to visit and arrived safely, once a week during our family prayer meeting. We prayed. And prayed. And prayed. "We've been making our requests known for years."

"Son." His voice filled with warning as he bent down and picked up the cane.

"I'm only saying, we can't avoid the Japs—we can't avoid them anymore." I expected him to smack me on the back of the leg again. Still, with the military showing up at the schools, I couldn't keep quiet. "There must be something we can do."

Father walked behind his desk. He turned to stare out the window. "We're already doing it."

No. We weren't doing anything. Long before I was born, Father had joined a resistance movement to attempt to push the Japs out. I'd heard him brag once to Mr. Thomas that participating in the March 1st Movement had confirmed his belief in God. What had happened to his strong spirit?

I remembered hearing parts of the Resistance Treaty of 1919, and the words were burned into my heart. *We herewith proclaim the independence of Korea and the liberty of the Korean people.* I wished Father would shout those words from his pulpit.

The Resistance of 1919 hadn't worked. Thousands had been arrested, tortured, killed. But today was different. We were all sick of Japan. At least, those of us with a brain larger than a soy bean. We were disgusted with their Emperor who pretended to be an all-loving God while he ordered the raping and killing and possession of country after country.

"People will try to push you this way or that." Father turned to face me, bringing his thick fist to his chest. "But when you feel something deep in your heart, it's your duty to respond."

I closed my eyes. I agreed a dozen times over. Too bad our heartfelt emotions didn't point to the same response.

"My duty…" He clasped his hands together, nodding to me. "Our duty as a family is to God."

"What about Korea?" I clenched my fists. "What about us?"

He waved these issues away as though shooing gnats from his rice bowl. "The Bible says— as perhaps you recall from yesterday—*Consider the sufferings of this present time are not worthy to be compared with the glory which shall be revealed in us."*

"But…" Damn it. I shifted from one foot to the next, my limbs shaking. "Wouldn't it be even better—uh, more glorious to God— to get rid of all this suffering? Now?"

"It's in God's hands." He patted the worn cover of the Bible. "The Lord brings peace in times of chaos. He offers hope when there is none." Father reached into his drawer and brought out a pack of matches. He struck the wooden match with his thumbnail, the flame spitting and hissing. Then he lit the candle on his desk. "The Lord lights the way when all is dark."

He came to me, resting his hand on my stubby scalp as he did with other parishioners, passing the peace of the Lord through his palm. "Our only mission, Son, is to help others feel His glory."

My scalp itched. My blood itched. I closed my eyes, grit my teeth. "There must be something more—"

"Enough," he commanded, letting his hand drop to his side. Then he went to the closet, opened the door, and returned the cane to its place on the top shelf. Our discussion was over.

Father sat behind his desk and reached for his reading glasses. He would open the Bible and read until He-Dong called him for dinner. He would finish Mother's food before the rest of us had even raised our chopsticks, and he'd come back here to his Bible. I stared at that little black book which held such power over him. Over our entire family. I gave a quick bow, my heart pounding in my ears.

I should have been elated. I'd never left his office with just one swift thwack on my calf. But the certainty I'd had that Father would take action and stop this craziness had disappeared like a thin wisp of smoke from his candle, making my throat burn.

Brothers-in-arms! Japan has come to help us realize our ideals and aspirations and establish an economic, cultural and spiritual confederacy of Oriental nations known as the Great East Asia Co-prosperity sphere. Let us shake off the yoke of white domination forever, and find a dignified place for us among this concert of Oriental nations.
—Japanese propaganda leaflet dropped on American Commonwealth Country of Philippines

Monday, March 2, 1942—one week later

Mother (Uhmony)

I stood at the kitchen counter, arranging cups of boiled water on a tray. I could hear my dear friends, Gong-Tae *uhmony* and Min-Kook *uhmony* out on the back porch. Their wooden stools scraped against the deck as they sat down to the table and unloaded the ingredients they had brought.

Gong-Tae *uhmony* had one son who was my He-Seung's best friend. Min-Kook *uhmony* had three grown daughters and only one son, all of whom worked far away in the countryside. In-Young, the fourth and newest member of All Holiness Ladies, was not yet the mother—the *uhmony*—of any children. She had not yet arrived.

We were a unique group of friends, different in our ages and status, yet held together in the Lord's palm. We gathered for traditional events, like *kimchee*-making or Christmas and Easter feast preparations. I hurried to the front door to take one more look down the path. A woman with a child on her back hurried past. A group of men in their white balloon pants and long white shirts pushed and pulled a cart of radishes down the road. But there was no In-Young. She was a thoughtful soul always willing to stop to help an old lady with too many bags from the market, a child who'd lost his rubber ball, a stray cat who looked hungry. She could get delayed by the request of a cricket. What had delayed her this morning?

I hesitated a moment, noting He-Dong had missed a spot sweeping the porch this morning. Or the spring breeze had already brought the dust back. Perhaps if I just swept up the dirt, In-Young would be here.

I grabbed the broom from the side of the house and set the bristles to the wooden porch. Dear He-Dong had been reluctant to go to school this past week. I was sure he was still disappointed about losing his job as Class Monitor, especially since the position was given to a boy only half as clever. The Japanese were afraid of clever boys like my son, like my husband. I wished I could tell him so. But I didn't want him disrespecting the Japanese like his older brother, saying something that would get him or all of us in trouble. I leaned on the broom, looking out toward the front again. His brother gave us all enough trouble.

Yesterday when I walked home with the boys after church, He-Dong made the mistake of saying Dr. Lee was going to have puppies.

"Ha!" He-Seung, despite his running around, kicking stones, had heard. "Dr. Lee can't have puppies, you fool."

"I mean Dr. Lee's dog," He-Dong corrected himself. "Mee-Won is going to have puppies." He tilted his head to the side, his eyes wide and imploring. "Can we have one of their puppies? Please, Mother?"

"Stop your whining." He-Seung punched He-Dong in the arm.

He-Seung as the elder brother had the responsibility to teach and discipline his younger brother. But often he just bullied He-Dong. If my eldest son, He-Chul, were at home, he would certainly giggle at He-Dong, but with that gentle laughter in his voice.

I squeezed He-Dong's small hand. His warm fingers in mine made my heart feel lighter than butterfly wings.

"Does that mean yes?" He-Dong looked up at me. "I'd take care of the little fella so well you wouldn't even know it was around."

"You couldn't take care of a bedbug." He-Seung reached up to hit He-Dong again.

"Boys, boys." I wrapped my arms around He-Dong to protect him.

There was some truth to He-Seung's words. He-Dong was still young, still needed help to button his shirt properly or fold his bedding or remember his lunch. Besides, now didn't feel like the right time to take on such a responsibility. Still, dear He-Dong. He would love a puppy.

A strong wind blew, scattering dust and leaves back on the porch. It would make no difference to keep sweeping. I gave one last look down the path. An old lady hobbled by with the aid of a walking stick. Then came two young Japanese soldiers, marching past the old woman as if she wasn't there. She stumbled out of the way narrowly avoiding their steel-toed boots. What rudeness, treating this woman like garbage in the path.

My dear said we were all God's children, but when I saw things like this, I felt a sharp pain in my chest. I wished I was closer to the woman so I could help her. I wished to tell those Japanese soldiers to mind their steps. I watched the woman hobble along, hoping she could feel my encouragement. Then I put the broom back against the side of the house, closed the front door and went back through the kitchen to the back porch.

"You look worried." Min-Kook *uhmony* looked up from straightening a small pile of cabbages. "Is In-Young still not here?"

"No, she's not." I set cups of boiled water on the table for them to drink. I sat down to join them. I didn't want to mention the soldiers almost knocking that poor woman down. I could already hear Min-Kook *uhmony* railing against the Japanese. "He-Dong wants a puppy."

"You're thinking of puppies?" Min-Kook *uhmony* blew a strand of hair from her face. She gestured to the table which held a small stack of tiny cabbages, a handful of garlic cloves, a sprinkling of green onions and red peppers. "I'm worried this *kimchee* won't even fill our pickling jars this year."

"We should have enough for a good batch." Gong-Tae *uhmony* folded her hands in her lap. She sat hunched over, her back rounded like a hook. "The Lord will provide."

"Yes, of course." Min-Kook *uhmony* picked a worm-eaten leaf from one of the small cabbages. "But the last thing our Revered Lady needs now is another mouth to feed. I wouldn't go getting a puppy—"

"But you have one." Gong-Tae *uhmony* shifted on her stool and raised her eyebrows at Min-Kook *uhmony*.

"Correction." She shook her head, still scanning the table as if she might discover more cabbage hidden somewhere. "I have a watchdog. For the protection I know my husband is incapable of giving." She picked up the cleaver, tapping it on the side of the table. "You both have strong men in your house."

Gong-Tae *uhmony* cleared her throat to signal she didn't want to hear more. She didn't appreciate the way Min-Kook *uhmony* spoke of her husband.

Min-Kook *uhmony* looked out in the yard, then back at the cabbages. "Shall we get started then?"

"What about In-Young?" Gong-Tae *uhmony* frowned.

"She said she wouldn't be late." Min-Kook *uhmony* pulled the stack of cabbages in front of her.

"She should be along." I pushed Min-Kook *uhmony*'s cup of water closer to her. "Surely she just got detained."

"For what?" Min-Kook *uhmony* turned to me, her brow furrowed in concern.

I regretted my choice of words. A choice that would have meant nothing last year, but which now had a sinister sound, conjuring images of policemen and torture and blood. "I just mean...well, you know In-Young."

Gong-Tae *uhmony* pulled at a thread from her skirt. "Yes. In-Young has just not yet learned to be responsible."

"Well." Min-Kook *uhmony* dropped the cleaver on the first head of cabbage, her movements precise and fast. Then she tossed a handful of chopped cabbage in our direction. "She needs to learn to be."

Gong-Tae *uhmony* pursed her lips. I too wanted to stop Min-Kook *uhmony* from chopping. We'd never started the ritual of *kimchee* without all the members present, without a prayer, a cup of hot water and some laughter to get us going.

I grabbed my small Bible from my skirt pocket and put it in the center of the table. Then I took hold of Min-Kook *uhmony's* hand before she could pick up another head of cabbage. I reached over to hold Gong-Tae *uhmony's* hand. I bowed my head. "Lord, we are humbled in Your presence. Thank You for providing us with all that You do. For bringing us together on this fine spring morning. For Your continued guidance and protection. In Your name we pray. Amen."

"Amen," Min-Kook *uhmony* and Gong-Tae *uhmony* echoed.

"Speaking of protection, I've been thinking." Min-Kook *uhmony* wiped bits of cabbage from the side of her cleaver and looked over at me. "We should take a picnic to Mount Nam San."

Gong-Tae *uhmony* sputtered, choking on a sip of water.

Mount Nam San was where the Japanese had erected a Shinto Shrine. Everyone was expected to pay respects to the shrine, but that was one visit our family, the followers of All Holiness, had not made.

"We could just go," Min-Kook *uhmony* continued. "Just to pretend."

"Visiting that mountain, that Shinto shrine would be a sin against all sins." Gong-Tae *uhmony* said, sitting up tall.

"I'll tell you what's a sin against all sins," Min-Kook *uhmony* leaned forward, emitting her words through gritted teeth. "The way these foreigners have turned our country into a nightmare." She sat back and gave a quick glance around her. "Besides if we went to their foolish shrine, they'd record our royal visit at the Neighborhood Office."

"That office is just to keep track of the number of people in a house, so they can distribute ration cards." Gong-Tae *uhmony* flopped a piece of cabbage back and forth. "They only take down information like ages, professions, and so forth."

"The *so forth* is what worries me." Min-Kook *uhmony* tapped her finger on the table. "Like your new Japanese name. Then it was whether or not you'd planted a cherry tree. Now I understand they record and reward visits to the shrine."

My heart drooped like the wet cabbage. Trust in God had never been easy for any of us. Most people in the city thought we were strange, and crossed the street to avoid passing us. Some even pointed and called out names. These days, though, our love for the Lord seemed even more difficult. Was that why our rice rations had been cut in half over the last month?

Min-Kook *uhmony* looked over at me, her brow set in a stubborn frown. I picked up a clove of garlic, peeling the fragile skin from the cloves. The pungent odor filled the air. I wished my dear or my eldest son, He-Chul, were here by my side. They would give me the wisdom to respond to Min-Kook *uhmony's* idea. I felt as thin and useless as the skin I peeled from the garlic.

"I'm telling you they're targeting Christians." Min-Kook *uhmony* slapped her thighs. "Besides, what's the harm in having a picnic? It's not as if we're going to pray to the shrine. And just by being there, we might get a good mark with the Neighborhood Office. In fact, we might be able to take the pressure off the whole congregation."

"Be not afraid," Gong-Tae *uhmony* said, sounding a lot like my dear. "This war nonsense will soon blow over like a rotten smell from the sewer."

"Don't be so sure." Min-Kook *uhmony* waved her hand back and forth at Gong-Tae *uhmony* as though shooing at a fly. "It's getting worse. But you know that." Min-Kook *uhmony* chopped the bits of cabbage so small that I thought they'd disappear in the water. Then she looked up. "Is Gong-Tae going to join up?"

"What?" My mouth dropped open.

"Let me guess." Min-Kook *uhmony* frowned at me as she continued chopping. "You don't know about the visit to the high school."

"The Military is taking our boys?" My heart beat hard.

"Don't worry." Min-Kook *uhmony* set her cleaver down long enough to reach over and rest her cool fingertips on my arm. "Your He-Seung is too young. At least for today." Her voice was filled with sarcasm. "It's supposed to be voluntary, although I heard the army has been harassing families whose sons do not join. That's why I wondered about Gong-Tae."

"Moses said to the people." Gong-Tae *uhmony* dropped all the cabbage into the bowl of water at her feet, leaning down and pushing the thin green pieces under the water. *"Do not be afraid. God has come to test you, so that the fear of God will be with you to keep you from sinning."*

Min-Kook *uhmony* handed the remaining chopped pieces of cabbage to Gong-Tae *uhmony*. "Meaning?"

"We are not afraid of the authorities. Not tempted by the devil's gifts." Gong-Tae *uhmony* swished the cabbage leaves around so hard, my insides churned. "The Lord will prevail."

My dear had emphasized the same in his sermon yesterday. So why did my head spin? Why couldn't I breathe? Why did I have the urge to run to He-Seung's school and hold onto him?

Just then a loud knock sounded on the front door. Gong-Tae uhmony sat up straight, opened her mouth wide and whispered the Lord's Prayer.

My heart stopped. Would Japanese Army Recruitment officers be standing on the porch eager to harass me or Gong-Tae *uhmony*?

"Surely it's just In-Young." Min-Kook *uhmony* said, but she reached up to hide my Bible beneath her skirt just the same.

I went off to answer the caller.

In-Young stood on the front porch in her wrinkled and faded *cheemar,* a bulky bag in her hands. I smiled, letting out a small sigh. Of course it was only her. Then I noticed her red face, her swollen eyes.

"In-Young?" I reached out and grabbed her arm. Perhaps today her delay was caused by more than a cricket. "Are you all right?"

"I meant to get here earlier." Her eyes brimmed with tears as she bent down and slipped off her rubber *gomushin*, still new from her wedding.

I glanced outside for signs of a Japanese soldier who might have caused her such anguish. "We wondered where you were."

"Is that little Miss I'll-Be-On-Time?" Min-Kook *uhmony* called, her voice shrill.

Surely, the two women were still standing in back, praying. I held In-Young's hand, as we went to join the others. Her palm felt small and cold against mine.

Gong-Tae *uhmony* glanced up at In-Young's swollen eyes. "What happened to—"

"I knew this would happen." Min-Kook *uhmony* tapped her cleaver on the table. "Didn't I tell you? Didn't I? You got detained, didn't you?"

"Yes." In-Young sat on the stool next to me. She lowered her head and covered her mouth.

"*Aigo.*" Gong-Tae *uhmony* patted In-Young's arm. "Oh, dear."

Where was Deacon Nam? Was he being questioned? What about my dear? A shiver ran down my spine.

"Tell us." Min-Kook *uhmony* stood up, looking from side to side, as if ready to dart from the porch at any moment.

In-Young took a deep breath. She stared down at her feet, her eyes pooling. "My husband commanded I stay back so he could talk to me."

Min-Kook *uhmony* gave a hoot. Her knees buckled, and she fell forward, stumbling onto her stool. "Did you—did you say your husband?"

In-Young nodded. Her lower lip trembled. A tear rolled down her cheek.

Min-Kook *uhmony* settled her skirt around her stool. "What a relief."

I had to agree, even if In-Young did look miserable. Compared to the violent scenarios I'd imagined, a bit of matrimonial discord was nothing. I poured her a cup of water. "Well, you're just in time—"

"But wait." Min-Kook *uhmony* pulled her stool close to In-Young, the feet scraping against the deck. "He commanded you stay back and talk about what?"

Min-Kook *uhmony* was so abrupt. Not allowing people the space to process their feelings, but reaching in and grabbing, like a child after a piece of candy.

In-Young fingered a hole in a cabbage leaf. "His shirt got ripped."

"Did the Japs do it?" Min-Kook *uhmony* whispered.

Gong-Tae *uhmony* made a sound in her throat. Min-Kook *uhmony* was badmouthing the Japanese worse than He-Seung.

"No, no." In-Young shook her head. "It's just, well, he ripped his shirt—I don't know how—and I fixed it. Or tried to. He thought I did a poor job of mending the rip. He thought I was trying to shame him on purpose."

Deacon Nam was older than In-Young, almost twenty-seven years to her nineteen. He had patience for every churchgoer who forgot his Bible or left out a verse in a passage. Was it possible he had none for his dear wife? Dear In-Young. I knew her heart was full of sorrow.

"Were you?" Min-Kook *uhmony* asked, a mischievous look on her face. "Trying to shame him?"

"No." Tears filled her eyes again. "I can't cook like any of you. I could never get my dress as white as yours." She fingered Gong-Tae *uhmony's* skirt. "I'm not a seamstress like He-Seung *uhmony*. You all have so many talents." In-Young's voice broke. "My husband is just unlucky."

"Nonsense," Min-Kook *uhmony* said.

"Don't say that." I patted In-Young's knee. I handed her a pile of cabbage to drain.

"You should be known for the beauty that comes from within," Gong-Tae *uhmony* quoted the Bible. "*The unfading beauty of a gentle and quiet spirit, which is so precious to God.*"

In-Young nodded, offering us the flicker of a smile. She took a deep breath. Then she squeezed the water from the cabbage leaf.

"You can get more water out of there than that." Min-Kook *uhmony* reached over and picked up the pile of cabbage, wringing the leaves so hard water fell back into the bucket like rain.

"You're a gentle one." I quickly handed In-Young a piece of ginger to chop. I wanted to take her under my wing and protect her. I'd show her how to sew her impatient husband's shirts. That was certainly what was in the bag she'd left at the door. "Don't worry. Marriage is not easy."

"That's the truth." Min-Kook *uhmony* snorted.

"You know when I first married," I said, "I was so afraid of the husband my parents promised me to, I kept my eyes closed." I could remember my mother coaching me the day of my wedding, warning me to talk in a soft, thin voice to my husband only after I'd made my mind undisturbed. To avoid attracting attention to myself. To avoid coughing or sneezing or making other indecent noises. To keep my eyes low, head straight, hands polite and posture virtuous. "I didn't sneak a look at my husband for five days."

Gong-Tae *uhmony* chuckled as she gathered the chili peppers. I knew she had done the same, keeping her head lowered so she only saw her husband's stocking feet when he came home, closing her eyes tight when her head hit the pillow at night.

"That's ridiculous." Min-Kook *uhmony* tapped her fingers on the table. "Not me. In fact, I defied tradition and looked right into my husband's eyes."

Min-Kook *uhmony's* parents, elderly and ill, had married her off in a hurry to a man below her station. She reminded him of this every minute.

"In fact." Min-Kook *uhmony* held a limp piece of cabbage in front of her. "I told him—"

"Wait." I knew what she was going to say. How she had told her husband he was lucky to have someone like her. But those words certainly wouldn't help In-Young. "Will you take a look at that?"

"What?" Min-Kook *uhmony* stood, glancing to the left and right.

"See? Two sparrows are circling the cherry tree." I pointed at the first thing I could think of. "Aren't they lovely?"

"I hate those damn cherry trees." Min-Kook *uhmony* shook her head. "They look like bombs ready to explode. On us."

The birds made the cherry buds jump up and down on the branches. I used to think these trees were so delicate, so peaceful. But with Min-Kook uhmony standing next to me, talking about the army visiting the high school, and pretend visits to the shrine and rice rations, with her so nervous about gathering for the simple ritual of making kimchee that we all raced through the motions and assumed a friend's tears were caused by more than her husband's anger, I could imagine what Min-Kook uhmony saw. I could almost hear the tiny cherry buds ticking.

If we fight we will win; if we retreat we will be destroyed.
**—General Douglas MacArthur in letter to unit commanders,
Philippines, 1942**

Sunday, March 8, 1942—six days later

He-Seung

I sat in a pew next to Gong-Tae. Father towered over us, his fist pounding the pulpit. I was determined to listen to this week's sermon, in case Father quizzed me on the contents. I would show him that I wasn't just a dumb hothead, but someone who could concentrate and understand. Then maybe he'd listen to me.

Since the military had visited our school two weeks ago, our student population had dropped off. All the fifth-and-sixth year high school students were gone, except for the kid with a lame leg and the one who wore finger-thick glasses. Our fourth-year class was now considered top dog.

Each day Watanabe *Sensei* read out the list of brave students who had volunteered from our classroom, as if we hadn't heard him the first dozen times. Then he listed brave volunteers still eligible. In our class, Gong-Tae and Han-Joo were the only names left on that list.

Now, seated around us in the church, I counted only fifteen men. Fifteen. Last year, Father had had to borrow a bench from Mr. Kang to handle the crowds coming to worship. This morning not only was the bench empty, Mr. Kang hadn't even come to be our look-out man. Sixty-one-year-old Mr. Im, the oldest man in the congregation, maybe in all of Korea, had offered to watch out for the Japs. Father had to do something more about this situation than pray.

A few women sat behind us. Mother's *Kimchee* group, Gong-Tae's beautiful sweetheart Myung-Hae and Purple Face. As if they'd heard me thinking of them, I heard skirts being rustled. I had the urge to look. I already imagined the sight of Myung-Hae's ankles beneath swirls of pink fabric. Gong-Tae wasn't looking, though. So I didn't either.

Instead I cocked my head, forcing myself to hear Father. He was in the midst of some passage about glory. I'd already missed the beginning.

"Han-Joo is coming back to school tomorrow." Gong-Tae nudged me. He indicated his foot, gave a thumbs up.

Han-Joo. Our buddy who had stepped on a nail during a game a few weeks back. We all thought he was a goner. Too bad he'd survived just in time to be offered a volunteer position in the Youth Corps.

"At least you won't be alone, now." I whispered.

"I never was." He patted my shoulder. "I had you."

"What?" I shrugged my shoulders.

He made a kicking motion, banging the pew in front of us. Gong-Tae wasn't thinking of Watanabe *Sensei's* volunteer list. For Gong-Tae, the darkest year in Korea was not in 1910 when the Japs took over our country. It wasn't this month when the army was ransacking our school and taking away our buddies. It was the other day when FIFA called off the World Cup games rather than allow Germany to play host. Gong-Tae was only concerned for his beloved soccer. I laughed.

A couple of nosy coots in our row cleared their throats and glared. Father looked over in our direction. I kicked Gong-Tae in the calf. Why did he have to get me going when I was on my best church behavior?

At least Gong-Tae had given me a praise to offer up at the end of the sermon. My uncle on Father's side whom I'd never met had a son whom I'd also never met who stepped on a nail and was dead within a week from Lockjaw. We hadn't been invited to pray or mourn with the family. Mother had heard about it at the market. The fact that Han-Joo's foot had healed was a small miracle. Father would be impressed I had a praise to contribute.

Suddenly, Mr. Im, the lookout man, coughed long and hard. A woman cried out. A man in our row dropped to his knees as if he could hide his bulky self under the pew. We turned, expecting a band of Jap soldiers to march through the door.

"Just my old lungs." Mr. Im shook his head and patted his chest.

The congregation made sympathetic murmurings, a few women tittered. Father, his eyes still wide and defiant, finished his sentence, something about the love of God protecting us from all worldly threats. Despite this, a man in our row jumped up and scurried down the aisle and out the door. Now only fourteen men remained.

Those Japs were plucking every member from our church. Every coin from the donation plate. Every grain of rice from our mouths.

Mr. Im coughed again, beating his chest. He cleared his throat and spit out the door.

Gong-Tae coughed in imitation. "Why is he the guard?"

I patted Gong-Tae's back hard. I wish he hadn't picked today to be Mr. Funny Boy. "He was the last one to arrive at church."

"Last one in would get to be first one out." He raised his eyebrows. "I'm surprised you're not standing there." He elbowed me. "You offered, didn't you? I know you did." He snickered, covering the sound with another loud cough.

"Will you stop all that noise?" I hissed. The whole congregation—all fourteen plus female change—surely had figured out that Gong-Tae was making fun of Mr. Im. Father would not be pleased.

Gong-Tae gave me a look. I knew I sounded like a jerk. "Besides." I scratched my wrist, rubbing the skin so hard it burned. "It's not right to cough unless you're an old coot."

"It's not right to go rubbing yourself either." He gave a lecherous giggle followed by another particularly loud cough.

"Shut up. Please." I squinted my eyes hard, as if that might make Father's words stick longer in my ears. Salvation. Righteousness. God's Love. It all mushed around inside my head. I pushed my wrist between my legs, locking my knees around the sore, willing the itch to go away and counting the seconds until the final prayer when we all stood and shouted for forgiveness. My brain got tired of counting.

"Let us bring our thanks to the Lord." Father lifted his hands. Finally.

I stood next to Gong-Tae, waving my arms over my head, thinking that I'd had a praise I intended to offer. What was it? A man at the end of our row mumbled his thanks for another week of safety, and everyone added their *amens*. Pin pricks stabbed my wrist and shot down my arm. I expected to hear more shouts of praise, to have more time to remember what I was going to contribute, but there was a prolonged silence punctuated only by Mr. Im once again clearing his throat.

"In His name we praise." Father put his hands down. "Amen."

The old coots in our aisle pushed their way out. Father raced to the door, his black robe billowing, in order to greet them before they left.

"You'd think there was a fire in here." Gong-Tae gestured toward the men.

"There is." I nodded at the small congregation fearful of gathering, fearful of being arrested by the very people who were supposed to be taking care of us. "This whole country's on fire."

"Do you ever think of anything else?" Gong-Tae rolled his eyes at me.

"I do," I said, remembering my praise. The Japs hadn't taken everyone. We had health: Han-Joo's foot had healed. And happiness: Gong-Tae was still at home. "I think of you."

"Aw, shucks." He batted his eyes. "I think you need a bit of math. Perhaps you could tutor me this afternoon?"

"Ha!" I smiled looking at the red ball peaking from his jacket pocket. He always groaned about us not having regulation-sized soccer balls like in FIFA. At least our Korean soccer balls were small enough to hide.

Last week I had gotten permission from Father to chop wood with Gong-Tae, an iffy activity on the Lord's day, but one which Father sanctioned because it was helping a fellow Christian. Too bad I'd missed catching Gong-Tae's kick and the ball landed in a neighbor's window. *Tutoring in math,* while a quiet activity, would never work either. "Father would more likely believe I was going to fly."

"Then tell him that." His voice, as always, was insistent.

"I can't." I didn't have time to play with Gong-Tae. I had more serious things to accomplish. That thought sounded so much like my older brother it scared me. I shook my arm. It felt like an army of ants were traveling through my veins down to my hand. "Besides, my hand's asleep. I'm not in top goalie form."

"I'm used to that." He rubbed his hand across his upper lip, his non-existent facial hair.

"Right." I grabbed the ball from his pocket. "Not with me you're not."

"The park." He snuck a look over my shoulder. "Half hour?"

I followed his gaze. Myung-Hae stood with Purple Face and her mother waiting for us men to finish greeting Father. Her house was near the park. Would she come out and smile on the sidelines? She wore a pink-and-green striped dress, her thick silky black hair cascading over her shoulders. Whereas normally she would peek up at Gong-Tae, she kept her eyes to the ground. That was odd.

A man cleared his throat so loud Gong-Tae and I both jumped, turning toward the receiving line. All the men in front of us had left. Father stood alone, his temples pulsing. *It's not right to look at girls, especially in the Lord's house,* I could hear Father yelling at me.

Gong-Tae rushed forward and bowed to Father. "Thank you for the meaningful message."

"You're welcome." Father nodded to Gong-Tae. "It sounds as if you're ill."

Gong-Tae put his hands together and bowed again. "I think I just swallowed wrong."

"Are you sure?" Father furrowed his bushy eyebrows.

"I'm fine. In fact, I was just about to ask if He-Seung could, uh, tutor…" Gong-Tae looked over at me.

Gong-Tae knew my father better than that. There was no way I could bring up the idea of tutoring math when Father's temples were pulsing. It was a ridiculous notion from the outset.

"I'm so relieved to hear you're feeling fine." Father smiled, the sentiment not mirrored in his eyes. "Because I need you two to stay behind."

He motioned for the two of us to sit in one of the back pews. Surely he would question us to see if we'd been listening and not just hacking away in imitation of Mr. Im. I wracked my brain for a passage, anything that

Father had said. I turned to Gong-Tae. "What was the meaningful message?"

"Huh?" He stared at Myung-Hae as she, her mother and Purple Face all bowed to Father and thanked him for the sermon. Myung-Hae had a nice bottom. A nice everything. Gong-Tae was a lucky guy.

"The sermon?" I nudged him. "You thanked Father for the meaningful message. What was it?"

He shrugged still looking after Myung-Hae as she walked out the door without even a backwards glance. "I was just saying that."

Great. I spotted He-Dong cowering next to Mother. He would have listened to every word and been able to spit back each precise phrase. He was probably already repeating Father's prayers in his head, as if saying them twice made God more likely to listen. I wished I could nab the runt for ten seconds, so he could spit out some of Father's phrases.

Mother looked over at us, her eyes wide. She probably wondered why I wasn't waiting by the door to walk home. I wanted to. I'd rather suffer the annoying baby's whining about how Dr. Lee would have puppies soon than try to retrieve a meaningful message for Father. I could already hear Father's thousand questions, see his temple pulsing, feel his anger on my calves. He would never even hear the fact that our school, our church, our family was slowly being swallowed by the Japs. Mother and He-Dong bowed to Father and hurried out the door.

"Boys." Father came over, his hands clasped.

"Thank you for that meaningful message," I tried.

Father crossed his arms and raised an eyebrow. I nudged Gong-Tae. He could think of something to add, couldn't he?

Father looked down at me. "It's not right to…"

I knew Father would say it wasn't right to just say things, wasn't right to make fun of other people, wasn't right to stare at the girls. "I know—"

"Borrow something you no longer need." Father continued as if I hadn't spoken. He indicated for us to follow him to the door, stopping in front of Mr. Kang's bench. "Please return this, with thanks, to Mr. Kang."

Japan is the foundation and the axis of the world.
The world must be unified around Japan.
—**Professor T. Komaki, Kyoto Imperial University over Tokyo Radio,**
Feb, 1942

Sunday March 8, 1942—same day

He-Seung

I held one end of the bench and Gong-Tae took the other. He walked backward, while I directed him past the edge of the market. My shoulders ached so much I'd long forgotten my rash. Sweat slid down my arms. I almost wished Father had lectured us about making fun of Mr. Im, about staring at Myung-Hae's bottom. At least I'd be relaxing in the church.

An ox stood hitched to a cart by the right side of the road, his fur black with mud, his breath filling the air with steam. A sweet potato vendor pushed his wooden cart past us, calling for us to buy the warm treat. A bunch of old men sat on their haunches smoking long pipes and watching.

Gong-Tae groaned. "We need a break."

I pushed and pulled on the bench, making him wobble along. "We wouldn't be out here like a bunch of low-class fools if you'd just agreed with my father. In fact, we might even be playing at the park with pretty girls watching us, if you had just told him you were coming down with something."

"That would have been a sin against all sins." He glared at me, sounding so much like his mother, I expected to hear the rustling of a skirt.

I guided him down the road. On our left was a tall brick wall separating the road from the houses. From behind the wall, the sounds of chopping, the squish-squish of washing clothes, the whine of a small brat filled the air. All normal sounds. Only life didn't feel normal anymore—any day my buddy would tell me he was joining the war. Any day.

Too bad my elder brother He-Chul was off in Manchuria, writing us long-winded letters about producers and landlords, collectivism and other words that just made my brain feel emptier than usual. If he were home, perhaps he'd be able to convince Father to stop all this praying and pick up the fight. Perhaps he'd have an answer that would keep my classmates in school, would keep the congregation filling Father's church. "The fact we have to return this bench at all is a sin against all sins."

"I know what you mean," Gong -Tae grunted. "Since when are we a bunch of common laborers?"

"I'm used to Father's low opinion of me." The sun poked through the dark clouds, rays of light shooting out just like the Japanese military flag.

"What I mean is we wouldn't be out here laboring harder than that ox, wouldn't have to return the bench at all, if those stupid Japs would quit forcing their foolish Emperor down our throats."

His eyes widened. He looked around as though expecting a sword to fly at him from somewhere.

"At the rate they're pushing." I ignored his paranoia. "Father will be giving his sermons to just me, Mother, and He-Dong."

"You mean…" He squinted as if in deep thought. "Just your Mother and He-Dong."

"I'm not going anywhere." I shoved the bench, making him stumble backwards. "I'd rather burn in hell than help the Japs fight their stupid war."

"I know." He pushed back, smirking at me. "But you never listen to the sermons anyway."

He knew me too well. This guy who taught me to laugh when I was scratching myself to pieces, when my heart was burning from all the sins Father was sure I had committed. Tomorrow Watanabe *Sensei* would continue wheedling away at Gong-Tae. Or perhaps *Sensei* would have devised some other scheme, like saying that those eligible to serve could not attend school.

"He-Seung?" Gong-Tae knocked his fist on the bench. "You still with me?"

"I was just thinking, that's all." I looked at him. I wasn't going to get all mushy with him. "I mean who can concentrate on Father's sermon with all those lovely skirts rustling behind us?"

"Agh!" Gong-Tae cried out, flying backwards.

He looked like the nimble comic-book character, *Jangsah*, the way he tumbled and landed on his feet. I expected to see one of our friends having snuck up behind him.

"You jerk." He stood up, brushing his backside and pointing to the huge cinderblock in the middle of the road that had caused him to stumble. "Why didn't you say anything?"

"I didn't see it." I set my end of the bench down and flopped onto the hard wood, laughing. My stomach ached from the sight of Gong-Tae flipping. It was like a really neat soccer move without the ball. I wiped a drop of sweat from my forehead. "Really. I didn't."

"I'm risking my life here with you at the helm," he said, staring at the cinderblock.

"I wonder where that came from." Perhaps the cinderblock had fallen off one of the ox-carts. Somebody would soon be missing it. But before they did, perhaps we could play with it.

Gong-Tae looked up the road. To the right was an apple orchard. To the left was the road to the market. An old woman came rushing toward us. "Looks like whoever lost it has come to find it."

"Well, darn." She wore a white *cheemar*, trails of ink staining her skirt. "That's the woman from the print shop, knucklehead. Why would she be wanting a cinderblock?"

"Who knows?" Gong-Tae said. "But she's coming this way. Maybe she's spotted our bench and wants to take a rest."

I sat up. The woman's hair was held back just barely, and wisps of grey flew about her face. Her brow was furrowed as she looked at the bench, then us. I could imagine her asking if she might have a small rest. I could imagine us sitting here while she talked about how there used to be more apple orchards and less cherry trees, or how her grandson just had his hundred-day celebration when no one thought he would live that long, talking until my ears were numb from the noise. I stood, motioning for Gong-Tae to move. "Grab your end."

Before Gong-Tae responded, the old woman nodded at us, maneuvered around the cinderblock, turned the corner and hurried down the road.

"Well, that was unexpected." I looked after the woman. "The old lady has more energy than I thought."

"Either that or she left her soup on the stove." Gong Tae joined me on the bench. He leaned down with his head in his hands. He forced a laugh. "Speaking of unexpected, Dr. Lee's colleague is looking around for a suitable wife for his son."

I dissected his wobbly words. The only suitable match for a son of a friend would be a daughter. Dr. Lee's daughter meant Myung-Hae or Purple Face. But Purple Face was too young. I raised an eyebrow. "Huh?"

"Yeah." He took the red soccer ball from his pocket and tossed it back and forth in his hands.

"It won't happen." I assured him with greater conviction than I felt. "These are modern times. Myung-Hae will just say." I raised my voice an octave. "'No, Father. My heart belongs to Gong-Tae.'"

He stood up, volleying the little ball on the inside of his foot, then the outside. "She already tried that." He took in a deep breath of air, closing his eyes. "Dr. Lee doesn't think of these times as modern, but as troubled. And, in these troubled days, strict obedience is most important. He forbade any discussion." Gong-Tae leaned down as if to pick up the ball. Instead he swiped his hand over his face.

These troubled times. To hell with these troubled times. I wasn't going to stand here and watch my friend get all runt-like with me.

I heaved the cinderblock next to the stone wall. I pushed the bench a few feet away. Two firm goal posts. Then I grabbed his soccer ball. Was this little red ball in celebration of the Japs conquering Hong Kong, Burma or Singapore? Was it a reward for taking over the city of Beijing, Nanking or Shanghai? I wished it were in celebration of slaughtering the Japs.

"Times aren't troubled unless we allow them to be." I slammed the ball against the wall. "Let's do some *math*. Five shots each. Highest scorer wins."

"That's five goals I got off you." I wiped a drop of sweat from my cheek.

"I'm just getting warmed up." Gong-Tae said.

He didn't need warming up. He was a natural. He was off kilter today, playing almost as bad as He-Dong. Almost.

"At the rate you're warming..." I grabbed my suit coat from the bench. "The war will be over first."

The sound of labored breathing made us both turn. A woman came running toward us. She held her white *cheemar* up so she could move fast. The woman's eyes were wide, her mouth gasping for air. "That's the woman from the print shop again."

"You're right." He picked up the ball and pocketed it. "She's awfully busy today. I'm glad my family's not in that business."

We watched the old lady rush by us. Surely Gong-Tae wished his father was in the doctoring business so he could jump higher and reach the hems of Myung-Hae's skirt before another doctor's boy whisked her away. But watching the print shop lady, I was wondering if Mother could run as fast. And if she could, what would make her do so?

Just then a soldier came racing down the road. He paused at the corner, surveying the apple orchard to his right. He looked over and spotted us. *Oy!*"

"Who does he think we are, calling to us that way?" I cleared my throat and spit on the ground. "A bunch of oxen?"

"He-Seung." Gong-Tae's voice held warning. He picked up his end of the bench. "It's time to take this back. Time to go home. Time to eat dinner."

I crossed my arms. I thought of all the school fights I'd won. This would be no different. "But the bastard's alone."

"We don't know that." Gong-Tae kicked the bench to get my attention.

"What do you mean?" I twisted my head to the side, cracking my neck. "We see that."

"Do we also see his pistol?" Gong-Tae came over next to me.

The Jap swaggered over. Or perhaps that's what he thought he was doing. But he was young and scrawny. His hat fell over his eyes. His swagger looked more like a kid who'd messed his pants. Except for that pistol at his side which gleamed silver and was just a fingernail's reach away.

Gong-Tae stood behind me and bowed to the Jap, at the same time pushing my back down.

"Did you see a grandma running this way?" His voice came in short gasps.

Gong-Tae didn't respond. It wasn't like him to tell a story. That would be a sin against all sins. But surely he didn't want to get an old lady in trouble. I wanted the little soldier to move near me. Then I'd have no trouble beating the crap out of him. Gun or no gun.

I shrugged. "What?"

"Grandma!" He ran his hands down his brown pants pantomiming a dress. His big hat fell to the ground.

I reached for it. At least that would give me an excuse to get close to him. But Gong-Tae poked my backside. I could almost hear his voice. *I'm risking my life with you at the helm.*

I brushed dirt from the soldier's hat. I would have rather spit on it or tossed it over the brick wall in hopes it landed in a pile of dog shit. I grit my teeth and held out the cap. "Grandma?"

"Yes, you idiot." The soldier shouted, looking around. "Grandma? Aunty? Woman? Girl? What word do you understand?"

It dawned on me that this kid soldier assumed we were common laborers moving a bench, and that we didn't understand his language. "Girl?" I repeated the last word he'd spoken.

"Yes, girl." He nodded vigorously. "Where?"

"Yes, girl," I repeated, smiling. "Where?"

"*Bakayaro,*" the soldier shouted. Idiots.

"*Bakayaro,*" I repeated, staring at this short jerk who trampled on our country, enjoying the way that cruel word rolled from my lips.

The soldier made a growling sound that started in his puny chest. He put his hand to his gun. Despite his pock-marked face, his fingers massaged the top of that gun like an old pro. Gong-Tae sucked in his breath.

"Apples?" I pointed toward the orchard, pretending to show off more of my Japanese vocabulary. I smiled. "Girls. Apples. Idiots."

"Girls. Apples." Gong-Tae joined in, leaving off the offensive word.

"I don't have time for fools like you." The soldier grabbed his hat from me and ran off, pausing at the end of the road to look once more at the orchard.

I wondered what the old print shop grandma had done to irk this soldier. Did she have a son who had refused to *volunteer* for the army? Had she forgotten to print the latest Jap victory?

"Are you nuts?!" Gong-Tae lunged at me.

I grabbed his arm and twisted it behind his back. He pulled and jerked his body to get loose, but I wouldn't let go. Then he stomped his feet, trying to step on mine.

"Can't you ever think past the moment right in front of your nose." He turned his face towards mine, his eyes watery. "You may not mind getting shot, but I do."

"I'll remember that." I held him tight. "But up until now nothing in my life has felt better than calling that Jap an idiot. Not even scoring a goal compares."

Gong-Tae shook his head. "Well that's such a rarity, you probably don't remember what that feels like."

I laughed. He might have been angry with me, but he never lost his sense of humor. I let him go. "Don't forget I got five goals off you, easy as snapping my fingers."

"I already don't remember. My mind was just wiped clean as a slate here." He reached out to pick up his end of the bench. "Let's get out of here."

I picked up my side of the bench, and we started down the road to Mr. Kang's. Gong-Tae jogged backwards, pulling me away from the area as fast as possible. He probably worried the idiot would return, angry that we'd sent him the wrong way.

When it was obvious the soldier was not returning for us, he let out a deep sigh. "Actually, that was a pretty smart trick for a fool like you."

I shook my head. "Like getting rid of one ant."

Gong-Tae furrowed his eyebrows. "Got any thoughts on how to get rid of a son of a doctor?"

"Let me think on that." I had done something, even if it was small. Now, Gong-Tae was actually looking to me for advice. I felt warmth spreading in my chest, something akin to pride.

*There is a necessity of establishing a world peace
which reflects the light of the power and glory of the Emperor...There is
a spitefulness in the Europeans and Americans. This, too, is a reason
that Europeans and Americans should be annihilated.*
—**Professor T. Komaki, Kyoto Imperial University over Tokyo radio,
Feb 1942**

Monday, March 9, 1942—next day

Baby He-Dong

Last year, I was always one of the first boys to school. I had wanted to be at the entrance when my flock of students arrived, just as Father stood at the door of the church. Now, I waited until the last possible minute to trudge through the big gates. I couldn't bear to watch the new Class Monitor stumble up, his pants scuffed, dirt smudges on his cheek. I couldn't bear the way he bungled the Japanese national anthem, mouthing the words as though singing really loud, but really not saying a thing. I couldn't bear to see him in my spot.

I held tight to my *bento* lunch box as I walked across the trolley rails. Every day I prayed all the way to school, asking God to please give me another chance as leader. I would not mess up. Then I closed my eyes tight just before entering the gates.

This morning, when I opened my eyes, Bon-Hwa stood there as usual, his pant legs dragging in the dust, his shoulders not erect, his chin not high. Our class had gathered in front of him by the Japanese flag to sing *Kimi Ga Yo,* the anthem. I put my foot forward into the schoolyard, a bitter taste filling my mouth.

"What's your rush?" Kee Wok materialized from behind the wall and pushed me back outside the school yard.

Kee-Wok. He was the tough kid, the one who'd convinced the teacher to let me sit down the first day of school. These days we arrived about the same time, though he normally didn't talk to me. I felt a small thrill.

"Did you do the character practice?" He gave me a big smile.

My chest puffed out. The teacher had given us 51 characters to write. Ten times. Did Kee-Wok need my help? "Of course."

"Well, give it to me." He thrust his dirty hand out.

I didn't mind helping him, although now wasn't the time. I now spotted the principal crossing the courtyard, his strides long for such a short man. As soon as he reached his spot at the flagpole, everyone would begin singing the anthem. We would be late. I would be punished again, this time in front of the entire school.

"Your homework." He wiggled his fingers as though expecting me to hand over my work. "I didn't have time to do mine."

"We should get inside." I pointed to where all the students were inside the yard—the boys on one side of the flag, the girls on the other—standing tall, ready to sing. The principal would get to the pole any second. "I'll help you later. At lunch."

Kee-Wok laughed. He leaned against the entrance, smiling as if it was a Sunday afternoon and he was at a loss for something to do. "I don't want to waste my lunch time." He stuck his hand out. "Just give me yours."

"That's against the rules," I said, the words sounding stiff and prim.

"What a little bean-curd boy." He sneered.

My brother called me that. But that was because he was my elder and could say whatever he wanted. I wasn't a bean-curd boy, words that should be used only for a real weakling. I would tell Mother about Kee-Wok's bad behavior.

"Besides, since when do you—or anyone in your family—care about rules?" he asked.

I knew what he was referring to. The Japanese had a new rule that everyone must only worship the Emperor. Our family believed in God the Father and Jesus Christ our Lord.

"Our family cares about important rules." We never stole from the market, never lied, never cheated. Father didn't even drink alcohol like lots of other fathers.

"A rule's a rule," Kee-Wok said, his gaze lingering on the new Class Monitor. "Besides, now you have plenty of extra time. Now that you're no longer busy."

Here I thought he'd wanted to be my friend, wanted to talk to me because I used to be Class Monitor, was so smart, and had a big brother so important that the Japanese had sent him to study in Manchukuo. I felt chili peppers biting my nose, could feel my eyes burning. I moved forward to push by him.

"I didn't think you were an idiot as well," Kee-Wok blocked my path, pinching the tender skin on the inside of my arm.

I jumped back, my arm smarting. I wished I could be tough and take care of myself like He-Seung. I could hear his words in my head. *You couldn't even take care of a bed bug.*

"Everyone listens to Colonel Kee-Wok." He patted his chest. "Now, give me your homework."

"Am I late? Am I late?" The new kid, Ih-Duk, called out to us in Korean as he came running across the tracks. His face was flushed. His eyes filled with excitement. He held a long stick in his hand.

I knew the first language out of his mouth was always Korean, but I didn't want to get in trouble again. Kee-Wok obviously felt the same.

"Shush," we both said.

"Sorry." He switched to Japanese. We looked to the flagpole. The teachers stood erect in a line, waiting for the principal. They didn't even glance our way.

"It's just...well, my gosh." Ih-Duk held out the stick. He switched back to Korean, whispering, "Look what I found on the way to school. Isn't he lovely?"

"You like sticks so much, you talk like they're your friends?" Kee-Wok laughed. "What a lovely little branch he is."

I laughed, too. Perhaps in our unity against the new kid I would make it to the flagpole, even the classroom, with my own homework in my hand.

"Not the stick, silly," Ih-Duk said, lifting the branch close to our faces.

Silly. Did Ih-Duk actually call Kee-Wok *silly?*

I was glad I'd stayed away from Ih-Duk. I knew it hadn't been his fault I was punished by the teacher, but I couldn't help blaming him. I didn't want to know why his Japanese was so bad. I didn't want to feel him struggling to understand. If I had been his friend when he called Kee-Wok *silly*, we'd both be hanging by our toes.

I waited for Kee-Wok to grab the foolish new kid by the ears, push him back outside, pinch the tender underside of his arm. But Kee-Wok acted like he didn't hear a thing. He must have still been worrying about his homework, or the fact that the morning gathering was about to start, cause he looked from the flagpole to my hands, almost as if hoping my homework paper was there for him.

"Did you know there are 35,000 different families of spiders?" Ih-Duk said, searching the side of his stick.

"Ten of which are already extinct." I knew a bit about spiders.

"I hope I didn't extinct this one." Ih-Duk lifted the branch up in front of Kee-Wok's face. "Do you see—"

"Get that thing away from me, weirdo." Kee-Wok grimaced. He backed away, but not before ripping my lunch bucket from my hand and taking off.

I tried to act as if I didn't care that the bully had stolen my lunch, Mother's fresh *kimchee*, rice, an egg. I watched the stick, pretending to be fascinated by the small spider which I now saw traveling at the end of the stick. "I wonder which class of spider he belongs to?"

"Do you mean Lightning Feet here or Kee-Wok?" Ih-Duk looked up at me. "If it's Kee-Wok, I would say sedentary." He glanced down at my empty hand, the scrape on my finger. "Sitting in his burrow all day long waiting for food."

Over the burning lump in my throat, I felt a bubble of laughter. I nodded. "And homework."

"He wanted your homework, too?" Ih-Duk shook his head in disbelief. "And you were going to give it to him?"

I shook my head. Shame filled my being. It wasn't as if I wanted to give him my lunch, either.

As we hurried to join the others, Ih-Duk whispered in Korean. "My mother always packs me too much food. If you want, I can share with you."

I knew he wasn't being truthful. Nobody had too much food to pack these days. I felt another lump in my throat, this time a grateful one.

If it is the boast of India that she produced the Buddha, and the boast of Judea that she counts among her sons Jesus the Redeemer of the world, it is enough for Japan to boast that she has been from generation to generation under the sway of emperors who, in an unbroken line, ascended the throne of Imperial---that is to say, of Divine--dignity.
--Genchi Kato, Professor, Tokyo University, 1942

Monday, March 9, 1942—same day

Mother (*Uhmony*)

I sat on the back porch, a wash bucket between my legs. A gentle breeze carried the smell of blossoms through the air. The rooster clucked about in his pen. I had already scrubbed the leg of He-Seung's soiled trousers a dozen times.

"Good morning!" A voice called out. Min-Kook *uhmony*. She always knew where to find me. "You're still washing?"

"It's just these stains. I've washed them over and over—"

Min-Kook *uhmony* set her covered basket down on the porch. Then she pulled the pants from my grasp, staring at the offending stain which still looked small and round like a ball. I was sure she'd ask what He-Seung had been doing playing soccer in his Sunday trousers. And after my husband had gotten through with him, had He-Seung been able to walk to school this morning?

"You could cut off some soap flakes and let the material soak for a while." She handed the pants back.

I had tried that. I pushed the pants under the water.

"Or you could just cut them off and make a pair of shorts," she suggested. "Spring is almost here. They won't fit He-Seung next winter, and it will be years before He-Dong can wear them."

I hadn't thought of that. I stood. "Can I get you a glass of water?"

"I just saw Gong-Tae *uhmony*." She looked at me.

"Oh?" Min-Kook *uhmony* never stopped to visit Gong-Tae *uhmony*, unless there was an emergency. "Is she ill?"

"Same as always." Min-Kook *uhmony* tossed her hand up. "Quoting this scripture and that as if she could actually read."

I smiled sympathetically. I shaved some more soap flakes onto the material. "Someday you'll have to teach us."

Min-Kook *uhmony* brushed my words away. "You don't know, do you?"

My thoughts fled to the church. Both Min-Kook *uhmony* and Gong-Tae *uhmony's* husbands worked with my dear. Was there another new rule? "Know what?"

She put her hands on her hips. "Gong-Tae and your He-Seung had a close call with a soldier yesterday."

"What? But why? All they did was return a bench." I held on tight to the pants as if He-Seung were still in them. "I wonder why he didn't say anything."

"Did he even get a chance?" She sat down on the steps, brushing off an imaginary speck of dust from her arm.

I thought back to He-Seung returning, sweat staining his arms, dirt covering his pants. My dear had met him at the door, handed him the Bible and told him he needed to study for the rest of the night. Not to come back down. I had taken He-Seung a bit of rice and *kimchee*. He could have said something to me, but he didn't. I colored. "Maybe he didn't want me to worry."

"I don't want you to worry, either." She reached down and picked up her basket. "So I brought us a picnic. Would you join me?"

I knew what she was asking. Would I go to Mt. Nam San with her? Would I pretend to believe the Emperor of Japan was my god? "Is your husband going?"

She snorted at the thought. A very un-lady-like sound. Clearly she hadn't told her husband her plans.

"I would really like to come, especially on this beautiful day." I indicated the forsythia bush blowing gently in the breeze. "It's a lovely morning. But I'm not sure it's right. The Ten Commandments say—"

"Please, please." She dropped the basket at my feet. "You think Gong-Tae *uhmony* spared me the recitation of every pertinent passage? *Do not have any gods before me*." She raised her voice. "*Do not bow down to them or worship them*."

I tied the pant leg around the soap shavings and pushed the material into the bucket. The cool water massaged my hands, my thoughts. If Gong-Tae *uhmony* had already reminded her, why was she still coming to me of all people?

"This is no different than eating dinner with your father-in-law." She held up one finger.

"That was a lifetime ago." Min-Kook *uhmony* was one of the few people who knew about my dear's father.

"Or calling in the witch doctor to take a look at He-Dong and predict his future." She held up another finger.

"That, too, was years ago." I sighed.

"It doesn't matter." She dropped her fingers. "The point is just because we look at Mrs. Park's bean sprouts doesn't mean we're going to abandon our loyalty to the Kim's."

Min-Kook *uhmony* and I always browsed the new stalls at the marketplace, even though we knew we'd end up at the Kim's. The Kim's provided the crispest soy beans, the cheapest price, the kindest service. I understood Min-Kook *uhmony's* reasoning, but I was already shaking my head.

"Just looking at someone else's god, pretending a bit of respect, can't be wrong," she whispered.

If that were true than where was Gong-Tae *uhmony?* And why hadn't my dear suggested we take such a picnic? "I don't know."

"I do." Min-Kook *uhmony* put her hands in the dirty water and grabbed my fingers. "I know that now is the time to look at the other bean sprouts and feign interest in buying them."

I thought of the soldiers encroaching on every aspect of our lives: my son's school, the road outside my house, the road to our neighbor Mr. Kang's house. They were everywhere, and perhaps we could no longer sidestep their existence. Then again, this wasn't just about me. This was about my dear's calling, our life, our family—the small family that we were. I gripped onto her hands, promising I'd meet her by the staircase to the shrine in two hours. If my dear agreed.

Twenty minutes later, with my lunch basket in hand, I headed to the church. Min-Kook *uhmony's* words churned over and over in my head. *This is no worse than eating dinner with your father-in-law. It's time to feign interest in buying their bean sprouts.*

Most people we knew had large extended families with cousins, aunts, uncles, grandmothers and grandfathers. My dear and I belonged to a special family—all of our aunts and uncles were relatives in the Lord. My dear's parents had died, but by then we had long been banished.

My Father-in-law had held his thick finger a shoestring's length from my dear's face on the night of our final conversation. "Sitting at the same table with your wife? Not even opening this delicious rice wine? The white man has seduced you with their God like a song girl at the market."

My dear flushed, bringing his hands together as if praying. Perhaps praying that Father-in-law would come to understand. Would accept the Lord as Savior. Would stop speaking such rudeness in front of his new wife.

"The days of Confucius are over," my dear said. "The only words worthy of respect are those of our Heavenly Father."

"You needn't flatter me by calling me Heavenly." Father-in-law slapped his hand on his chest. "Oh, wait. But you're talking of someone else's father, aren't you? A white man's father." He finished off his wine, slamming the cup down hard. "You're a disgrace to our society, our family, our good name." He stood up and walked to the door. He leaned down, took my dear's shoes and mine and tossed them out the door. "Get out."

My dear rose and I quickly followed. I expected him to bow down to his father and ask forgiveness, although even then I should have known better. Still, I hoped he'd find some way to make things right. I didn't want to have children not knowing their grandparents, their aunts, uncles, cousins. I didn't want the neighbors to hear that we'd been cut off from our family. Besides, where would we live?

"Father?" my dear said.

"What?" Father-in-law looked up, expectant.

"God bless you." My dear hurried out the door, stopping only to retrieve his shoes.

I hobbled over the path, the stones cutting the soles of my soft feet. I turned one last time to look at my new Father-in-law, the man we'd lived with for six months since our wedding. He stared at us with such hatred, I thought we would burst into flames.

Now as I went up the steps leading to my dear's beautiful red brick church, my food basket felt heavy in my hand. I opened the wooden door and walked into the sanctuary, imagining the shuffling of shoes heading to the men's section at the front, the rustle of skirts as women arranged themselves at the back, little children leaning against their mothers, helping to turn the pages of the hymnal as the organist played songs of joy and gratitude. My dear had suffered so much to have this family in the Lord. How could I even suggest a visit to a shrine?

On the other hand, there were so few people attending church these days, we barely collected enough money to purchase salt and soy sauce. We needed to placate people's fear of us somehow.

I heard voices coming from my dear's office. He wouldn't be happy if I interrupted him while he had a parishioner, even if I had brought him lunch. I took a seat in the nearest pew and stared up at the bronze cross against the front wall. *Dear God. Help me find strength to do what is right in Your name. Min-Kook uhmony says it's necessary now to pretend. I sense my dear will not agree. What do you say?*

The voices in the office got louder, and I realized they were shouting in Japanese. I felt a sudden chill. The sound of scraping furniture made me stand.

The door to the office banged open. He emerged, his head held high. Two men in dark blue police uniforms pushed him forward. One of the officers carried a long metal chain over his shoulder. He had an angry red scar. The other officer had thick ruddy cheeks. I hadn't seen such cheeks since rice rationing began. They both wore pistols at their sides.

"*Oy*," called More Than His Share. He held a rolled-up parchment in his well-fed hands. "What are you doing here?"

A coldness spread across my heart. I could hear Min-Kook *uhmony's* voice again. *It's time to look at their bean sprouts and feign interest in buying.* "I brought a picnic." I held up the basket.

The other policeman stepped forward and grabbed the basket from me, prodding through the contents. I felt as if he were rifling through my *cheemar*. My legs trembled. He picked up one of the rice balls and held it inches from my dear's mouth. "Would that be for the tr-tr-traitor to our Im-Im-Im—"

"Imperial Emperor?" More Than His Share stepped in, grabbing one of our treats.

"He's not a traitor." The words tumbled out of my mouth. I wanted to mention that we were on our way to Mt. Nam San, but the words froze on my tongue as I glanced over at my dear. He had his eyes closed, his hands folded to his chest. Certainly he was praying. *I tell you not to resist an evildoer. On the contrary, whoever slaps you on the right cheek, turn the other to him as well.* "Would you like some tea?" I asked.

"Well, what a kind wife." More Than His Share wiped a grain of our precious rice off his chin. He looked me up and down as if I were a fish at the market. "Sharing her tea with any man who passes. Maybe this Christianity stuff isn't so bad."

My insides froze. My dear's eyes opened wide.

"I haven't had tea today." More Than His Share gestured to my body. He gave a disgusting laugh. He nudged his partner. "You want some?"

"Nah," the Scarred Man said. "Her tea belongs to the tr-tr-traitor."

He picked up the teapot and upended it over my dear's head. I sucked in a breath, praying for the liquid to have cooled already. My dear smiled, as calm as if a friend were pouring a bucket of water on him at the public bath.

"Get out of here." More Than His Share grabbed the teapot and threw it to the floor. The tin clattered, echoing throughout the sanctuary. "*Ike!*"

He shoved my dear down the hall and out the white wooden doors. I followed.

The Scarred Man took the huge chain he'd been carrying and wrapped the links around the sanctuary doors, once, twice, three times. Each slap of the chain against the wood made me flinch.

More Than His Share took out a nail and, using the butt of his pistol as a hammer, he affixed the parchment to the door. I didn't know what the characters said, but I was sure it was something to keep people away. They were closing the church.

"I expect now we'll be seeing you up at Mt. Nam San," More Than His Share said.

"Th-th-that's r-r-right." The Scarred Man pulled on the padlock testing its strength. "No more of this Ch-ch-christian crap."

"Honorable officers." My dear smiled at the men. I had a sudden fear that he would bless them. Not that they shouldn't have been blessed—we were all God's children. But some people didn't want to hear that, and these men looked as if they would do worse than just throw our shoes out the door and give us an evil glare.

"I thought I told you to keep your mouth shut." More Than His Share made a deep sound in his throat and spit in my dear's face.

My dear bowed. I did, too. But my heart burned as if there wasn't just a pool of tea and a glob of saliva dripping from my dear's cheek, but the officer had sent a bullet through my chest.

*The divine mission Japan has been called to fulfill from time
immemorial is, in a word, to permeate the whole earth with one cosmic
vitality embodied in our Divine Sovereign, so that all segregated national
units may be led to reunite themselves spiritually with the sincere feeling
of brothers sharing the same blood.*
—Prof Chikao Fujisawa, Tokyo, 1942

Wednesday, March 11, 1942—two days later

He-Seung

Mother insisted I play with the foreign kid, Jim. His mother had been schooling him at home, but I guess he was now smart enough to go the Korean school. Mother suggested I bring him along to play in our soccer games to introduce him to some friends. But I knew he wasn't good at soccer. I'd seen him outside trying to play on his own, and his feet were clumsy and large. Mother had suggested I practice with him.

Fortunately, clouds moved in and the wind picked up before I had to suffer through his miserable toe dribbling. Before a drop of rain even fell, he ran to his house, and I hurried to the dormitory where we stayed on the top floor.

All afternoon I stared at the rain, praying that it would stop and I could go play with my real friends. A popping sounded and I was sprayed with glass, little pin pricks of blood all over my knees and hand, warm liquid dripping down my cheek.

"My little one." Mother came running, pulling me away, dabbing at my cuts. "You can't sit in front of the window when there's a typhoon."

When the wind finally died down, and the rain tapered off, I went outside. Jim was already there, dragging a stick around. I showed him my wounds. His mouth dropped in awe. He said he had something really cool to show me, too. An ocean. He took me to our community garden.

"That's not an ocean," I said, looking at the river of water that flowed through our carrot bed. "That's just a puddle of water. Our carrots are drowning."

He raced over and put his stick in the middle of the river of water, trying to stem the flow. I laughed at him, searching around for a rock. The two of us dragged over the heavy reinforcement. Again, the water found its way around our obstacles.

A knocking sounded, first at the outer edges of my brain. Were my feet that loud in the garden? Was that a clap of thunder? The sound grew louder. My bedroom door?

"He-Seung," Mother called, banging on the door. "Rise and shine."

Now, I opened my eyes and sat up. Unlike my dream, outside the sky was turning light, an insistent brightening of the sky. The warm sweet smell of rice teased the air. The salty smell of *miso* soup. Surely Father was preparing his worship.

I lay back down on my *eebul*, pulling my comforter over my head. Such a strange dream. Jim. I remembered thinking of him as *the foreign kid*. I remembered thinking of him as such a klutz. I missed him now. And that typhoon. That stubborn typhoon. Now it reminded me of my father.

After the police locked the church, Father had gone door to door to visit each member, explaining what had happened and inviting them to services at our home from 5-6 am on Wednesdays and Sundays. Last night, he'd had Mother turn our living room into a mini-sanctuary, with the wooden cross on the wall, a black cover on the windows, the floor divided in half by a piece of string. One side for the women, one for the men.

Voices sounded from downstairs. I threw the comforter off. Surely parishioners were arriving. I couldn't be the last one to church when it was my own house.

I folded my comforter and the cotton *eebul*, stuffing them in one side of the closet. From the other side, I picked out my rumpled school uniform. I pulled on the trousers. With my jacket in hand, I walked down the hallway to the bathroom.

Part of me worried that someone—Gong-Tae's girl perhaps—might peer up the staircase on the way to the living room and see me walking down the hallway in my undershirt, small dark hairs poking out from beneath my underarms. Part of me hoped that she would.

I went in the bathroom and washed my face and hands. The water from our faucet was cold, always cold. But I smiled as I splashed my face, as if standing before an admiring group of girls. I scrubbed the sour-smelling salve from my arms.

I put on my jacket, buttoning it from the bottom to the top. When I got to the topmost button, I stopped. I didn't have to fasten that brass circle until I got to school. I stared at the horrible black uniform in the oval mirror above the sink. I hadn't bothered telling Father of my squelching the Japs one ant at a time. He was so busy trying to drown me with his Bible. He was so busy convincing the congregation that all would be fine. I hadn't even had a chance to ask him what to do about Gong-Tae's predicament. The bathroom door swung open and He-Dong marched in, already dressed.

I rubbed my fingers over my scalp. I put my collar up again. Then let it hang loose. I smiled into the mirror. I wasn't bad looking. How could Myung-Hae favor Gong-Tae over me when I was such a handsome devil?

He went over to the toilet, but he twisted to look at me. "Is there something wrong with your button?"

"No, little runt, there's nothing wrong."

Downstairs, I heard the front door open and close. More voices. He-Dong finished his business and came over. He pushed against me.

"What are you doing?" he asked.

I shoved the runt out of the way. Then I took a bit of water and splashed my face again. "Why don't you hurry downstairs and save me a space?"

"Mother already assigned spots. I'm closest to the hall, so I can leave early."

"Oh?" I glanced at him in the mirror.

"Mother said it was fine."

Droplets of water fell from my eyes. "I thought you weren't Class Monitor anymore."

He lowered his eyes, his cheeks coloring. "I'm not."

"Well, then, what's your hurry?" I grabbed a hand towel, drying my face and neck, making certain my eyebrows were flat. "Is there another new rule? You must all come to school an hour early to show respect for the Emperor? Or you're finally getting tired of church, too?"

"No." He looked up nervously, as if God might have heard my words. He kneaded his hands, that same irritating habit of Mother's. "I just need to get to school before—before someone else does."

Did the little runt like some girl? Already? That couldn't be. More likely he was helping the teacher collect homework papers or greeting the classmates as they came to school. The goody-two-shoes. I wondered if Mother would let me leave early, too.

"Who do you need to beat to school?" I looked at him in the mirror. His eyes met mine. "Who?"

"There's this boy in my class." He shuddered. "Mother says he's one of God's children."

I knew those code words. Mother and Father said it like a prayer. About the jerks who closed Father's church, about that fool of an Emperor, about anyone who did us wrong.

"Who is the *Manghal jarshik*?" I asked.

He-Dong didn't flinch, as he normally did when I cursed. Either he was growing up or this person really did deserve to be damned. Probably the latter.

"I tried Mother's advice, smiling every time I see him," He-Dong explained, his voice wobbling. "But, he still takes my lunch."

I turned to him. The runt was thinner than a broom handle. "Why do you let this jerk take your lunch?"

"I don't want to." His eyes brimmed with water. "That's why I'm going to try to get to school as early as I can. Perhaps the teacher will protect—"

"No." I threw my towel on the sink. "Don't rely on a Jap teacher. They're not your—" I looked at his trusting face in the mirror.

"They're not my what?" He-Dong asked.

I could think of dozens of examples of how the teachers could care less about us. It would crush the runt. He'd melt into a pool of tears on the bathroom floor and Mother would blame me. "Just tell the beggar who wants your lunch to go away. And don't smile. That's just stupid."

He-Dong rocked from foot to foot, his eyebrows set in a worried frown. I could see him trying to understand and failing.

"You *Manghal jarshik!*" I yelled, pointing a menacing finger at him. Then I relaxed and patted his shoulder. "You yell at the jerk just like that."

He nodded, taking in a big breath. He didn't look so sure. As if this was as confusing as a dog having puppies.

"Say it with me." I instructed to his image in the mirror. "*Manghal jarshik!*"

His lips mouthed the words. He nodded again. But his brow remained furrowed.

"Again. Louder."

"*Manghal jarshik!*" We called out together, although I could barely hear his little voice.

"That's it." I winked at his image in the mirror.

He wiped his hands over his eyes, brushing away his foolish tears. Then he put his shoulders back and turned to leave the bathroom. I heard his light footsteps on the stairs.

Perhaps the teacher will protect me. That would be a first. The teachers I knew were sacrificing my classmates left and right for their *noble cause.* Nishimura *Sensei* tried to convince Han-Joo that he could help out with the war, despite his bandaged foot. *A real hero doesn't feel pain,* that fool of a *sensei* had said. Then he'd turned around to complain about what savages the Americans were.

"Can you imagine?" Nishimura *Sensei* had thwacked his cane on the chalkboard yesterday even after the Principal had rung the end-of-school bell. "The American government ejecting poor Japanese civilians forcibly from areas where they've spent their entire lives? Treating them like criminals?"

"Too bad those American cowboys don't come here," I'd leaned back on my chair and whispered to Gong-Tae.

"Japan would never resort to such heinous acts." Nishimura *Sensei* shook his head. "We have a fundamental policy toward civilians in occupied areas, offering people all the freedoms possible."

"Liar," I whispered. Father certainly hadn't been given *all the freedom possible* to run his church.

Footsteps sounded on the stairs. But they were coming up, not going down. I would have guessed it was He-Dong coming back up to practice his bravery one more time. But the steps were too loud for him. I stepped out into the hallway.

"Your voice carries far." Mother stood at the top of the staircase, her chest rising up and down. "Your father is welcoming people for prayer and meditation." She whispered so fiercely I knew she was angry. "And you're up here cursing at your brother."

I closed my eyes and groaned. "But I wasn't—"

"Don't." Mother closed her eyes, gave a quick shake of her head. "Don't speak words you'll regret." Then she turned to go back down the steps. "Your Father has been ready to begin for several minutes."

I hurried to my room to get my bookbag. If Father had heard, he'd be furious. He wouldn't care that I'd been trying to help He-Dong. In fact, he wouldn't think of it as helping.

Stupid He-Dong. I remembered my disappointment when Father told me the little runt was born, and led me and He-Chul into Mother's room. That ugly little baby with his big fat head and wrinkled skin had taken my position as *mangne,* the youngest son. I wasn't the intelligent, respected eldest son like He-Chul. And I'd no longer be the spoiled baby. I was stuck in the middle…which is no position at all.

Why did I even bother with He-Dong? I should have just let him go off to school and hide behind the teacher or whatever he was planning to do. I looked out my bedroom window. Too bad I couldn't jump to the ground and sneak away in my stocking feet.

I took a deep breath and headed for the stairs. The wooden flooring felt unforgiving beneath my thin socks. Then again, maybe only Mother had heard me. She had awfully good hearing, waking when the rooster shook its feathers. Perhaps she had been standing near the steps and heard me talking to He-Dong. I had been talking, hadn't I? Not shouting.

I took my time walking down the steps. Relaxed. Not in a hurry. Not concerned. In the living room, Father sat in his rocking chair, the Bible open in his lap. A blur of black suits sat next to the window. I spotted a bunch of white skirts near the hall. The one saving grace was that I didn't see Myung-Hae or Purple Face's black school uniforms. No girls had witnessed my humiliation.

The runt sat next to Mother, biting his lip. He was probably praying for forgiveness and a million other sorries. That stupid brother of mine. I wanted to strangle him.

While everyone pretended not to hear me enter the room, Gong-Tae motioned for me to join him. He sat in the middle *row*, next to Mr. Yee.

Mr. Yee, perhaps to show his disapproval, did not budge when I tried to slip in next to Gong-Tae. So I stepped over the old geezer to a space next to the blacked-out window.

"Good idea," Gong-Tae mouthed to me, his thumbs up.

I wasn't sure if he was talking about my choice not to knock Mr. Yee over so I could sit where I wanted, the training I'd been giving He-Dong, or what. But this wasn't like our church. We couldn't whisper back and forth without everyone hearing. I couldn't even nudge or pinch him without everyone seeing. I sat down on the *ondol* floor. Unfortunately, I was in front of Mr. Im, who coughed on me, while Father's words fell on my head like cold rain, numbing my brain. I vaguely heard Father talking about the first thing God told Moses, the first commandment, that there should be no other god before Him. I'd heard the story before.

Instead of listening to Father drone on, I kept myself from falling asleep by thinking of Gong-Tae's predicament. I had come up with a couple of ideas. Have Gong-Tae study as a doctor's apprentice—and thus be some kind of a doctor— making him a suitable match for Dr. Lee's daughter. Or, have Father talk to Dr. Lee and suggest that his daughter's spiritual well-being was more important than anything else. I didn't have much hope for either of these plans. Gong-Tae wasn't that smart, and I already knew what Father would say, if he spoke to me at all. *It's in God's hands.* I didn't believe that. If everything was in God's hands, we should be enjoying a relaxing breakfast in our home instead of begging people to squish together on our floor. If I had the chance, I would point this out to Father.

"The Lord is My Light and Salvation." Father read from the bible. *"Whom should I fear?"*

I leaned forward, looked over at Gong-Tae and rolled my eyes. If we'd been in church I would have nudged him, whispering, "The Japs, Reverend Chai. The Japs."

Footsteps pounded up the steps and on our porch. A knock sounded. Father paused, holding up the Bible like it was a protective shield. The rest of us held our breath.

"Hello?" A female voice called. It sounded like Myung-Ja *uhmony.*

Mother stood and rushed to welcome this harmless caller. Still, we all sat up tall, straining to hear how many footsteps crossed the threshold, how many pairs of shoes were plunked into the entryway, how many voices filled the air. I again looked over at Gong-Tae. Huddled here in this small living room, it felt like we were playing a game of hide-and-find, and hoping the Japs wouldn't find us.

I heard the rustling of skirts and looked up. There was Mother and Myung-Hae *uhmony*. Behind them, in black school uniforms, stood Myung-Hae and Purple Face.

"I apologize for the cramped quarters." Mother whispered, but her voice carried in the small room.

Mother pointed to the few free spots on the women's side of the floor. And while it was technically the women's side—divided by a string—if Gong-Tae had reached out, he would have been able to touch Myung-Hae. Now he leaned forward and looked at me sidewise, with a huge grin on his face. I expected him to start wagging his tail.

"Let's bring some of our praises to the Lord." Father closed the Bible.

There was silence. What did we have to be thankful for? The Japs and their Emperor God taking over the world? No church? Sitting squashed together in our living room unable to breathe?

"Well, I was worried about not having enough food to prepare lunch yesterday." Gong-Tae *uhmony* coughed delicately into her handkerchief. "When I went searching through the garden, however, I discovered a giant tomato beneath a dead leaf."

"The Lord looks after us." Father nodded with enthusiasm. "Amen."

"Amen." Everyone echoed.

A small squeak sounded next to me. Gaseous Mr. Yee.

Amen, Mr. Yee, to that commentary on some damn tomato.

But the air soon filled with an odor that burned my nose so bad I opened my mouth to breathe. Mr. Im hacked behind me. Then I made the mistake of leaning over to look at Gong-Tae. His eyes were focused on the blacked-out window next to me, as if he looked hard enough he might be able to get to the other side and breathe fresh air. I bit my lip. My shoulders shook.

"He-Seung?" Father sat up tall in his rocking chair. "Did you have something to add?"

"I'm grateful for such..." I clamped down on my tongue, taking a deep breath through my nose, then regretting it. "Togetherness. A—" I opened my mouth to try another breath. I looked around at everyone, as though grateful for each. I spotted the runt, his hand over his mouth, his fingers pinching his nose. "A-amen."

"Amen." Everyone echoed.

I felt a finger on my back. Gong-Tae had reached around Mr. Yee. I snorted.

"I must say." Mr. Yee leaned forward, sending up another cloud of smelly air. "I'm usually grateful, but these past few days I've had a stomachache that just won't go away."

Gong-Tae poked me again. I wanted more than anything to roll around, slapping my hands on the ondol floor, kicking my legs and laughing out loud. My lower back ached, my stomach felt like it was bursting.

"It's good of you to bring this up." Deacon Nam wrinkled his nose. "I think we need to be more concerned." He gave his wife, In-Young, a long look. "With the preparation of the food we eat. Amen."

I let out a disgusted sigh, wishing I could fart loudly with as good timing as Mr. Yee. Deacon Nam's issues with his useless wife weren't God's business. Or ours. What we needed was for God to get rid of the Japs so we could have our own country, our own food back. Then we might be spared the aching stomach, the smelly air.

"I ask for guidance..." In-Young's voice was so small it sounded like a baby bird. "In becoming a good housewife like my dear sisters in the Lord." She looked at Min-Kook *uhmony* and Gong-Tae *uhmony* and Mother. "Amen."

"Amen," everyone echoed, her husband with particular vehemence.

"I also ask for guidance and wisdom." Myung-Hae *uhmony* put her hands together and bowed her head. I groaned. If all the women jumped on the housewife-guidance cart, this could go on forever. And all we really needed at this moment was some fresh air. "Guidance and wisdom as Myung-Hae leaves next week to work in a Japanese factory."

"What?" I gasped.

Gong-Tae reached over and grabbed onto my jacket. I leaned back and looked at him, expecting to see his mouth dropped open. Instead, he raised his eyebrows, nodding. Was this the *good idea* he'd mentioned when I first sat down?

"This is very brave," Father said.

"Amen," the group agreed, although not with the same enthusiasm they had over Gong-Tae's mother finding a tomato.

Gong-Tae's girl sat with her eyes closed, her hands folded in her lap. Purple Face also had her head down, but she had her hand on top of her sister's, clasping so tight her long thin fingers were white.

"Members helping the war effort will take some of the tension off the church," that idiot Deacon Nam said.

"Amen," everyone agreed, now with greater force.

"This is ridiculous," I said.

Gong-Tae pinched my back.

"He-Seung," Father's voice was filled with warning. He stared at me, waiting for me to bow my head and offer an "Amen."

But how could we sit here and praise Myung-Hae for going to help the same people responsible for closing Father's church, for making us all miserable?

Father gave up on me and put his hands to the ceiling. *"Tell the righteous it shall be well with them For they shall eat the fruit of their deeds. Woe to the wicked—"*

I stood, unable to listen even one more second. I stepped over smelly Mr. Yee. I ignored Gong-Tae's hand, his shake of the head, his voice in my head. *Walking out on a service? Your father will kill you.*

As I scooted between feet and knees and bottoms, I heard the sharp intake of breath. I felt all the parishioners' eyes on me. Father had stopped speaking. At the last minute, I remembered He-Dong saying, *I'm closest to the hall so I can leave early. Mother said it was fine.*

"School," I grunted, the word tasting acidic. I reached down and grabbed the little runt. I pushed his shoes and rucksack in his arms and dragged him out the door. I would be his personal escort.

"What's the hurry, Brother?" he asked when we got outside. He looked back at the house as if he'd left his prayer there.

How could I explain to the runt about Myung-Hae working for people who hated us? How could his little brain understand that Myung-Hae wasn't just going off to get a job which would bring more food on the table, but was going far away for maybe a long time? For a half a minute, I missed the eloquence of my older brother.

"I couldn't breathe in there anymore," I said. "Could you?"

"It did kind of stink." He-Dong said, still dragging his feet, looking back to the house. "Did Father signal we could leave?"

"You said you had to get to school early." I reached back, pulling him along. "Besides, Mr. Yee's signal was strong enough. In fact, I don't think he likes these morning gatherings."

"Well, next time, we could ask Mother to crack a window," He-Dong whispered.

This was another annoying habit of his. He would speak so quietly God wouldn't hear us. Or so He-Dong thought.

"If Father's forced to continue these home services, we need to get rid of the fartbag," I shouted just to annoy him back.

He-Dong looked around and whispered more urgently, "Or we could try making him some anti-smelling medicine."

I laughed, despite my annoyance. "What an idea."

"Isn't it?" He smiled. "This new kid at school showed me a reader about the American scientist Mr. Benjamin Franklin who tried to come up with such a thing."

"He-Seung!" Gong-Tae called from behind. "Wait!"

I glanced back, watching him run, stopping twice to shuffle into his shoes. Wait for what? To hear him make excuses about why it was a good idea for his girl to help our family's biggest enemy?

"Should we wait?" He-Dong asked.

"You were saying something about a scientist?" I pushed He-Dong forward. "Something about inventing a fart pill."

"He didn't invent it. He just thought about it." He-Dong looked from me back to Gong-Tae, his eyebrows twitching with anxiety. He rubbed his hands together. "I remember one funny line from the reader. *Imagine the ease and comfort every man living might feel by discharging freely the wind from his bowels. Especially if it be converted into perfume.*"

"He-Seung," Gong-Tae called again.

I leaned down and picked up a stick. I didn't want to hear Gong-Tae's noise. "Your school sounds a lot more interesting than when I was a kid."

He-Dong looked thrilled for just a moment, then his chubby face clouded.

"Don't worry about the bully." I handed him the stick. "You're ready for him now. I want you to practice what we learned this morning."

"About the Lord being our light and salva—"

"No, runt," I said. "Pretend the cherry trees are that bully who keeps taking your lunch. I want to see you wave that stick and yell at each tree. *Manghal Jarshik.*"

He-Dong stood there, his mouth hanging open, staring at the branch like he'd never seen one before.

"Well, go on," I said.

"He-Seung!" Gong-Tae rushed up in front of us, his chest heaving from the exertion.

"In fact." I looked away from Gong-Tae. "Why don't you practice it on Gong-Tae? *Manghal—*"

"Stop it." Gong-Tae got right in my face.

"Oh, so now you're giving orders." Blood rushed to my head. I flexed my fists.

"Everything isn't good or bad, right or wrong." He stepped back.

"How can you say that?" I pushed his shoulder. "This is like kicking my father in the nuts."

"Dr. Lee was being considered for a government position—"

"He's a doctor." I pushed Gong-Tae again. "Not a politician."

He-Dong waved the stick in front of us, like it was a white flag or something. "Do you see a spider on here?" he asked.

"Yeah, I don't get it either." Gong-Tae shrugged, ignoring the stick and my silly brother. "Only that the job has something do to with helping the government. And Dr. Lee's loyalty was, well—"

I stopped pushing. "Questioned?"

Gong-Tae looked away. His color deepened.

When would Father see that his enemy wasn't the devil? His enemy was the Japs. There could not exist a world with both God's children and Japs. "What does this have to do with Myung-Hae?"

"One of the officers suggested that if Myung-Hae worked for the army, it would show the family's loyalty," Gong-Tae said.

I felt my nose wrinkling as if I'd just smelled Mr. Yee's expulsion. I covered my eyes, as much to block out Gong-Tae's hopeful face as to not have to look at He-Dong waving his stick around like a girl dancing with a colored ribbon.

"If you think about it, it's a great plan." Gong-Tae put his arm around my shoulder. "Thanks to her, her father will get this great job. He will be so grateful that, when she comes home in a few months, she can ask for a favor in return."

"Are you the favor?" I shook my head at him.

"Don't I look like a favor?" He stood back, hands on his hips.

"Never in a million years."

"You say that now," Gong-Tae said. "But just wait until you get home and your father decides not to kill you."

I cocked my head, raising my eyebrows.

He nudged me. "I told him we all needed to hurry to school early today and you had forgotten to mention this."

"That sounds like a sin against all sins." I mocked his mother's voice.

He blushed, but only a little this time. "You can thank me, the favor. Anytime now."

I nodded my thanks, a short nod. However my brain felt numb, and this time it had nothing to do with Bible passages.

Japan captures capitol of Burma (Myanmar), attacks New Guinea with the goal of establishing a base of operations in Australia, and fights for control of the Dutch East Indies (Indonesia) —March 1942

Wednesday, March 11, 1942—same day

Baby He-Dong

A few students stood by the flagpole. Kee-Wok, of course, wasn't there. Fortunes of all fortunes, the Class Monitor Bon-Hwa hadn't arrived yet either. If my brother would leave, I could go to the flagpole and pretend for a moment that I was still the leader.

"Where is this bully?" He-Seung looked around, straightening his shoulders, cracking his neck.

"I don't see him." I looked around, tapping my stick as if I knew how to take care of things now.

I never worried about my eldest brother being near my friends, my school. He-Chul was intelligent and thoughtful. People admired his brilliance and thus treated me better. With He-Seung, though, I felt myself holding my breath, hoping he wouldn't do something embarrassing.

"Hey." Ih-Duk rushed over. Had he come to keep me company or had he just not found any interesting spiders on his way to school?

"Is this him?" He-Seung grabbed Ih-Duk.

"No, no." I didn't know what to call Ih-Duk. He was interesting, but he'd also gotten me in trouble with the teacher that first day. If it weren't for him, I'd probably still be Class Monitor. Besides, he wasn't a Christian. "This is a new—"

"I'm his new friend." Ih-Duk rubbed his arm where He-Seung had grabbed him. Then Ih-Duk bowed to my brother.

He-Seung nodded, giving Ih-Duk a once-over. His glance paused at Ih-Duk's shiny buttons, the billowing arms of his jacket which suggested a weak, bean-curd body. I prayed He-Seung wouldn't say anything.

"Well, where is the bastard?" He-Seung looked around.

"He's not here yet," Ih-Duk answered.

He-Seung looked back at Ih-Duk, reassessing this new kid. "Well, I can't wait all day. When he gets here…" He-Seung spoke to Ih-Duk rather than me. "You tell him he's playing with fire, understand?"

I furrowed my eyebrows as if listening intently to He-Seung's words, not that it mattered. He went to join Gong-Tae. They were already arguing about armies and factories. I cringed watching them, sure that Ih-Duk would think me just as quick-tempered.

"I wish I had an older brother," Ih-Duk said, watching the two of them push one another down the road.

I didn't know what was so great about it. He-Seung had shouted *Mangal Jarshik* for the parishioners to hear, yanked me from my prayer, and called out *Where is the bastard*? I repeated what my father always said about He-Seung. "He's kind of a hothead."

"Is that why he wanted me to threaten stuff about playing with fire?" Ih-Duk asked, motioning for us to hurry to the flagpole.

"I don't know." I shrugged, dropping the stick. "We probably don't have to do that."

We got in our positions by the flagpole. Kee-Wok showed up at the last minute, but he was so far behind me I couldn't even feel him thinking about grabbing my rice and fried egg. For once I had my lunch and my homework in hand as I walked to class behind the sloppy Monitor.

"This morning, before we practice our characters," Ito *sensei* said, standing in front of her desk, looking at us, "I want to teach you a new ritual."

All sixty-four of us shuffled in our seats. Rituals were fun, like receiving packets of money for New Year's. Or silly, like the rabbit-hopping song Mother had me sing on the long walk to market.

"San toki, toki-ya urdero kanunya." Ih-Duk leaned forward and sang softly in Korean. Little Mountain rabbit, where are you going?

"Shh," I said more sharply than I intended. Obviously he was thinking of the same ritual as I. Still, I didn't want the teacher to hear him. I nudged his arm, smiling to take the edge off.

"Watch me," Ito *Sensei* said. *"Tenno Heika, banzai."* She raised her arms toward the ceiling. *Imperial Emperor. Live for Ten Thousand Years!*

She called out this wish three times. Each time when she asked for eternal life for the Emperor, I thought of Father's church. People who came to worship each week always raised their hands to heaven crying out about how happy they were to be children of God.

"Now, you try." Ito *Sensei* turned to us.

I pretended to say the words, instead praying to God. *Dear God, Live Forever.* The words matched the timing perfectly. I raised my arms as if I were doing a stretching exercise, just as He-Seung would have done.

Ito *Sensei* asked Bon-Hwa to lead the class. But he was incapable of saying the words and moving his hands at the right time. For once I didn't look down on him, but was pleased that he was so bad at his job.

"This is a very simple—yet important—sign of respect for our Father, the Emperor." Ito *Sensei* frowned at us. "Can I get a volunteer to show everyone how to do it right?"

Normally, I would have shot my hand into the air. I waited for any and every small opportunity to lead the class. Now, I put my head down, hoping the *Sensei* would catch someone else's eye.

"I know who can do it best." I heard Kee-Wok's voice, his gleeful tone. I knew, before I even looked, that he had his finger pointed at me. "Our ex-class monitor."

Ito *Sensei* nodded, walking over to my desk. "An excellent idea."

The Emperor was certainly a very nice man—he always sent us red rubber balls. But this felt wrong. Just this morning Father had preached to us about what Moses said, that we should not worship any other Gods. This was worshipping.

"Well?" Ito *Sensei* tapped her cane on my desk.

"*T-tenno Heika…*" My tongue dribbled over the words *Imperial Emperor*. I could not finish this praise. The class giggled.

"What's wrong with you?" Ito *Sensei* nudged my arm with the end of her cane. "I expect you to say the words like they're engraved on your heart, not trip over them like you can't remember."

"I can do it." Ih-Duk called out, waving his hand in case *Sensei* didn't recognize his heavily-accented Japanese.

The *Sensei* turned away from me, concentrating on Ih-Duk's pronunciation, his posture, his timing. He performed the ritual to perfection. She nodded, happy at last.

I clasped my hands together underneath my desk. *Thank you, God. Thank you, Ih-Duk.*

Over 200,000 Asian women and European POWS conscripted to serve as sex slaves *(Comfort Women)* to the Japanese military. —1942-45.

Saturday, April 3, 1942—three weeks later

He-Seung

I sat naked on a small wooden stool at the public bath. Although we had a white porcelain tub in our bathroom, water was precious. Mother insisted we come here to bathe at least once a month. She and He-Dong were on the other side in the women-and-baby section. Normally Gong-Tae and I came together.

There was a small changing area, a washing area with a row of spigots, and the soaking area which held two large wooden baths filled with clean hot water. The air was thick and humid, making my rash itch.

On my left, a wrinkly old man kneeled with his hands under the running water, cleaning his nails. On my right, two men took turns scrubbing each other's backs. I wondered if Gong-Tae and I would be like that when we got to be old farts. I poured a bucket of warm water on my body. Then, taking out the sliver of soap from my washcloth, I soaped my legs.

I didn't get to see much of Gong-Tae outside of class these days. He hadn't come to play soccer lately. He hadn't shown up for Father's Wednesday prayer meetings. Then again, not many people came anymore. Dr. Lee's family had stopped coming. Min-Kook *uhmony* and her husband, Deacon Mah. Mr. Yee. They all were suddenly otherwise engaged or ill.

I wondered if my old friend Jim and his family were suffering the same problems. Were Christians hated in California? Was Jim being asked to join the army?

It was strange to think of Jim. Two years ago, he sat on the stool next to me, albeit embarrassed and in his underwear, trying not to look around at all the naked men. Two years ago we were neighbors, friends even. Now we were official enemies. At least our countries were. Father said he wasn't allowed to post letters to Reverend Thomas anymore.

"What's so funny?" Gong-Tae swatted me on the shoulder with his washcloth.

I felt a rush of relief seeing his crooked smile. At least he hadn't forgotten me altogether. "I was just thinking of Jim."

"How shocked he was to sit naked with the rest of the city?" Gong-Tae looked at the coots around us.

"Yeah. After sitting naked with the soybean seller, I don't think he ever went to the market again." I splashed some water at him. "What's your excuse? Why have you been hiding?"

The two old men next to us stood to move further away.

Gong-Tae took on of their vacated stools. He turned the water on and filled his bucket. "I think I pulled a hamstring."

"Doing what?" I asked. "Running to catch the mailman?"

He scrubbed his neck, then paused. "It feels wrong to go out and play knowing Myung-Hae is off working hard for us."

"Eeww." I splashed more water on him. "You're starting to sound like an old geezer."

The back scrubbers and the nail cleaner, perhaps trying to escape us altogether, headed for the bath.

"You know the last story she told me?" Gong-Tae asked.

"David and Goliath?" I suggested, motioning for us to go to the hot bath.

"No." He frowned.

He dipped his toes in the water, his calves flexing. I always wished to be half as strong.

"We were walking outside in the park just before she left." He stepped into the bath, sinking beneath the hot water. "She pointed out the stars. Do you know the story of the Princess and the Cow herder?"

I shrugged. Was this one of Father's Bible stories that I'd missed? "I don't think—"

"I'd never heard it either." Gong-Tae sighed. "It's—"

"A lovely story." The old Nail Cleaner looked over, putting his washcloth on his head. "About the star Jingnyeo, the beautiful daughter of the heavenly lord, who could have any husband she wished."

One of the back scrubbers, a man with bushy eyebrows, added. "Instead of choosing some wealthy man, the Princess fell in love with a lowly cow herder."

"Yes," said his friend. "The heavenly lord allowed the wedding, as the cow herder was kind and intelligent."

I rolled my eyes at Gong-Tae. But he was smiling, happy that all of these strangers knew the same story.

"But." The Nail Cleaner winked at us. "When the two young lovers were together they had such fun they never did any work."

Gong-Tae nodded as if he were remembering Myung-Hae telling him the story. I went up next to him and batted my eyelashes. He cupped his hands together, scooped some hot water and splashed me.

"The heavenly lord got so angry." The Nail Cleaner lifted his wrinkly arms up to the sky as if he saw the lovely princess and not just a moldy wooden ceiling. "He sent his daughter to the eastern end of the universe and his new son-in-law to the western end, only allowing them to meet only once a year in July when the Milky Way forms a bridge across the sky."

Gong-Tae watched the old man's arms, as if he could see Myung-Hae. My old friend missed his girl. He was turning batty.

"Maybe I remember some kind of story like this," I said. "Isn't there a holiday or something for it?"

"July 7th," said the Nail Cleaner.

"I don't want to only see her once a year," Gong-Tae said.

"I don't even see the connection here," I said.

Gong-Tae dipped his washcloth in the water and draped it over his face. "I'm thinking of going to the army office."

I stood, my rash itching, my blood itching. "What do you expect the army to do? Offer you a position in the factory right down the hall from where she works?"

"No." Gong-Tae pulled the washcloth from his face and tossed it at me. "But, well, maybe."

"Right." I wrung out the cloth, balled it up and and threw it back to him.

The three men sat forward, as if we were a small gathering of friends.

"I just want to be near her." He passed me the 'ball.'

"Well that's about the dumbest way to go about it I've ever heard," I said. "What about your future?"

"Yeah," Bushy Eyebrows spoke up. "Those Japanese soldiers can be…" He looked around to make sure he wasn't overheard. "Well, they'd think no more of slicing off someone's head than cutting down a sweet persimmon."

"They lay the enemy on sharpened bamboo sticks as punishment," said the Nail Cleaner. "They torture men by putting toothpicks under their fingernails."

"They cut off the enemy's male parts or tongue or both," said Bushy Eyebrows.

We all sank our male parts further beneath the protection of the water. These men spoke of things I'd never have dreamed of. Were they real or part of another fairytale?

"I can't just sit around and do nothing." Gong-Tae said, his whispered voice sounding as though he were shouting at us.

"Give her some time to get settled." The Nail Cleaner rested his wrinkly arms across the back of the bath.

"Yes," I agreed. "Some time to start sending you flowery letters with her address about the stars and other nonsense."

"She may just be down the road for all we know," said Bushy Eyebrows as if even he knew Myung-Hae.

"And then you'll have worried about joining the army for nothing," added his friend.

"Well—"

"And if you go, you know I'll have to," I said.

"What?" Gong-Tae laughed. "And leave He-Dong alone to fend off the bullies?"

I stared at him. "Wouldn't that be a disaster?"

He swatted me on the shoulder again with his washcloth, now wet and cold. "Well, I just wanted you to know I'm thinking about it."

"Why don't you think about coming out to play soccer instead? It might help your hamstrings."

"Yes," said the Nail Cleaner. "You look like you play some mighty good ball. I used to play soccer when I was a young one. I could score a goal from across the play yard."

"We played in our bare feet, rain or shine," Bushy Eyebrows said.

While the old farts compared their prowess from the good old days, I stepped out of the bath. Everyone had acted like Myung-Hae's job was a simple thing. No big deal. Amen. My gut feeling had told me otherwise. It had been more than two weeks, and there was still no word from Myung-Hae. Now, my gut was warning me again to keep an eye on Gong-Tae or I'd lose him, too.

*There is virtually no other country in the world other than Japan having
such a superb and lofty mission bearing world significance. World
history is moving largely and impressively. The ideal of the construction
of a world of moral principles based on the historic mission of Japan
have been on a fair way toward fruition through the construction of a
new East Asiatic order.*
—**Japanese Education Ministry, early 1940s**

Saturday, April 18, 1942—two weeks later

Baby He-Dong

All week, Ito *Sensei* had been talking about going to Mt. Nam San. I
assumed it was to see the blossoms on the cherry trees. Mt. Nam San had
the most Cherry Blossom trees in the city, all of which were now in full
bloom. Ih-Duk told me, though, that it was also to visit the Shinto Shrine.

I'd asked Mother if I should stay at home on the day the school went
for the outing. She told me it was best to participate with the class. But
maybe she hadn't really heard me. Sometimes she just said things without
too much thinking.

I'd asked He-Seung. He said that it was a fun hike, to count the number
of stairs to the top of the mountain. There were always more on the way up
than on the way down. He said that the shrine held 800 gods, and to see if I
could count that many. I couldn't understand why neither Mother nor
Brother was too worried.

This morning, I awakened early and hurried to find Father. When I
went downstairs, I was happy to spot him sitting in the rocking chair. I
walked into the living room as quietly as possible, so as not to disturb his
thinking. I kept my eyes down. It wasn't until I stood next to Father that I
heard another voice.

"We haven't heard a thing from her." It was Dr. Lee. Mother said he
looked older these days, but he looked the same to me, with cold fingers
that would grab my wrist, piercing dark eyes that would scare the
sicknesses away. He cleared his throat, like he had something stuck there.
"She's been gone 29 days."

They must be talking about Myung-Hae. She'd left to work in the
Japanese factories a long time ago. Everyone had been so excited when
she left, talking about more food and a greater future, a new job for Dr.
Lee. Now, though, he didn't look so happy. I didn't think it was a good
time for me to talk to Father, so I bowed to them as I walked through to the
kitchen.

Mother fluffed the cooked rice in the pot on the stove. She dished a few scoops into my metal bowl.

"Do you think Dr. Lee will stay long?" I asked.

"I don't know." Mother handed me my bowl. "Why?"

"No reason, I guess." I used my chopsticks to shovel the rice to my mouth.

However, the more I thought about visiting a shrine, the slower I chewed. What if God struck me down in front of the class and let the devil poke me with his fork and throw me into his fire pit? The warm rice kernels tasted like glue. The thought of offending God made me want to throw up. The thought of the devil poking me into his flames made my heart bang so loud my chest hurt.

"*Aiya.*" My rice bowl was jerked from my hands.

I looked up to see He-Seung standing in front of me with my bowl of rice. How long had he been standing there watching me? Where had Mother gone?

"I asked you a question." He-Seung nodded toward the living room. "Did you hear them talking about Myung-Hae or just—you know— praying and stuff?"

I looked at my bowl of rice which he held dangling above my head. What was the big deal about Myung-Hae? "I don't know."

"You mean you haven't been standing here listening?" He-Seung took a bite of my rice, a grain falling on my face. "What are you still doing here then? Why aren't you off to school?"

Mother came back inside, an empty pot in her hand.

"I don't know." I thought about our possible outing to Mt. Nam San. I looked down at my stocking feet. "I don't feel so good."

Mother set down the pot, dried her hands on her *cheemar,* and came over to feel my cheek. She cocked her head to the side. "You don't have a fever."

"It's my stomach." I leaned over. "And my heart."

"You've got the Christian cold, too?" He-Seung snorted.

Was there a cold that only we Christians were getting? Why hadn't Mother warned me?

"The only difference between your cold and the Christian one is that your calves will hurt when Father hears your nonsense." He-Seung shoveled the rest of my rice in his mouth. Then he dropped my bowl on the counter, the chopsticks clattering to the floor.

"He-Seung!" Mother hurried to clean the mess.

"What's going on in there?" Father called out, his warning that he and Dr. Lee could hear us.

"Ask the runt," He-Seung shouted back. Then he walked out of the kitchen. The front door slammed.

"Oh, dear." Mother shook her head at Brother's thunder. She ran her palm over her eyes.

I imagined Father standing, his face flushed as he apologized to Dr. Lee for He-Seung's behavior.

What had I done? I shouldn't have made up this silly story about feeling not so good—this lie—which just made He-Seung loud, Father angry, and Mother sad. God would get angry, too. "Mother, I'm sorry—"

"Let me get Dr. Lee." Mother put the back of her hand to my forehead, then my cheeks.

I could imagine Dr. Lee's piercing eyes looking through me and seeing no sickness to scare away. "Maybe I just need to, uh, lie down for a bit."

Mother was so flustered about He-Seung, she didn't insist. She loaded a tray with tea for Father and Dr. Lee, then pushed me off toward her room. "You go rest."

Mother's room smelled of talc. Normally a comforting smell, now it made my throat feel thick. I got on my knees, held my hands together and closed my eyes tight.

Dear God,

Forgive me for not saying true things to Mother and He-Seung. I won't ever do it again. I'm not trying to make excuses, but I couldn't visit the shrine and show respect to another God. Or 800 of them. Please don't be angry. Please don't send me to hell. Please. Amen.

I opened one eye at a time. There was no yawning pit of hell waiting to swallow me. No bed of spiky burning nails ready to poke me. No Devil with horns reaching out to grab me.

Thank you, God.

A tingling sensation made me jump. Something brown crawled across my leg. I brushed it away. The spider scurried across the floor toward the wall. I inched forward, peering close to the little brown fellow. Was this a Sedentary Spider?

I lay down and watched the little brown spider, wondering who Kee-Wok would steal food from today. I wasn't good at smiling or yelling curse words. But, getting to school early and finding spiders worked most of the time. I'd only lost my lunch to him twice this past week.

If only I was bigger, I wouldn't have to worry about Kee-Wok. Next year, I'd be big. I'd move up to the men's floor and sleep with He-Seung. Then I'd be strong. Watch out, Kee-Wok. I kicked at the air, gave one punch, then another. The spider scurried up the side of the wall. That's how I wanted Kee-Wok to react to me.

The spider continued to the ceiling. How could a spider walk on the side of the wall, even upside down, without falling? Maybe the little fellow had sticky paste on the bottom of his long legs, like the smooshed rice Mother used to glue stamps to the letters she mailed to He-Chul in Manchukuo. I hadn't seen any white stuff hanging off the spider's legs, though. He didn't seem to be having trouble pulling his feet up, which would be the case if the bottoms were sticky.

I flopped on my stomach. My stomach which didn't hurt. I bet Ito *Sensei* would know what made spiders stick to the wall. Why did she have to make the class do stupid rituals and visit a shrine? Why couldn't we talk of insects instead? Or Ih-Duk would know. He knew things like that.

Yesterday he'd told me about another experiment by that fart-curing scientist. Apparently, this Mr. Franklin noticed how armies of ants found their way to his sticky-sweet molasses even when he moved the jar to different spots in the room. So he shook all but one of the ants out and hung the jar by a string. He watched the one ant which had been left behind crawl out of the jar, up the string, then down the wall to find the others. Not long after, the rest of the ants were eating from the same jar again, proving those ants must have their own language. Ih-Duk and I wanted to try the experiment. In fact, I'd promised I would ask my mother if we could use our honey jar.

I got up and went looking for her. I would explain the truth. I would tell her I had said sorry to God. Surely she wouldn't have to talk about it with Father. He was probably still angry about He-Seung slamming the door. Besides, Mother always said he had enough on his mind.

Nobody was in the living room. Surely Dr. Lee had left and Father had gone up to his study. I looked in the kitchen, but Mother wasn't there. I stepped out on the front porch. Perhaps she'd gone to the market.

Dark clouds covered the sky, like big blankets, as if the sun had decided to stay home from school today, too. Perhaps God would make it rain on all the students who dared visit the shrine.

The broom stood next to the door. It was my job to sweep the porch clean each day. Perhaps if I swept the porch, Mother would know I was feeling better. I wouldn't have to explain. I picked up the broom and put the bristles to the floor.

Footsteps crunched up the dirt path behind me. I wasn't quite finished with the porch yet, though. I hurried to sweep the last of the leaves and dust away. Mother would be pleased. Or would she? She didn't call out to me as usual. I backed my way down the five steps. One step. Two steps.

The sound of someone clearing his throat made me stop. Had Dr. Lee returned to check on me? I turned to look.

Two Japanese policemen stood on the bottom step dressed in dark blue uniforms. I had seen policemen on the streets but never this close. They wore blue caps with visors. They each had big black pistols at their hips. I felt a tightness in my throat. Had they come to arrest me for lying? I bowed.

The big man stepped forward. He had thick cheeks, like he got a lot of rice. "Is your father Yamamoto Hirosaki?"

Father's real name was Chai Suk-Mo. But the Japanese called him Mr. Yamamoto. "Yes," I said.

"Where is he?" the big man asked, his speech blunt.

Maybe they wouldn't take me away, but would just tell Father that I was nothing more than a faker, a liar, a sinner. I bowed again, hoping to prove that I wasn't so bad.

"B-b-boy." The words tripped from the other officer's mouth in broken Korean as if I had not understood the first officer. As if I never went to school. "Wh-wh-where's your father?"

This man's voice stopped at the beginning of his words the same way I got stuck on saying *Emperor Live Forever* at school. Was he nervous about speaking a foreign language or about talking to Father? Father could look scary and had a big voice. His voice would get even bigger when he realized I was a faker, a liar, a sinner. "He's—"

"Go get him." The big man thrust his chin up. An order, not a request. He cleared his throat and spit on my clean wooden step. "Obviously closing the damn church wasn't enough."

A strange feeling tingled down my insides which had nothing to do with my being a faker, a liar, a sinner. I looked past them up the path. I wished I were like an ant and had a secret language that could call Mother home quickly, or I could close my eyes and pray and these men would disappear. I set the broom against the side of the house and ran inside to find Father.

He sat at his desk, the Bible open in front of him. His glasses were perched on top of his head. He massaged his eyes.

I stood at the doorway and bowed. "Excuse me, Father."

"He-Dong." He put his glasses back on and looked at me. "Is your stomach better?"

I put my hands to my mid-section. "About that—"

"That's good." He put his glasses back on and picked up his pencil. "Can you go down and get me a glass of water? I'm so thirsty. I was blessed with lots of *kimchee* this morning, but not enough rice."

"Father." My voice wobbled. "There are two men downstairs who want to talk to you."

"Already?" Father looked up.

I was so relieved Father was expecting these two officers. I let out a big sigh. Maybe that big man and his nervous friend just didn't know how to behave. Maybe they had come to Father for advice.

"That's Reverend Park." Father smiled. "And one of the deacons from his church. Will you tell them I'll be done in just a—"

"These men…" I looked over my shoulder as if the rude men had followed me up the stairs. "…are police."

His eyes widened. He took off his glasses, folding them and setting them on his desk. Then he shook his head.

"I could tell them you're busy preparing for an expected guest," I said, although my stomach cramped at the idea.

"No, son." He closed his Bible and let his hand rest on the black leather cover. "I've been expecting them, as well." He stood. "Where's your mother?"

"Maybe at the market," I said.

"Why don't you go back to your room and rest?" He patted my head, as he walked past me down the stairs.

I wanted nothing more than to return to observe the spider on my wall. But I couldn't leave Father. I followed him to the front door.

The policemen stood outside on the porch, their hands resting on their guns. I waited for them to bow to my great father. Instead, Father bowed to them. "What can I do for you?"

"We need you to come with us," the big man said.

"I was just in the middle of some work—"

"Your-your-your work can wait." The nervous talker moved his hands from his gun towards a pair of handcuffs at his waist.

"Is it so urgent?" Father's voice shook.

I'd never heard Father's voice shake. Not even when he stood before all those people on Sunday. He was King of the community.

"Get your father's shoes," the big man ordered me.

I waited for Father to explode. To tell these disrespectful officers to leave and not come back. Instead, Father kept his head bowed.

I grabbed Father's black leather shoes from the rack beside the door. The black leather shoes that he wore each Sunday when he preached to hundreds of people. The black leather shoes he wore when he went visiting church members who loved him. Why were these men treating him worse than the dirt on the soles? I set the shoes down in front of Father. Pressure built up behind my eyelids.

"Good boy," the big man nodded, as if I were an obedient dog.

I knelt before Father and tied his shoelaces, my hands trembling. Father leaned down and covered my hands with his. His palms were damp, but big and strong.

"Hurry up." The big man shifted from one foot to the next.

Father gave my hands a squeeze. Then he stood and walked out the door. I followed, wanting to go with him all the way to wherever they were going. But at the bottom of the porch steps, the big man turned. "Your father will be fine with us."

Father walked between the two policemen. Anyone seeing them would think they were on a walk, perhaps out admiring the cherry blossoms. But looking closer you could see that they all kept their eyes on the road. The nervous talker kept his hand on his gun.

My knees trembled. An angry breeze slapped me in the face. A drop of rain fell. What had I done? I could imagine He-Seung yelling at me. *You idiot! Why weren't you resting? Why didn't you tell the damn Japs to go away?*

He-Seung would have protected Father. He wouldn't have let these strangers treat Father like dirt and bully him into going somewhere. He would have taken his slingshot and fired until the Japanese men ran away.

I should have stayed on the *eebul* with the spider. No. I should never have pretended to be sick in the first place. I shouldn't have sinned.

All the prisoners (of war) have a very happy life. They are grateful to the
Japanese Government for the just and good treatment accorded them.
—**Domei, Japanese official news agency, 1940s**

Saturday, April 18, 1942—same day

Mother (*Uhmony*)

I carried a tray to my boys in the living room. I moved slowly, focusing on the three bowls of steaming rice, three bowls of miso soup, a dish of *kimchee*, and the broiled mackerel that Mrs. Byun, the fish seller, had given me from her private stash this morning. But while my body moved forward, my mind replayed the past. I could see myself coming up the path, He-Dong crying. *The police took Father. The police took Father.*

For the millionth time that day my chest felt tight as I thought of all the time I'd wasted at the market listening to the soy bean woman talk about her unhelpful husband, the pot seller describing her *kimchee* jars, the fish lady complaining about the Japanese requisitioning all the fresh food.

I should have just stayed at home with He-Dong. Then I would have been here when the policemen knocked. I don't think I could have done anything. But at least I would have been here.

"Aren't we going to wait for Father?" He-Dong looked out the window into the darkness.

"Fool!" He-Seung grabbed his comic book and hit He-Dong over the head. Why were He-Seung's words always so heavy? Especially tonight.

"But—" He-Dong looked to me for help. "Father will be angry if we eat without him."

Their voices sounded like jars clanging in my brain, threatening to break. Min-Kook *uhmony,* who had come over this afternoon, said this incident might take time. She told me of a man imprisoned a week for keeping his Rose of Sharon bush instead of planting a Cherry Blossom tree. Still, He-Dong was only a child. It wasn't unreasonable—certainly not foolish—for him to believe that his father had already been gone with the police long enough. I felt the same. I couldn't imagine what we'd do without my dear for a whole week. My head hurt.

I placed the dishes on the table, each one feeling too large in my small hands. Then I knelt down and closed my eyes. My eyelids felt so heavy. "Please, He-Seung. Please. Say the prayer."

"Dear God." He-Seung sighed. "Bring Father home safe. Amen."

Was that all my second son could think of to say? Even little He-Dong kept his eyes closed tight, whispering words into his clasped hands.

In my head, I heard my eldest son's strong intelligent voice taking over. *Thank you, Lord, our Provider and Protector, for watching after our father, for keeping him safe, for giving us this precious food. Please show the policeman Your grace and understanding. Protect our father from cruelty. Bring him home—*

"Hmmm, delicious." He-Seung smacked his lips.

I stared at my bowl of rice. The metal chopsticks looked cold and foreign. These chopsticks had been a wedding gift from my in-laws. I remembered how I'd so wanted to impress my new husband, rushing back and forth from the kitchen serving my best dishes. On the second night of our marriage, as I put a dish of rice in front of my dear, he put his hand over mine.

"Sit with us." He handed me these chopsticks. "Let's eat together."

"What?" My father-in-law choked, spitting bits of rice in my face like hail. He stabbed at my dear's hand with his chopsticks. "Have you gone mad?"

So much had happened since then with my in-laws, the church, our children. Still, my dear and I had always prayed together, always ate together. I wondered if my dear could feel me praying for him all afternoon. Praying for him now.

With my eyes closed, I could still imagine my dear sitting in the rocking chair, his glasses perched on his nose as he read from the Bible. *"Blessed are the meek, for they shall inherit the Earth. Blessed are those who hunger and thirst for righteousness, for they shall be filled. Blessed are the merciful, for they shall obtain mercy."* Was my dear obtaining mercy?

"Mother?" He-Dong tapped me on the arm. "Aren't you going to eat?"

"Of course, Little One." I looked at the food in front of me, listening to the ticking of the grandfather clock, the sound of He-Seung's clicking chopsticks, the beating of my heart. I could imagine my dear lifting his bowl of rice, his eyes finding mine.

A knock sounded at the front door. He-Dong jumped to his feet, his face flooded with relief. He-Seung dropped his chopsticks, pushing He-Dong out of the way as he rushed to answer the door. My dear would have used his key. Unless he'd been so badly beaten he couldn't manage. Perhaps it was another well-wisher. Min-Kook *uhmony* had been by already. So had In-Young, dear child.

"Boys," a deep voice at the door said. "Can you help an old man?"

My throat felt thick. It wasn't my dear.

An old man in disheveled clothing stood at the door. He held his dirty hand out, his hand shaking up and down. His feet were bare. His eyes were covered with a white film.

"Can you help an old man?" He asked again when we didn't respond. "All my children have gone off to fight in the Imperial War."

"Yeah?" He-Seung sneered. "Well our father was just arrested by those people your children are helping."

"I'm sorry." The old man nodded his head, putting his hand down.

I pulled He-Seung away. "I'm sorry for my son's behav—"

He-Seung slammed the door before I could say more. He returned to the table and I followed. I took my bowl of rice and added a small portion of fish.

"What are you doing?" He-Seung looked up, a grain of rice dangling from his lip.

Even if my dear wasn't here, and He-Seung was now the man of the family, I could not abide this. "That's no way to talk to an elderly gentleman."

I returned to the front door, looking for the man. I spotted him not far down the path, his shoulders hunched over with disappointment.

"Come," I beckoned.

I held out the bowl, and he sprinted up to the porch like a runner in a race. He cupped his dirty, swollen hands together and held them up to receive the food.

"God bless you," I said.

"Who blesses me?" The old man took a moment to look up from the food.

"God," I said. "God blesses you."

"Thank God and thank you." The old man bowed again and again, his eyes on the food, a string of drool falling from his lips. As soon as he turned away, he brought his hands to his mouth and shoveled the food down.

"Why did you do that?" He-Seung slammed the door again. "It's not as if we have lots to eat."

"We have enough." I hoped the small amount I'd given the old man would fill his stomach for a while. "Besides that man is someone's father. If your father showed up somewhere hungry, wouldn't you want others to help him?"

"Do you think Father is somewhere being hungry?" He-Dong tugged on my skirt.

"Now that old man will go tell all his friends." He-Seung batted his brother's hand and question away. "And we'll have every beggar in town knocking at our door."

"Then you better hurry up and finish your meal." I patted his shoulder.

"Mother?" He-Dong grabbed onto my skirt again.

"No, He-Dong." I led him back to the table. "Your Father's fine." I choked on the words, a salty burning sensation filling my throat. I swallowed. "God is watching after him."

"If this is God's idea of watching." He-Seung snorted. "Then—"

"He-Seung," I dropped my bowl with a clatter loud enough to interrupt him. I wasn't the disciplinarian in the family. That was the man's role. But I wouldn't sit by while he blasphemed the Lord, while he frightened He-Dong. Besides, my dear would be protected. God loved him.

Mercifully, He-Seung didn't continue. He picked up his chopsticks and shoveled rice into his mouth.

"Mother," He-Dong looked at his bowl full of rice, then over to my empty one. "Would you like some of mine?"

Another knock sounded.

He-Seung gave me a long look. As if this was an example of what he had just said. "If I were you, runt, I'd hold tight to my rice before Mother gives it to the next beggar."

"That must be Father." He-Dong dropped his bowl and ran for the door again. I ran after him. He-Seung followed.

"He-Dong," a female voice called out in greeting. Gong-Tae *uhmony*?

She stood at the door with her son, Gong-Tae. They bowed to us.

"We heard what happened." Gong-Tae *uhmony* rushed over to where I stood. She held a jar of *kimchee* in one hand. She latched onto me with the other.

"Thank you," I mumbled, suddenly realizing that maybe her husband, Deacon Mah, had been taken to the jail, as well. It was selfish of me not to remember until now. "Is your husband safe?"

"Yes, yes." She nodded. "We didn't do any of those pretend picnics at Mt. Nam San, but instead spent all our energies with prayer in the Lord."

"We didn't go to that stupid shrine either." He-Seung looked over from where he stood with Gong-Tae.

For once I was happy for his outspokenness.

"Well, then. Who can explain this?" Gong-Tae *uhmony* pushed the *kimchee* jar into my hands. "Remember, we made this together just a few months ago. When your husband was still home, when the church was still open, when we thought this nasty business would end quickly. Eat this and pray. He'll be home soon."

He-Dong clasped tight to me, his body exploding with joy. All he heard, I'm sure, was her last sentence. He-Seung scoffed at his brother.

"Remember also." Gong-Tae *uhmony* put her hands together. "*When the wicked spring up like grass, and workers of iniquity flourish, it is that they may be destroyed forever.*"

I know she didn't mean to be preaching to me, a Minister's wife. I know she only meant kindness. I nodded, leaning against the door.

"The righteous shall flourish like the palm tree. And grow mighty like the cedar of Lebanon."

I had no more energy to talk. I smiled.

"We're praying for you." Gong-Tae *uhmony* bowed. Then she glanced outside to the left and right before pulling her son out the door with her.

We watched them disappear down the path. I closed the door. We returned to the table.

"It's a good sign that Deacon Mah wasn't—" He-Seung paused. "Is still at home."

"Maybe we should pray again." He-Dong put his hands together. "Like Gong-Tae *Uhmony* did."

"No. We've done enough praying." He-Seung reached for He-Dong's bowl. "If you don't hurry and finish your dinner, I'll eat it for you."

"Mother." He-Dong looked up from his bowl. "What did Gong-Tae *uhmony* mean about wicked spring grass and the seaters of... where did they sit?"

He-Seung laughed, choking on his soup.

"Cedars, Dear One, Cedars. Of Lebanon." I patted his arm. "Your Father often says those words."

He-Dong shrunk back, as if I'd criticized him for not listening.

I gave his arm a squeeze. "It means the sinners will be punished and the righteous will remain strong and be saved."

He-Seung erupted into another wave of laughter. "Where did they sit?"

He-Dong looked to me, as if he was replaying Gong-Tae *uhmony's* words and they still didn't make sense. Then his eyes widened. He burst into tears.

"What's the matter?" I put my arm around his heaving shoulders.

"What if—" He took a big breath. "What if God took the wrong sinner?"

"What are you talking about?" He-Seung scowled.

"Well, today." He-Dong's lower lip trembled. "Today I wasn't really...wasn't really."

"Sick?" He-Seung poked his brother in the stomach. "We knew that already."

"We did?" I sat back, surprised.

"Maybe the policemen should have taken me." He-Dong looked into his lap.

"Yes, they should have." He-Seung took a scoop of his brother's rice. "Life would be a lot easier without your sniveling. But God didn't have the policemen pick Father instead of you by mistake."

He-Dong looked to me. His eyes were full of sorrow. Tears streamed down his cheeks.

"Your brother's words hold truth." I patted He-Dong on the arm, thinking how even He-Seung's kindness was sharper than a knife.

"Ha!" He-Seung raised his chopsticks in the air, triumphant. "Even mother thinks you're a sniveler."

"No, that's not the truth I meant." I put my hand out to shush He-Seung. "Your father being –being…" I couldn't say the word *arrested*. "This business with the police has nothing to do with your pretending to be sick."

"It doesn't?" A fresh batch of tears poured down his cheeks.

"Just don't go tricking me again." I held him tight, rocking him back and forth, the tears flowing down my cheeks, as well. I felt as fragile as Mrs. Hong's *kimchee* jars at the market. As if a breeze would blow me over and smash me to pieces. We had prayed very hard for my dear's safety, too. My dear had said God would protect us. Why was this happening?

This (Japanese led) Asiatic continent has the fundamental energy of the world's civilization, and the world is slowly recognizing this fact.
—**Professor T. Komaki, Kyoto Imperial University, 1942**

Sunday, April 19, 1942—next day

He-Seung

Months ago, Gong-Tae and I would have been sitting on a pew watching Father in his billowing black robe as he read from the Bible, and counting the minutes until our souls could be released to play soccer. Weeks ago, I would have been sitting on the living room floor counting the few brave souls who had come to the house. Today, before Mother asked me to read the Bible while she and He-Dong sat with their eyes closed tight, I wanted to look for Father.

I wasn't sure where to start. However, last night when Gong-Tae came over, he reminded me of our encounter with the Japanese soldier. He reminded me that most of the Japs were stupid and not to worry. It made me think of the print shop lady. If someone had access to information, she was a good bet. So, while Mother and He-Dong still slept, I went looking for her.

As I neared the edge of the market, I heard the clanging of the presses. The noise was so loud, I felt like the machines were inside my body, shaking my brain loose. I rounded the corner, and stepped inside the print shop.

A young girl about He-Dong's age stood behind the counter folding the city's two-page Jap newspapers. She had thin dark hair that was cut short. Smudges of ink decorated her face making her look like a homeless urchin.

"Is your mother here?" I asked.

She didn't even glance up. The machines clanged.

I waved, shouting, "Mother? Here?"

"The papers aren't ready yet," she called out as she continued folding.

"I don't want your propaganda sheets," I said as loud as I could, putting my hand out to stop her. "I want to speak to your mother."

"Does my mother want to speak to you?" she shouted back.

What nerve. "Yes." I nodded my head vigorously. "I'm sure she does."

She folded her hands across her chest. "How do I know that?"

Why did I need to tell an 8-year-old my business? "Once I helped her escape from a Jap—from a soldier."

She raised her eyebrows and gave me a hard stare.

"I did." I stepped closer. "I tricked him, acting stupid, acting like I didn't understand his questions. He was chasing your mother."

She pulled the papers from beneath my hand and continued folding. The machines clanged over and over again, as though pressing my brain further against the sides of my head.

"I'm Reverend Chai's son," I added, hoping Father's position mattered to her.

"Mother's not here," she called out as she added the newly folded paper to the finished pile.

I left the noisy shop. My throat burned, as if I'd swallowed a spoonful of chili paste. I realized it wasn't just Mother and He-Dong that needed Father back. I did, too. Soccer would not put rice in our mouths. My status as the 'tough guy' would not protect Mother and He-Dong. I didn't know how to keep our family going. I closed my eyes and leaned against the building.

"What do you want here?" A deep voice intruded.

I opened my eyes. The print shop woman stood in front of me, her steely dark eyes searching my face. She held a copy of the newspaper in her hands. I'd forgotten how deep her voice was. Gong-Tae and I often joked that she was a man wearing a *cheemar*.

I pushed away from the building, wondering if I looked the fool that I felt, crumpled like a dejected baby in the corner. Wondering if she'd heard me talking so rudely to her daughter.

"My father was arrested yesterday. I just—I just—I need to know where the prison is."

She snorted, a disgusting, unfeminine noise. "Why would I know that?"

"I think." I scratched my arm. "Don't you know a lot of things?"

"I wish I did, young man." She looked away, tapping the newspaper against her palm as Father often did with his Bible. She looked at me, as though finally remembering where she'd seen me. "You have a friend."

"Yes." I nodded. Most people remembered Gong-Tae, his athletic body, his kind face, before me. "We were moving a bench—helping my father—the day that Jap—"

"I remember." She gave a slight nod of her head. "They're everywhere."

Was someone watching us? I turned my head to look.

"Don't look around." She held the paper up in front of me. She opened to an article on how the Japs had recently *liberated* the Filipinos from evil American Colonialism. She smiled and pointed with exaggerated motions.

I pretended similar excitement, moving closer to the print shop woman and grabbing onto the paper, as if amazed by this liberation.

"I heard there were a lot of prisoners taken to Serdamoon." She smiled broadly as if we were celebrating the Japanese victory.

"Serdamoon?" I repeated the word, as if it were a magic key that would open the cell doors and release my father. Serdamoon.

"But who knows about political prisoners?"

"Political prisoners?" I jumped back as if slapped. "My father was as non-political as they make them."

"Shhh." She held the paper up again, showing a black-and-white of a soldier with his sword brandished. The sword looked dirty. Or bloody. "One man who might be able to tell you is Dr. Lee."

That sounded wrong. "He's a family friend, and he hasn't said anything."

"Well those prisons aren't places for young men," she said, pointing to the article and looking wide-eyed and impressed. "Even brave young men such as yourself. Perhaps he was concerned for your safety."

"I can take care of myself," I said.

She closed her eyes. She let out a deep sigh. She shook her head, whispering. "Those Jap—Japanese. You just stay safe. Keep your mother and brother safe. Your father will take care of himself." She looked down the road. An officer stood smoking and watching us. She handed me the paper and smiled. "He always has."

I accepted this newspaper with both hands, as though being given a bar of gold. I wanted to shake the woman up and down and see if she didn't have just any teensy bit of information left for me. This was nothing. And Dr. Lee? He certainly knew nothing more than my pulse rate.

Just stay safe. Keep your mother and brother safe. I didn't want to be safe. I just wanted Father home. I turned the corner, tossing those sheets of lies to the ground and stomping all over them.

**The U.S launches first air strike on Tokyo, Japan: the *Doolittle Raid*
—April 18, 1942**

Sunday, April 19, 1942-same day

He-Seung

I walked up the path to our home. Mother would surely be awake by now. Breakfast would be ready. I would wait until later and see if Gong-Tae had any bright ideas.

Two females stood by our door—Myung-Ja *uhmony* and Purple Face. Perhaps they had come to offer their sympathies. Either that or they had received a letter from Myung-Hae, finally.

"Hello." I hurried up the steps to the porch. I wiped a trail of sweat from my forehead.

"I was just about to knock." Myung-Ja *uhmony* turned. "Looks like you've been off having fun."

I moved to the door and lifted the key to the lock. "I was at the market."

"Of course." Myung-Ja *uhmony* looked at me, her eyes searching. Her thin black hair was arranged in a tidy bun.

I realized then that I had no fresh fish or tofu or anything to back up my words. I was tempted to mention the print shop, but had no information, not even a newspaper to show. I felt as shameful as if I had been out playing soccer with Gong-Tae.

"You must be tired and thirsty." Purple Face's voice filled the air behind me. There wasn't a questioning lilt in her words like most girls had.

Myung-Ja *uhmony* cleared her throat. I looked up to show my agreement that this ugly girl had no right to talk directly to a boy. But instead of glaring at Purple Face, she stared at my hands. As if she wanted to take the key and open the door herself. Quickly.

I don't know why I was such a fumble fingers. The door opened before I had a chance to fumble further.

"He-Seung? Is that you?" Mother grabbed onto my hands, as if I'd been away for years. Then she turned to greet our guests.

"Last week, you asked us to come for the dress." Myung-Ja *uhmony* bowed. "I hope this isn't a bad—"

"Of course." Mother looked bewildered. "Come in."

Mother was a better seamstress than Sim's Tailor at the market, and friends were always asking for her fine hand in making their clothes. But now? When we were all worried about Father?

I leaned down and took off my muddy shoes. The nerve of some people. Why didn't Mother tell them to go away? Then again, how could she? She was the Reverend's wife.

Mother had me seat them in the living room, while she brought out water as a refreshment. Mother served us each a cup, then bowed her head, offering thanks for everything. She thanked God that our visitors had arrived safely, that He-Dong and I were safe at home, that the sun still shone, ants still crawled. She asked for wisdom and guidance and lights to illuminate God's path, for God's hand to protect Father.

I heard a small sigh. Was it He-Dong or Purple Face? I opened my eyes. He-Dong's face was scrunched in concentration. Purple Face, as was custom, sat behind her mother. I couldn't see her. Perhaps the noise had escaped my lips, as I sat there wishing the prayer would end before the water in the cups evaporated.

"Amen," everyone said.

I gulped down my water and sat forward to stand. I wanted to go find Gong-Tae. He might have some idea as to what I should do next about Father.

"Now that we're inside, I wanted to tell you." Myung-Ja *uhmony* looked around as if maybe our walls were too thin. "Reverend Chai is safe."

"He is?" I asked, plopping back down.

"Where is he?" He-Dong asked, his voice eager. "We were waiting—"

"Psshhht." I hit He-Dong on the shoulder. "Where is he?"

"Don't worry about your father," Myung-Ja *uhmony* said.

Mother's voice trembled. "It's kind of you to come cheer us up."

All these weeks when she didn't hear from her daughter, Mother had listened to Myung-Ja *uhmony*, had assured her of God's love. Was Myung-Ja *uhmony* offering the same sisterly support? I groaned, leaning forward to get up.

"It's not just cheering." Myung-Ja *uhmony* re-positioned her water cup. "My dear's new job takes him to the prison when someone has been—" She glanced at He-Dong. "Hurt. He hasn't seen Reverend Chai."

She was using euphemisms to protect us, although I understood. Maybe the print-shop lady had been right. Dr. Lee would know where Father was. Perhaps even Myung-Ja *uhmony* would know.

Mother grabbed onto Myung-Ja *uhmony's* hands. Water flowed from her eyes. "Oh, thank God." She wiped at the tears, but the water kept coming. "Thank you for telling me—us—this."

"Next time my dear visits the prison." Myung-Ja *uhmony* patted her hand. "He'll try to look in on Reverend Chai."

"Thank you." Mother put her hands together, bowing forward. Her shoulders shook. "Thank you."

"Mother." He-Dong cocked his head. "If Dr. Lee knows the prison where Father is, why doesn't he bring Father home?"

"How does your brain ever come up with so many idiotic thoughts?" I swatted his arm.

Myung-Ja *uhmony* inhaled sharply.

I looked over at her. "Where is the pris—"

"He-Seung, please show kindness to your brother." Mother looked sharply at me.

He-Dong's face lit up. He looked around the room and spotted the *Bahduk* board in the corner. "A game would be kind."

"You must be joking." Playing *Bahduk* with him was worse than watching carrots grow.

"That's a wonderful idea." Mother smiled, handing me the board.

He-Dong grabbed onto it and set it between us.

I sighed. The object of *Bahduk* was to place stones in different positions on the board, building up an army to surround your opponent. He-Dong may have been smart, but I'd been playing Chinese Chess long before his fat head came into the world. My only challenge in playing with him was suffering through his hand rubbing and foolish moves. Still, if I stuck around, I would make Mother happy. On top of that, I might have a chance to ask Myung-Ja *uhmony* about the location of the prison. "One game."

"This will be a good one." He-Dong rubbed his hands together in anticipation.

"Any word from He-Chul?" Myung-Ja *uhmony* asked Mother.

Mother briefly smiled, glancing over toward his latest letter. "He's fine. Studying hard."

"Surely he'll be offered a fine job as an Economics professor when he returns." Myung-Ja *uhmony* loved He-Chul, wishing the boy were her own son. But then she probably wished anyone were her son. Well, almost anyone.

"That would be an honor. Although in his most recent note he said..." Mother scrunched her eyebrows, looking over at the rocking chair, as if trying to picture Father reading to her. *"I've joined a special group which follows the teaching of the most important man in the world."*

"Really?" Myung-Ja *uhmony's* mouth hung open.

"That certainly must be code for Jesus. I'm sure he has to be just as careful over in Manchukuo as we are..." Mother's voice trailed off.

"You must be so proud of him." Myung-Ja *uhmony* reached over and touched Mother's arm.

"Yes." Mother fussed with the water cups, arranging them and re-arranging them.

"He's a smart boy." Myung-Ja *uhmony* wrinkled her nose, her eyes falling on me. "And a brave one at that."

So maybe I wasn't the *smart one*. I was brave. The print-shop lady had just called me that this morning. I looked over at Myung-Ja *uhmony*. "Have you ever heard of Serdamoon—"

"Since you've come all the way here." Mother stood. "Shall we take a look at that dress?"

"No, no, no." Myung-Ja *uhmony* protested, at the same time allowing Mother to take her and Purple Face to the front bathroom to change.

I sighed again, wondering where this prison could be.

"Wait, wait." He-Dong took his white stone back. "Here. Let me go here."

He-Dong made yet another foolish move, exposing a whole row of his white 'soldiers' to me. We'd be finished with this stupid game in no time. "Great move."

"You can tell, can't you?" He-Dong stared at the board, his lips moving as he silently counted his men. "I've been practicing."

I put down a black stone, further trapping his men. I scratched my wrist. If Myung-Ja *uhmony* continued not to hear my question about the prison, I would escort her and Purple Face home, and talk with Dr. Lee.

He-Dong quickly put down another white stone in the absolute worst position on the board. There wasn't a dumber move. I snorted.

He looked up me, misinterpreting the noise as one of praise. "If I win, will you show me how to use your slingshot?"

The Japs would truly become peacemakers before that happened. I picked a black stone from my wooden bowl and held it up with a flourish. "Of course."

"Wait!" He-Dong's eyes widened as he realized—finally—that I had his men almost completely surrounded. "No."

"You can't keep re-taking your turn." I tossed my black stone up and down in my hand. "Besides, it won't make a difference."

He-Dong's lower lip quivered. His eyes filled. He hugged his arms tight to his chest.

Mother and Myung-Ja *uhmony's* voices sounded in the hall. They would see He-Dong bawling like a baby. Myung-Ja *uhmony* would make more disappointed noises, lament the absence of the intelligent, brave He-Chul, not tell me anything about the prison, even if she knew it.

"Oh, go ahead." I picked up his white stone and handed it to him.

"Thank you, Brother." He sniffed, brushing at his eyes with the back of his hand. Then he stared at the board so long, surely he was delivering a

Mother-length prayer filled with wisdom and guidance and light and protection. Finally he put his white piece down.

"I told you it made no difference." I swatted his hand away just as Mother came into the room. "That was the second stupidest move."

He-Dong pulled his hand back, staring at the board, gnawing on his lip. He saw that he was trapped yet again. "No," he squeaked, looking up for Mother.

"Your daughter's grown in just the week since you came." Mother bent down to her sewing basket by the window, oblivious to He-Dong. "Perhaps I need to let the hem out a bit."

"I think the dress is lovely as it is." Myung-Ja *uhmony* went over to join Mother. "The colors are so nice. They put a sparkle in her eyes."

I smiled to myself. *A sparkle in her eyes?* Was that all her mother could think to say?

"Maybe just a fingernail's extra length will do." Mother sat down and picked up her pin cushion. Her voice sounded normal for the first time since Father was taken.

"You fuss too much over her," Myung-Ja *uhmony* said.

"Oh, no." Mother rearranged needles in the pin cushion in front of her. "It's a pleasure to make dresses every once in a while."

I did have sisters, three of them. But none of them had lived to see their hundred-day celebration.

"You know." I stretched loudly. "You could make He-Dong a dress or two."

Mother shot me a disappointed look before worriedly glancing over at the runt. "That's not kind."

"Please, Brother." He-Dong put his hands together, begging. "Can I try one more time? I see where I should have moved."

I held the black stone high. Then I let my hand drop slowly, slowly, whistling as it fell like a bomb.

"Please, brother." He-Dong rocked back and forth on his knees. His hands were clasped so tight his fingers had gone white. He squeezed his eyes shut.

Just then, Purple Face walked past me. The cotton of her new dress swished against my arm. A flowery scent filled the air. I looked over to where she stood in front of Mother.

Mother had Purple Face turn this way and that, the pink, green and yellow fabric swirling around her ankles. Her small wrists poked from the sleeves. She stopped and pulled her long black ponytail over her left shoulder and smiled at us. So bold.

I stared back, realizing that with her hair tied back so that it fell partially over her right eye, I couldn't see the mottled skin, the tightness, the purple scar which long ago had earned her the nickname. She had high cheekbones, a small nose. If it weren't for that scar, she'd be even prettier than her sister. I looked away.

"Have you gone yet?" He-Dong opened one eye and peeked at the board. Then he looked over at me.

"I'm thinking." I wanted to look back at Purple Face in the dress, but my neck felt stiff all of a sudden. "I'm thinking."

I ran my palm over my scalp. I rolled my shoulders back, twisting my head to the side and cracking my neck. I put the stone down somewhere, anywhere.

He-Dong clapped his hands together, putting them up to the heavens. "Yes!"

I looked down. I hadn't placed my stone in the winning position, but in the one next to it. Damn. Oh, well. He wouldn't be able to escape my army.

"Are you sure the length feels right?" Mother asked.

I jerked my head in their direction as Mother kneeled down next to Purple Face and lifted the hem of the dress, revealing pale ankles. Purple Face had small, delicate feet.

"It's perfect." Myung-Ja *uhmony* ran her hand over the front of Purple Face's dress. "It's so beautiful."

My throat felt dry. I closed my mouth.

"No, no." Mother pulled at the hem, cocking her head to the side. "It's just a heap of cloth until she puts it on. She's the beauty."

Myung-Ja *uhmony* lifted her arm, shooing her daughter away to change. "She would be if only her face—"

"She's blossomed like a lovely flower," Mother interrupted.

Purple Face blushed as pink as the fabric of the dress. She knew what her mother was going to say. Purple Face hurried past me, and I fought an urge to reach out and touch her pale ankle.

"It's your turn again." He-Dong tapped my arm to get my attention.

I stared at the board, but only saw high cheekbones and small lips, the colorful fabrics of the dress, the pale ankles beneath. I put down a stone.

"Yes, yes, yes." He-Dong bounced up and down on his knees as if he had to take a piss. He hugged himself. Then he put his white stone down. "Look at that move. Ha, ha."

He had blocked off part of my army. He thought he was so smart. I rubbed the back of my neck and tossed down a black stone. Back and forth we went, but I couldn't focus on anything except the soft patter of feet when Purple Face finally returned. My breath came in short gasps. What was the matter with me?

Purple Face walked by our game, looking down at the board. She brushed a wisp of hair from her forehead, curling it behind her ear. Then she went over and kneeled on the cushion behind her mother.

"Your turn," He-Dong sang, shaking my bowl of stones.

"I know we've already imposed on your hospitality too much. Especially today." Myung-Ja *uhmony* gave an embarrassed smile. "But can I trouble you for another cup of water?"

"Certainly." Mother stood, rubbing her hands together.

Another cup of water? This was an odd request. Perhaps Myung-Ja *uhmony* had news for my manly ears, no matter how pathetic. Without looking, I put another stone on the board.

"Ha-ha!" He-Dong shouted, pointing to the *Bahduk* board as though he had an imaginary slingshot in his hands. "I've got your men trapped."

I looked at the board. A barrage of white soldiers surrounded my black ones. Heat rose to my face.

"Mother!" He-Dong jumped up. "I won. I beat Brother."

I tossed the *Bahduk* board over and reached for his scruffy neck. He was like a soggy branch in my hands. But then I remembered Purple Face and her mother sitting just a few feet away. Thinking of me as pathetic, stupid, not brave at all. I held onto He-Dong with both arms, squeezing his shoulders. Then I gave him a firm slap on the back and pushed him away. He tripped off to the kitchen.

"You're a kind elder brother to let He-Dong win." Purple Face giggled. "Especially when you had him so clearly beaten."

Kind? Nobody had ever called me that. Besides, what did Purple Face know about *Bahduk,* and why had she been watching us? I pulled at the sleeves of my shirt.

"Isn't it strange how all of our games are miniature versions of war?" she said.

Myung-Ja *uhmony* cleared her throat, frowning at her daughter. It wasn't right to be speaking out so.

"That's ridiculous." I frowned along with her mother.

Then I thought of the army beneath my fingers. The *men* I was strategically positioning to *kill* the other side. I glanced up. Myung-Ja raised her eyebrows as if she could hear me thinking.

Myung-Ja *uhmony* pulled an envelope from beneath her white blouse. She reached over and handed it to me. "Give this to your mother."

I looked at the thick envelope. Was it information about the prison? Or money?

"Your mother is always so kind to sew for us, but now—"

I felt as if I'd been punched. If she was suddenly paying for Mother's sewing services, she obviously didn't think Father would be home anytime soon. No matter how *safe* he was. I pushed the packet of cash away.

"Where is it?" I asked. "Serdamoon?"

Myung-Ja *uhmony* cocked her head, a blank look on her face. Either she didn't know where her husband worked or the print shop lady had given me wrong information.

"For your mother." Myung-Ja *uhmony* handed the money packet back to me and stood before I could ask anything more. "I insist."

She pushed her daughter down the hall toward the door. I would have to follow them home, ask to speak to Dr. Lee.

At the entrance, Purple Face leaned down to put on her rubber shoes. I realized there was a scuff mark on the left one. I could have fixed that with my pocketknife. Not that I wanted to.

"Thank your mother again for us." Myung-Ja *uhmony* cleared her throat. I was staring at her daughter.

"Can I walk you both home?" I offered.

"Thank you." Myung-Ja *uhmony* gave me a funny look, as if I she'd tasted a sour plum. "We've got errands to run."

I watched them disappear down the path. Myung-Ja *uhmony* said Father was safe. Min-Kook *uhmony* said this would take time. I stared at the thick packet of money in my hands. For the first time I wished my *brave genius* of a brother, He-Chul, were here. He would easily find the right answers.

Japan is firmly determined to fight, in close collaboration with Germany and Italy, even a Hundred Year War, to crush the United States and Britain.
—**Colonel Hideo Ohira at a Singapore victory celebration, 1942**

Sunday, April 19, 1942—same day

He-Seung

I raised my fist to knock on Dr. Lee's door. I could still hear the runt whining, *If Dr. Lee knows where Father is, why doesn't he bring Father home?* Even the lady from the print shop had told me to come here. Why did my stomach feel jittery?

A high-pitched cry sounded from the back of their house. I waited, expecting to hear voices. Instead another cry filled my ears. I'd never heard such a sorrowful noise. *The Japs lay the enemy on sharpened bamboo sticks as punishment,* the man from the public bath had said.

Why would the Japs harm Dr. Lee and his family? Hadn't they just given Dr. Lee a nice new job at their prison? Perhaps Dr. Lee had already contacted Father and displeased the authorities.

Panic made my heart pound. I looked about, grabbing the nearest weapon I could find—a broom leaning against the front of the house. I held the handle tight. I snuck into the backyard.

A long wooden pen lined the back of the dirt yard, half of it for their dog, Mee-Won, the other half for their rooster. A couple of rows of sad cabbage grew along the fence. There was that stupid required cherry tree in the corner. An iron smell filled the air. Like water from the well. Or a fresh cut on my lip.

Again, I heard the crying. This time I knew it was coming from the pen. Had the Japs come here and tied up the family in that wooden pen?

I ran over expecting to see Purple Face, her eyes grimacing in pain. I peeked through the slats of the pen. There, laying on a few pieces of old newspaper, was their dog Mee-Won.

"Geez!" I laughed so loud at my stupid self—my overactive imagination—that Mee-Won sat up. Next to her lay four small pups. Their wet fur was pasted against their bodies, making them look like rats.

I looked down at the broom in my hand. What was I thinking, planning to defend myself with a broom against a bunch of Japs with guns and swords? I could see Father shaking his head at me. Telling me I had no brain.

"He-Seung?" Behind me a door opened and closed. It wasn't Dr. Lee or even Myung-Ja *uhmony*, but Purple Face. She walked up next to me. "You're the help Mother was talking about?"

"Excuse me?" I frowned.

She no longer sparkled, but wore a plain white *cheemar*, the sleeves of which were frayed. Still, she had a sweet smell, like flowers, a welcome relief from the stink of blood.

She looked at the broom in my hand. Her brown eyes twinkled with amusement. "What are you doing here?"

I looked at my hand as if it wasn't really part of my body, as if I was just as shocked to see their broom in my sweaty palm. "It's just I heard crying and—"

"You thought you'd sweep it away?" She giggled, putting her hand over her mouth.

The idea that a bunch of Japs had been torturing the family now seemed embarrassing. As embarrassing as me cursing in front of Father's prayer group. As embarrassing as losing a simple game of *bahduk* to the runt. But this was only Purple Face. Why did I care? I stabbed the bristles to the ground. Mee-Won let out another cry.

"Poor Mee-Won." Purple Face brushed past me, her cotton dress soft against my arm. "She's been in labor for hours, and there's just one more pup. She can't get it out."

"How do you know how many pups there are?" I sounded like my stupid baby brother, asking anything that came to mind.

"I can feel them." Her long hair was pulled back with a pink ribbon. She leaned down and reached out to touch Mee-Won's stomach. "Here, you feel."

Who did she think she was, ordering me around like a servant? I had more important business than playing with a crying dog. Still, I rested the broom on the pen. Then I reached through the wood and patted Mee-Won's head. The iron odor made me swallow hard.

"Not her head, silly." Purple Face giggled.

I felt heat rising to my neck. This girl irritated me more than I could stand. I put my hand on Mee-Won's thick furry middle. A squirming in Mee-Won's belly made me jump.

"Well, I guess you're not going to be much help." Purple Face laughed. Not a mean laugh, but a soft sound, like birds calling out.

Now I understood. Perhaps her mother had gone to find a neighbor who knew how to help make Mee-Won give up the last pup. What about Dr. Lee? "Where's your fath—"

"I hope Mother hurries." She looked back toward the house. "Mee-Won is getting so tired. My friend's dog got so tired, she never woke up."

"That wouldn't be good. Come on, girl." I put my hand on Mee-Won's tummy again. "Get busy. You can do this."

I pushed down hard on Mee-Won's slick fur. She let out a long, wounded cry. I pulled my hand back. Out slithered the last puppy. Its body was covered with slime like a fish that had sat too many days at the market. Its tiny limbs moved back and forth as if on a bicycle. It made a mewing sound. A real live puppy.

"You did it." Purple Face jumped up and down, putting her hands together as if in prayer.

I didn't think I'd had anything to do with the puppy being born, but it felt good to hear praise. Even from her.

"You're amazing." She smiled at me. Then she leaned down to watch Mee-Won bathe her last pup.

Purple Face's neck was long and pale. I felt a strange tingling in my stomach, as if one of Mee-Won's puppies was in there. I cleared my throat. "Is your Father home?"

"No." She looked up at me with concern. "He was called on an emergency."

My mind flashed on the prison. *My dear is called to take care of the prisoners who are hurt,* I remembered Myung-Ja *uhmony* saying. My mouth dropped.

"Mr. Im fell off a ladder this morning." She shook her head, as if she'd heard my thoughts. "He was trying to repair his roof and toppled down onto Mrs. Im. They're both injured."

"Oh, thank God." I blushed. How insensitive could I sound? "I mean, I'm glad it wasn't—"

"I know." Purple Face raised her hand. She had long, delicate fingers.

"Where is the prison?" I kicked at the dirt. "Do you know?"

"What are you thinking?" She pulled her ponytail to her right shoulder, patting the ends with her long fingers. "You could get in big trouble there."

"It's just that I've never seen my mother so, so…" I didn't say *crazy,* but that's the word that came to mind. Maybe Dr. Lee wouldn't be able to bring Father home, as the runt hoped, but perhaps I could visit and make sure Father was being treated well. He might have some ideas on how I could earn money until he returned. "She prays for his return every second of the day…and night. He-Dong is just as bad." Why was I spilling all my thoughts to her? "They need to know—we need to know—that he's safe."

"You can't just walk to the prison and talk to your father." She took a step closer, shaking her head at me. The top of her head reached my shoulders. I felt heat from her body. I felt a strange heat in my own. "You're not afraid of anything, are you?"

I was. I was afraid of guns and swords and what would happen if Father never came back. I was afraid of standing here so close to her.

"I'm not afraid of jerks." I picked up the broom as though ready to fend off an army.

"Myung-Ja *yah*?" a voice called.

"Mother." Purple Face stepped back, her voice filled with panic.

I'd forgotten about her mother. We would be in trouble if she caught the two of us alone here in the backyard.

"I'll talk to Father." Purple Face whisked her hands back and forth as if to push me along. "Stop by tomorrow night. After sunset."

I hurried down the path with the broom in my hands. Crunch. Crunch. Crunch. I ran back. "Pssst."

"What?" she mouthed, her eyes wide with alarm.

"This is yours." I lifted my hand, the broom slipping from my sweaty palm.

She grabbed the handle from me and my fingers brushed against hers. I felt a jolt, the same way I often did when the fuse-box needed changing and I got my fingers too close. She must have felt something, too, for her cheeks turned deep pink. Like the Rose of Sharon.

I wanted to say something more. I looked into her eyes, having a sudden ridiculous urge to touch her pink cheeks. I turned away, crunching down the path, my heart beating hard. My fingers vibrated from the memory of her fingers against mine. For the first time since those bastards had taken father, I felt a lightness in my heart. Purple Face would help me. Myung-Ja.

Japan's war aims are the liberation of Asia and the destruction of America and Britain.
—**Professor Tokuyomi Sanya of Kyoto Imperial University, May 8, 1942**

Monday morning, April 20, 1942—next day

Baby He-Dong

I sat in the entryway, staring at my untied shoes. What if the police came while I was gone and, this time, took Mother? I didn't want to leave.

Mother picked up my *bento* lunch box from the floor and handed it to me. "You're going to be late."

Even He-Seung had left. I knew I should hurry. But my shoelaces felt like giant snakes which might reach up and bite me.

"Today is a glorious day." Mother opened the door for me.

How could she call the day glorious? Father was still gone. My insides swirled. I turned to her.

She bent down to tie my laces. "Go on now."

I walked down the dirt road. Flies swarmed around a pile of ox dung, a discarded candy wrapper, an old cabbage. I turned back to look for Mother. She had already closed the front door.

When I arrived at school, I saw my class leaving the gates in single file formation as if they were going on a field trip. *San toki, toki-ya urdero kanunya.* Little mountain rabbits, where are you going? I didn't want to go anywhere today, except back home to wait for Father.

"*Sensei*, we have a straggler." Kee-Wok shouted, pointing to me.

Ito *Sensei* rushed over, grabbed me by the ear and led me to the front of the line. "You're late."

"Where are we going?" I asked.

She swatted her cane against her thigh, the signal for me to keep quiet and move along.

"It rained on Saturday, preventing our outing," Bon Hwa said with authority.

It did? I couldn't remember. I knew it had rained all day inside me. That's all I knew.

His outfit was dirty and wrinkled, and for once I wondered why. Maybe he didn't have a mother at home.

"If we wait until next Saturday," Bon-Hwa continued. "The cherry blossoms will have fallen."

Cherry blossoms. Mt. Nam San. The Shinto shrine. I wanted to disappear and slink home. But Ito *Sensei* stayed next to me as we walked down the city streets, passing trollies, bicycles, oxcarts. Everybody looked so normal. How could they all go about their normal business when Father was in jail?

When we got to the steps to Mt. Nam San, I broke out in a sweat. *Thou shalt have no gods before me.* I could hear Father quoting the first Commandment. "*Sensei,* I can't go up there."

"Of course you can." She prodded me with her cane.

I dragged myself up the first step. Would God remember to punish me this time? Or would he pick on Mother?

Ih-Duk nudged into a spot next to me as we trudged up the steps. "I heard your father was put in jail," he whispered, glancing around to see if anyone was watching us. "I'm sorry."

"Mother said he will be home soon." I counted the steps. Fifty-eight. Fifty-nine.

"That's good," Ih-Duk said. Then he started singing the rabbit-hopping song, making me lose count of the steps.

At the top of the mountain was a small funny-looking red-and-green house with a slanted tile roof. I looked around for the shrine, but didn't see anything large enough to house 800 gods. Maybe Ito *Sensei* had decided to take us on a different outing which had nothing to do with gods and shrines. Around us, tiny cherry blossoms fluttered like pink snow. *God's miracle*, Father would have said.

"Now, watch me." Ito *Sensei* walked up to the small house.

I couldn't imagine anyone living up here, so far away from the shops. In front of the house was a rope with a bell attached to the bottom. She rang the bell. Then she bowed to the bell, as if someone important, like Father, had just answered her call. Bubbles of laughter erupted in my throat.

"Don't laugh," Ih-Duk whispered.

"She looks silly bowing to the bell." I covered my mouth.

"It's not just any bell." He frowned. "It's the shrine bell."

This little place? This was the shrine? I swallowed, whispering, "I shouldn't be here."

Ito *Sensei* clapped her hands twice and bowed once more. *Thou shalt have no other gods before me.* Maybe if I didn't look, God wouldn't be angered by my being here. I closed my eyes. I could hear my classmates approaching the shrine and ringing the bell, one after the other.

"Next," Bon-Hwa called.

"That means you, bean-curd!" Kee-Wok yelled.

I opened one eye. The whole class stood next to the shrine, waiting. Only Ih-Duk was behind me.

"Let me go first." Ih-Duk moved in front of me. He went up to the shrine and swung the rope back and forth so wildly, I thought the bell attached to the end would fly off. Actually I hoped it would. Then maybe we could leave this funny house.

"You only need call the gods gently." Ito *Sensei* grabbed onto the rope. "Now, make your wish."

Ih-Duk must have had lots of wishes, for he stayed bowed so long the whole class giggled. Everyone except me. I would have been happy for him to stay there until the sun set.

When he finally stepped from the shrine, he said to Ito *Sensei*, "I prayed for lunch now. Can we eat?"

"What about our ex-Class Monitor?" Kee Wok said. "We wouldn't want him to miss out on his turn."

The ground beneath me felt hotter than the gravel by the pond in the afternoon sun. Perhaps this wasn't just ground. Perhaps it was a bed of burning charcoal on the path to hell. *You know what's right, Son.* I could hear Father commanding me to follow the path of righteousness. I imagined him, not behind bars in prison, but standing behind his pulpit at the church. He held his large palms out to the sky.

The teacher pushed me forward. "Hurry up."

I approached the little house, wondering if lightning would strike or God would call down from the heavens. Sweat rolled down my cheeks. I couldn't get enough air in my chest to breathe.

"Haven't you even been watching?" Ito *Sensei* came up behind me. She put my hands on the rope and swung the bell.

I shuddered. Surely not only would the 800 gods hear me, but God the Father would see I was here breaking His commandments. I ducked, awaiting the strike of lightning.

"Not like that." Ito *Sensei* pursed her lips. "You need to clap your hands and bow."

I took a deep breath. *Dear God.* I put my hands up as though clapping. *I really don't want to be here.* I bowed. *Please forgive me.*

"That's right," Ito *Sensei* said. "Now that shouldn't have been so hard, especially for a smart boy like you."

Normally such praise would fill my chest with pride. I would feel taller than our oak tree. But at that moment, having disobeyed Father and God, I felt tinier than a cherry blossom.

As we climbed down the hill to a flat grassy section lined with cherry trees, I kept waiting for God to blow me into the burning pit of hell. We sat in a circle on the grass, our *bento* boxes in front of us. My brain felt numb.

"This is my favorite time of year." Ito *Sensei* stood on the inside of our circle. She bowed her head and closed her eyes. "At this time, our dear father, The Emperor, is out appreciating the blossoms, too and perhaps listening to these words:

"A flower blooms alone
Destined to fall alone
And never return
To its branch."

I looked around at the trees. My heart beat hard. Where was God, and why wasn't he throwing me into the hell fires?

"At every stage
It embodies life
The voice of the flower
We softly hear
The faith of the flower
We greatly feel."

Maybe God had laughed at that silly little house, too. Maybe He knew I didn't want to be here. Maybe that's why He hadn't struck me with lightning. I let out a deep sigh.

"The joy of eternal life
Shines within
The silent blossom blooms
Without regret."

Ito *Sensei* bowed to show she was done. She opened her eyes. "Now, you may all enjoy your lunches."

I opened my *bento*. The rice looked moist. To the side were Min-Kook *uhmony's* black beans and some cucumber pickles Gong-Tae *uhmony* had brought us. I took my chopsticks from the top of the box. Ito *Sensei* sat in the middle of our circle and talked about her days growing up, how each year her family would go to the park and watch people sing and dance beneath the cherry blossoms. She got tears in her eyes thinking of her family. I thought of Father. How it would be fun to sing and dance and have a picnic with him here.

A breeze blew. Fluffy pink blossoms landed on my arm, my thigh, my shoe, their delicate touch painful. I lifted the white grains of rice to my mouth. I didn't taste a thing.

After lunch, we formed a line and started down the mountain. This time Ito *Sensei* walked at the front of the line.

"We often compare our valiant samurai to the cherry blossom." Ito *Sensei* turned and pointed to a large blossoming tree.

"Flower boys." Kee-Wok snickered right behind me. "Sounds like you."

I ignored his dumb comments. He couldn't bother me. I would just count the steps. One. Two. Three.

"We often think the short life of the cherry blossom is similar to the short, yet spectacular, glory the samurai experience on the battlefield." Ito *Sensei* looked back at us. "When we say, 'the cherry blossom has flowered,' we mean some great success has happened. Like earlier this month when we succeeded in capturing Bataan."

Bataan, Philippines. Bataan was a place we had just learned about located in an American Commonwealth country. A Commonwealth country meant, Ito *Sensei* had explained to us, a country that wasn't really America, but was a place America had seized for its own use.

"What do you say when you fail," Kee-Wok called out.

"When we fail?" Ito *Sensei* turned, wearing a tight-lipped smile. "We don't fail enough to have a saying. However, when the life of one of our soldier's expires, we say, 'The cherry blossom has fallen.'"

That sounded so beautiful. So gentle. I looked around at the blossoms fluttering to the ground.

"Cherry blossoms remind us Japanese of the successes and failures of life," Ito *Sensei* continued. "The short life-span of the cherry blossom— about one week—is testimony to the impermanence of the material world."

I raised my hand. Then realizing she couldn't see me, I called out, "What is imper-impermints?"

"Imperma-nence." She turned around. "It means, 'not permanent.'" Then, seeing my hand about to shoot up, she added, "Passing quickly in and out of being."

I nodded. Father had said something about this in one of his sermons. About how this world was not the end, but only a quick stop. So we shouldn't worry about money or rice or things. Maybe the Japanese gods weren't so different from our real God. Maybe I had not sinned too badly. I let out another deep breath.

Just then, someone pushed my shoulder. I tripped down the fifty-fifth step and ran into Ih-Duk. "Excuse me."

"What's imper-imper--impermints?" Kee-Wok snickered, pushing me.

I ignored him, hurrying forward until I was walking on the heels of Ih-Duk. Fifty-eight, fifty-nine, sixty. We were surely almost back down the mountain.

"Impermanence means dead," Kee-Wok whispered in my ear. "Like your father."

Blood roared through my body, making my heart pound, blocking out the noises of the other boys marching down the steps, Ito *Sensei* chattering on. I gritted my teeth, clenched my fists.

"Manghal jarshik," I shouted from the depths of my being. You bastard!

The whole line of students stopped moving. "*Sensei's* coming," a classmate called.

I wanted to grab a cherry blossom branch and swat Kee-Wok until his whole body was pink. I turned, raising my fist to hit Kee-Wok's bulldog face. He grabbed my arm and twisted it behind my back.

"*Sensei*'s coming," Ih-Duk warned, his voice close by.

Kee-Wok kicked me in the back of my legs. I fell to the ground, the cement burning my knees.

"*Sensei!*" The boys around us whispered.

"Is there a problem back here?" Ito *Sensei* asked. She stood over us, her cane up in the air.

"No, no." Kee-Wok laughed. "Yoshimitsu is just not used to hiking all these steps. He fell. Poor kid."

"That's not true," Ih-Duk said. He was by my side, helping me up.

"That's not true." I stood on trembling legs.

"It's not?" Ito *Sensei* gave that smile that covered her teeth. "I was under the impression that this was your first time to the shrine."

"Well, yes, that…" I brushed tears from my eyes. "But Kee-Wok…"

"I don't want to hear anymore." Ito *Sensei* slapped her cane to her side for emphasis. "Let's keep moving."

God had punished me. My shorts were torn. My right knee was bleeding. I tasted dirt and the salt of my tears.

Men went mad overnight.
—Richard M Gordon, survivor of march imposed by the Japanese, in which 75,000 American and Filipino POWS were forced to walk 60 miles to prison camps with no food or water in what later was referred to as the *Bataan Death March*.
A quarter of the POWS died. April 12-24, 1942

Monday, April 20, 1942—same day

Baby He-Dong

I sat on the floor of the living room, copying Ito *Sensei's* poem. *The faith of the flower, we greatly feel.* I wish that was all I felt. My whole body ached from Kee-Wok twisting my arm behind my back and kicking me to the ground. *Impermanence means dead like your father.* I could still see his leering face.

The air smelled of our dinner. I tried not to think about the hard yellow bits of grain Mother had added to our rice tonight, made even harder to eat with my swollen lip. *Chickenfeed,* He-Seung had called it, slamming upstairs.

I looked up from my half-filled paper, twisting my pencil in my hand. I don't know why God was always so angry with me. I never meant to disobey His word.

I caught sight of He-Seung's comic book on the floor. *Jangsah,* the tough man. How I dreamed of being like him. He wasn't afraid of a growling tiger, was able to throw a monkey high in the air and catch it with one hand, had even saved a boy from the clutches of a giant snake. He obviously knew how to behave so that God helped him.

I pushed down on the paper with my pencil. My pencil tip broke. I'd have to ask He-Seung to sharpen it again with his pocket knife. I held up my pencil as he trudged into the living room.

"That's enough study." He threw the pencil on the table. "Come with me."

He went down the hall to the front door. Did he want help bringing in the firewood for the kitchen stove? I didn't want to carry wood when it was almost dark outside. The wood always had lots of bugs on it. I liked bugs, but I didn't want them crawling all over me. I heard him fumbling with his shoes and opening the front door.

"Hurry up," he called.

I put the half-finished poem aside and hurried to the door. He was already walking down the front path toward the main road. So we weren't collecting wood. I grabbed my shoes and slipped them on.

"What are we doing?" I caught up to him.

"Didn't you say you wanted a puppy?" His voice sounded proud. "Mee-Won had her litter."

"Really?" I looked back to our house. "Did—did Father say I can have one?"

"Don't worry." He pushed me along. "I'm sure he'd be fine with a puppy. That is, if you take care of it."

"But Mother isn't coming with us?" I paused. "Won't Dr. Lee be offended if we visit without her?"

"Gosh, but if you don't always find something to worry over." He reached down and picked up a pebble. He tossed it from hand to hand. "How will you ever be able to take care of a puppy if you worry about every little thing?"

"I will." I could imagine my puppy—a small, furry, brown boy with big eyes— waiting for me each day when I came home from school. His small, pink tongue licking my hand. "I will."

He-Seung threw the rock so far I couldn't see it land. "Without forgetting your other responsibilities."

Other responsibilities. A sliver of warmth puffed up my whole body. He made me sound so grown up.

"Maybe you're too young," he said.

"I'm not." I walked to school by myself. I did my homework by myself. I swept off the porch. I carried in wood…sometimes.

"What would you do if that bully Kee-Wok came to take your dog?"

I lowered my head. When I had come home, Mother just assumed I'd fallen down, and was happy to sit and sew my shorts. But He-Seung knew. Had his school been out cherry-blossom viewing at the same time, or was it news that was all over the schools? The city? The world?

"Well?" he asked again.

"I'd fight him until he ran away." I clenched my fists, angry at the thought. "I'd punch him in the face."

"Like you did today?" he raised his eyebrows.

My knees ached where Kee-Wok had tripped me on one of the 108 steps. My swollen lips burned with shame. "Well…"

"Show me." He stopped in the middle of the road.

"I don't want to hurt you."

He barked with laughter. My insides boiled. I raised my fist. He grabbed my arm and twisted it behind my back, just as Kee-Wok had. Then he let go of my arm.

"I wasn't concentrating." I took a big breath. Then I turned and threw another punch. Again, he grabbed my arm.

"Anytime you try to hit me, I'll be looking to stop you." He pushed off an imaginary enemy. "You have to be faster. You have to learn to anticipate my moves. Just like in the game of *bahduk*."

"I beat you at that," I reminded him.

"Well, then." He put his arms out, offering me an open target. "Try again."

But I was out of breath. My arm hurt. Already the light in the sky was fading. We'd have to hurry if we wanted to get home before dark. "Can we just get the puppy?"

"First I want to show you a place." He nodded up the road. "It will be a great place to take the puppy on walks."

He led me to Dr. Lee's house, glancing up the entire time toward a window on the second floor. The light was on, and through the curtains I could see the form of Myung-Ja sitting at her desk. But we didn't go to the door. We didn't even walk up the well-swept dirt path. Instead he took me down a road behind the house toward the hills where poor people had shacks made out of boxes and tin. I'd heard Gong-Tae *uhmony* and Mother talk about the sad people that lived back here. The beggars and market sellers. Surely Myung-Ja didn't walk her dog here.

"Why are we going this way?" I followed behind him.

To the right a woman roasted what looked like grass over a small fire. Her face in the firelight was lined with sweat and grime. In the hut further on, a man and woman shouted at one another.

I pulled on his sleeve. "Maybe we should look at this puppy-walking-place tomorrow."

He shrugged my hand away. "Keep going."

We passed the shack loud with anger. Then we were in a small grove of trees. The sky was darkening. A sliver of moonlight shone through the branches.

He pushed me forward. "Go stand by that tree."

Was this a tree the puppy would like? The puppy would be lucky to have a brave owner like me, willing to bring it here. I didn't think I'd be able to come here all by myself, though. "Will you come with me to walk the dog? Sometimes?"

He-Seung shook his head at me. He had his hands on his hips. "Just repeat after me. 'I'm not afraid of the dark.'"

If he wasn't going to come here with me, I would walk the puppy at the nice park during the day when the sun was bright. Not in this creepy place where it was dark and filled with strange animals, angry people. Maybe even ghosts.

"I'm not afraid of the dark." I glanced around.

"Say it louder."

"I'm not afraid of the dark," I called out, hoping no ghosts would hear me and appear to prove me wrong.

"Again."

"I'm not afraid of the dark," I shouted so loud my throat hurt. Then I whispered, "Can we get the puppy now?"

"Stay here." His voice was like ice. "I'll be back in thirty minutes."

My insides melted. He-Seung's word was law, I knew. But thirty whole minutes? "Brother, please don't leave."

He turned and walked away.

I stood rooted to the spot. My legs shook, despite the warmth of the night. He-Chul would never have done this to me.

The sky grew darker and darker until I couldn't even see my own feet. I stared up at the sliver of light glowing in between the tops of the trees. I imagined ghosts coming to take me away to the moon.

Finally, when I felt like I'd been standing by this tree forever, not just thirty minutes, I heard footsteps and voices. Perhaps He-Seung had brought his friend, Gong-Tae. I didn't care if he'd brought his whole class, as long as he was there. I wanted to grab onto him and go home. I hated being brave. The footsteps neared.

"I heard some fool yelling that he wasn't afraid of the dark," a man's voice said. "If I find that idiot, I'm going to squeeze his neck so he won't be yelling anymore."

The voice didn't sound like He-Seung or Gong-Tae. A shiver ran down my back.

"Oh, come now," another voice said. Again, not He-Seung's. "Perhaps his mother is tired of leading him to the woods to pee."

The two of them laughed at this. I listened hard for a third voice. I prayed with my hands clasped so tight that my fingers hurt, as I strained to hear He-Seung's deep laugh. I prayed that I would soon feel his arm on my shoulder.

The footsteps sounded louder coming towards me. A sour smell filled the air, like the drink Uncle brought to our house one time which made Father angry. I didn't think He-Seung was making those steps. If I didn't move, these men who were not He-Seung would walk right into me. Grab me. Squeeze my neck.

I turned from the sound and walked one foot in front of the other. The leaves beneath my feet crackled. Each step thundered in my ears. I took another step and hit my head on something solid—the tree. I grabbed hold, hoping that there were no snakes or lizards or spiders waiting to bite me. I felt my way around to the other side.

The footsteps stopped. Had the men heard me? I held my breath. The bark crumbled beneath my trembling fingers. My heart pounded so hard I thought my shirt would burst open.

A sprinkling sounded. An earthy smell filled my nose, like the salve Mother made to cure the sores on He-Seung. Warm liquid splashed on my leg. I wanted to move, to shout out, "Hey, buddy. Go pee somewhere else." But I was frozen. How could He-Seung have left me like this?

Another forever later, I heard another noise. The rustling of leaves. The men who peed on me had long since left. Had one of them come back again? Or was it an animal, a hungry animal coming to bite off a chunk of my wet leg? Perhaps a man's pee was as delicious as chili sauce to the wild animals. I grabbed onto the tree. There was no escape for me. The rustling stopped.

"Where are you?" a voice called.

That voice was the most wonderful sound I'd ever heard. All the muscles in my body relaxed. I ran towards the voice and grabbed onto He-Seung's hand. "I'm here."

He dislodged his hand from my grip and patted me on the shoulder as we walked down the path. "Now, that wasn't so hard, was it?"

I thought of those strange men who peed on my leg, of all the funny noises, of the ghosts who might have taken me away. My eyes stung. "It was so dark."

"It's not that bad." He nudged my shoulder. "Look over there. You can see the Weaver and the Cow Herder."

I rubbed the tears from my eyes. Even the dirty woman who'd been sitting by the fire had gone inside. "I don't see anyone."

"In the sky." He-Seung pointed. "See the stars? There is the Weaver up there."

My brother was talking crazy. Wasn't only God up there? I was tempted to mention this, but I was so grateful he had come to rescue me instead of those men who would have squeezed my neck. "Can we go home now?"

"What about the puppy?" he asked.

I'd forgotten about the original reason we were out here wandering around in the dark. Still, would we really stop at Dr. Lee's home so late without Mother? When my pants were soaked with pee? Heat rose to my face.

"You already forgot about the puppy?" He pushed my shoulder.

"No, it's just..." I wanted to be home, surrounded by the warmth of our bright lights and listening to mother's voice humming out-of-tune hymns. I reached for him. "Maybe Mother misses us."

"Sure she does." He batted my hand away. "Come on. Your time in the woods has made you stink."

My time in the woods. I had actually spent time alone in the woods in the dark, something I never would have thought possible. Brother had turned me into a tough guy so I could protect my puppy. Maybe I would even be a *Jangsah* someday. I let out a deep sigh, my eyes stinging again. My legs burned as I tried to keep up with He-Seung, my bright star in the dark night.

That the majesty of our Imperial house towers high above everything to be found in the world and and that it is as durable as heaven and earth is too well known to need dwelling here.
—**Baron Oura, former Japanese Minister of Agriculture and Commerce, 1942**

Tuesday April 21, 1942—next day

Baby He-Dong

I sat in the living room next to Mother. She had her lap filled Myung-Ja's dress, letting out the hem. She hummed *My Gracious Redeemer*. At least I thought that's what it was. It might have been *Amazing Grace*. Upstairs, He-Seung banged around his room.

I leaned over my reader, trying to focus on my homework. I no longer felt like a tough guy. Last night those men might have done more than just pee on me. They might have broken my neck. And what if an animal had gotten me? What if I'd wandered so far from those dirty men I'd gotten lost?

I sighed and put my finger under the next line in my social-studies reader. The chapter talked about how the Japanese were fierce warriors. How they were going to take over the world. How Koreans were proud to have them as leaders.

I heard another bang, a drawer slamming. What was He-Seung doing up there? Perhaps he was searching for a pencil or had lost his pocketknife. Or he was changing his clothes to take me to another dog-walking place.

"Mother?" I would tell her. She would scold He-Seung for being so careless. She would protect me.

"Hmm?" Her voice made a noise, but she didn't look up from the cloth in front of her.

"Mother?" I said again.

She cleared her throat and started in on another tune. Her eyes followed the careful stitches she made.

I looked back to my reader. It was good she wasn't crying. Her eyes weren't even swollen today. Maybe I shouldn't bother her. Besides, if I told on He-Seung, he might get so angry he wouldn't get me the puppy.

He had talked on and on about how the puppy was so tiny it would fit in his hand. How it had big brown eyes. How its fur was softer than new grass.

If he was planning on another puppy-training mission, I just wouldn't go out with him. I'd tell him I didn't feel so good. No, I couldn't tell that lie again. But, then, it wasn't a lie. My stomach burned.

He-Seung's footsteps thundered on the stairs. I could imagine Father shouting, "Stop all that un-Godlike noise." Mother, however, didn't even look up.

I stuck my head in my reader. *The Japanese are fierce warriors. The Japanese are fierce warriors. The Japanese are fierce warriors.*

He-Seung strode into the room. I spotted his brown stocking feet next to my elbow. Something sharp poked my cheek.

He-Seung dangled his slingshot in front of my face. "Ready to try?"

Even though I'd won the *Bahduk* game, won our bet, I hadn't really expected him to let me touch his slingshot. Maybe I'd proven to him that I was tougher and more grown up than he thought. A warmth spread through my chest.

"Then again." He tapped the reader in my hands with the tip of the slingshot. "Maybe you're too busy."

I closed the social studies reader and tossed it on the floor. "I'm done."

The sun was already falling low in the sky. But instead of going to the backyard and setting up empty cans, so we'd have as much practice time as possible before it got dark, he took me down the street. We walked past Dr. Lee's house again. With each step, my heart felt heavier. What if he made me stand in the forest alone again?

"I've changed my mind." It was difficult to catch my breath. "I really should go back—"

"Oh, quit your whining." He Seung pulled me along. "We're here already."

We turned into the nearby park. The sound of croaking frogs filled the air. I forced myself to breathe.

A large pond took up most of the area, and we walked down to the edge. The dark waters rippled, probably from the night breeze. But maybe from something worse. Ih-Duk told me about a monster who had dragged a little girl down to the bottom last summer.

He-Seung pulled the slingshot from his pocket, picked up a pebble, and aimed for a large rock in the middle of the pond. His pebble hit the target. He smiled. "Bulls-eye."

I stepped closer. I tapped his arm.

"What?" He looked back, as though surprised to see me.

The pebbles crunched beneath my feet. "I thought you said you were going to show me."

"I am." He held out the slingshot. "You sit there on the ground and watch for twenty hits. If you don't move—not even the hair on your scrawny arms—I'll let you try."

I nodded, sitting down on the gravel, crossing my legs and putting my hands on my thighs. How hard could it be for me to sit still for twenty tries? He-Seung's lips were clenched together in concentration as he aimed the pebble. His eyes looked fierce and angry, as if he were in a fight. He never missed.

Perhaps if I looked fierce like that, I too would be able to hit the rock. He-Seung picked up another pebble, the fifth one. Fifteen more to go. Then it would be my turn. He glanced back at me, his eyes wide. He probably thought I couldn't sit in one place so long.

"Is that a stink bug?" He looked at my legs.

"Where?" I shook my legs up and down, brushing them with both hands.

"Ha." He pointed the slingshot at me. "You moved."

I groaned. But He-Seung went back to picking up pebbles as if I wasn't there. I closed my eyes—so that not even my eyeballs moved—and counted the sound of the pebbles hitting the rock. One, two, three…fifteen, sixteen.

A tickling sensation ran up my thigh. Was He-Seung trying to get me to move again? Clack. But how could he tickle me and shoot rocks at the same time? I opened my eyes and peeked. Something big and black crawled up my leg.

"Get off me," I shouted, jumping up.

He-Seung looked over, laughing. He stepped close to me and flicked the giant black bug off with the tip of his slingshot.

"Looks like we're starting over again." He made a big sigh. It sounded pretend. "Have a seat."

I thought of Mr. Ben Franklin's experiment with the ants. How one ant told another ant who told another ant where all the good food was. What if that giant black bug did the same, coming back to find me with all his friends? I didn't want to sit on the ground again.

"It was only a beetle," he said.

I wanted to try the slingshot. But I didn't want to be eaten up by beetles or anything else while I waited for my turn.

"I am strong." He stood in front of me, his shoulders back, head high. "Say that."

"I—" I looked at my shoe. Was that another bug?

"Say it." He tapped my chest with the slingshot.

"I am." I hopped to a different part of the ground. It was an ant. That little guy would give my location away to the whole ant community. "Strong."

"Louder." He thwacked my calf with the rubber end of his slingshot.

"I am strong," I shouted.

"I can do anything," he said.

"You can?" I stopped hopping around. "Can you bring Fath—"

"Repeat."

"But Ito *Sensei* said I can't do—"

He thwacked me again. The back of my leg burned.

"I can do anything," I shouted.

"Now sit down," he ordered. "And don't move."

Blood coursed through my body. I could do this. I cleared a spot beneath my feet and sat back down. I slowed my breathing, hoping that the less breath I took, the less likely other living things would hear me and come visit. This seemed to slow He-Seung, as well. He was on his eighth shot. But he couldn't seem to find rocks he liked. He would pick one up, hold it in his hand. Then drop it and look for another. My neck ached. My legs itched to move. He-Seung had just made his fifteenth shot. I wanted to stand up. The sun was getting lower in the sky.

"That's twenty." I jumped up. My legs were so stiff from sitting that I tumbled into him.

"Are you sure?"

"He-Seung." I grabbed onto his arm.

He handed me the slingshot, showing me how to grasp the leather strap, pull it back and let it fly. I put a pebble in between the leather strap, my fingers trembling with excitement. I pulled back and released. The pebble landed right at my feet.

"Don't be so nice." He-Seung took the slingshot from me. "Hold tight, pull back, release. It's simple."

I tried again and again, but my pebbles always landed near my feet. A baby could have tossed a rock further.

He-Seung pointed in the distance. "Pretend you're aiming at the Japs, hoping to hit one of them in the eye."

Was that why his eyes looked so angry and determined when he was shooting? What would Father say about such thinking? I thought he'd feel disappointed.

"Go on, hurry up." He motioned back and forth with his hand. "The sun is going to set."

I picked up another pebble. Across the water, beyond the trees, the bright orange globe of the sun had started to drop. It would be dark soon. Darn sun. I aimed at that orange globe, willing it to stay up longer. I pulled back the leather and let the pebble fly. Splash. My pebble landed in the water.

He handed me another pebble. "Nice shot."

I looked to see if he was being sarcastic. But he was already waiting for me to try again. I was glad I hadn't told Mother about He-Seung leaving me in the woods. I'd been brave enough to survive that, and now here I was shooting a real slingshot. I let the pebble fly.

The dynasties created by men may collapse
but the Heavenly-created throne is beyond men's power.
—**Baron Kiichiro Hiranumu, Home Minister of Japan, 1941**

Tuesday, April 21, 1942—same day

He-Seung

I was ready to find Father now. It had been three long days with no news. Last night while He-Dong had fended off ghosts in the woods, Myung-Ja had talked so long of stars I hadn't had a chance to question her about the prison. I wasn't risking that again. I'd take He-Dong with me.

"Why are we going this way?" He-Dong asked.

Instead of passing Myung-Ja's house, we headed up the path. "I thought we'd stop and see the puppy."

"It's dark already." He-Dong's voice wobbled. "How will we see them?"

"Just follow me. Quietly." She had told me to meet her outside by the puppies. As I walked down the front path, though, I could see her silhouette in her bedroom window. Her long hair was tied up. Her small frame sat up straight at her desk.

I wondered if Father was far away or just a short walk from here. After I discovered the location, I would take He-Dong home, and then make a quick trip to the prison. Did prisons have closing times like the stores in the marketplace? I ran a hand over my stubby scalp.

"What are we doing now?" He-Dong whispered.

I knelt down and felt around for a few pebbles. I wasn't very good at baseball, but I had a pretty good pitch. I threw a pebble, a tingle of pride filling me when I heard the windowpane tinkle. Myung-Ja didn't look up.

I threw another pebble, this time a bit harder. A thwack sounded. Myung-Ja rushed over to the window and looked out. The sky was now pitch black, though.

"Who's out there?" she called.

He-Dong pulled on my sleeve. "We're scaring her."

I wished for a candle or a match to light my face. I called up to her. "It's me."

"Oh." Her expression softened.

"Did you…" I swallowed. "Did you find out about—"

She slammed the window shut. I felt as if Father had hit me with his cane. Had I offended her by not asking about stars or puppies or other pleasantries? I saw another figure walk across the room. Her mother.

"Maybe we shouldn't be watching," He-Dong said.

"A little watching is good for you," I replied.

Last night I'd gotten stuck listening to her silly stories about stars, pretending I hadn't ever heard the tale of the star-crossed lovers, watching her feathery lashes blink again and again. Today I'd waited all afternoon to come here. Now her mother was gumming away about something. I felt blood coursing through my body. Surely my temples were pulsing like Father's with frustration.

"How much is a little?" He-Dong asked.

"Just be patient," I said.

Myung-Ja and her mother left the bedroom. I heard the slamming of the back door. Voices.

He-Dong latched tighter to my hand. "We better leave."

I shook He-Dong's hand loose and hurried around to the back. Myung-Ja held a candle as she hurried along the path.

"I'm here," I whispered.

"Ah," she cried out, the candle falling from her hands.

I reached forward and caught it. The flame flickered in the dark. We both waited for the sound of footsteps, another light. He-Dong came over next to me.

"Sorry," I whispered, holding the flame up to her face. "I didn't mean to frighten you." I didn't want to get lost in her small mouth and sweet brown eyes. I'd come here for information about Father's whereabouts. I cleared my throat. "What did you find out?"

She nodded at my little brother, taking the candle from me. Her soft fingers brushed against mine. "Come."

We followed. Her skirt swished. Her small feet padded on the dirt. The smell of fresh flowers filled the air.

Myung-Ja rested her candle on the top of the dog pen. Mee-Won raised her head and looked at us. Then she lay back down, four pups nuzzled up to her stomach. One puppy lay off to the side by himself.

"Look at all those little guys." He-Dong marveled. "They're just like you said."

I put my hand around He-Dong's chubby fingers and stuffed them through the wooden slats. The one pup that lay by himself sniffed the air, stood on shaky legs, and wobbled towards my brother's shaky fingers.

"That poor little puppy was the last one born." Myung-Ja explained. "You remember. You delivered him."

He-Dong looked up from where the puppy slobbered on his fingers. "You did?"

I shrugged.

"Didn't he tell you?" Myung-Ja asked.

My lips twitched. Heat rushed to my cheeks.

"This little fella never fights for himself," she said.

"I think this one likes me." He-Dong leaned closer.

"That's strange." Myung-Ja said.

I laughed. "Definitely strange."

She made a tsk sound like her mother. She leaned down to stroke the defenseless puppy. I watched her small bottom, wishing the candlelight was stronger. "That fella never acts like he has a will of his own. He's always getting pushed away by that fat puppy." She patted He-Dong's shoulder. "You demonstrated that although he's little, he does have a will."

He-Dong's face lit up when she put her sweet fingers on his shirt. I couldn't blame him. I took a deep breath. Bringing He-Dong along was not helping me concentrate. "What else have you learned today?"

"A lot." She turned to me, pulling her pony tail to the side. "It takes an oxcart to get there."

So the prison was not nearby. I would need to wait until tomorrow. I would skip school, although I could imagine Father frowning. Nothing was more important than our education. I paced back and forth in front of her. "And?"

She looked at me.

"That's it?" The air exploded from my lips.

"Don't make it sound like that." She snapped back as if I'd slapped her.

"An oxcart can go north, south, east or west." I pointed in every direction. "Can plod along for minutes or hours."

"Or just stand still," He-Dong said, looking up at us as if we were discussing some scientific theory.

I wondered if Dr. Lee was home now. I looked to the house. I would just knock on the door and ask him, myself. In fact, that's what I should have done in the first place. Not relied on this silly girl.

"He's not here," she whispered. "And no, he wasn't called to the prison. It's Mr. Im again."

"I can't believe that's all you found out," I whispered back through gritted teeth.

"Myung-Ja? Are you still out here?" Myung-Ja *uhmony* stepped outside with a candle in her hand.

I dropped down on the ground behind the pen, pulling He-Dong with me. The smell of rooster shit filled my nose. A piece of grass tickled my neck. I yanked until it came out of the ground.

"What are we doing now?" He-Dong asked.

"Practicing being quiet," I whispered. "And not moving even an inch. Just like you did so well in the park."

"Are the puppies all right?" The sound of Myung-Ja *uhmony*'s footsteps plodded on the dirt path towards us.

I had visions of my runt brother popping up to brush off a stink bug the moment she came over. I put my arm around his shoulders, holding him tight.

"I'm still checking." Myung-Ja busied herself, making noise in the pen. I imagined her leaning down and petting the runt puppy.

I couldn't believe I was laying here in rooster droppings. Couldn't she shoo her mother inside? Couldn't she find out the location of the prison? Couldn't she do anything? I reached out with the long piece of grass and poked at where I thought Myung-Ja's ankles were.

"Ah," she cried, swatting at the air next to her.

"What happened?" Her mother called.

"Nothing." Myung-Ja held the candle up to her face, smiling in the direction of her mother.

"Come on inside." Myung-Ja *uhmony's* footsteps retreated toward the house. "It's late."

"Yes, Mother."

Myung-Ja had been promising me for days that she could find out where Father was. What was she so busy doing that she couldn't ask her Father? I poked at her ankles again.

"You may be able to bully others." Myung-Ja's voice sounded right over us. "But not me."

Myung-Ja stomped toward the house. Dust flew back in my face. The back door slammed. Had she been talking to the fat puppy? Or me?

I stood, my legs wobbly from having the door shut in my face. Or perhaps it was from almost being caught with Dr. Lee's daughter. I brushed dirt from my pants. "Let's go."

"But we can't leave this little guy," He-Dong said.

He probably had his hand back in the pen, getting kissed by that runt of a puppy. I reached over him, feeling around for the soft mound.

"He's probably worn out from licking you to death." I put the puppy on its mother's stomach. "Let him rest."

I grabbed He-Dong, and pulled him away. I set the pace, jogging back home.

"You fooled me, Brother," He-Dong called, his voice filled with excitement. "You were both training me, right?"

"Huh?" I turned toward him, as if that would make his idiotic comment clearer.

"I've never heard you call her Myung-Ja before." He practically shouted.

"What are you talking about?" I pushed him to run faster.

"You've always called her—" He sucked in a breath. "Well you just never said her name before."

I flushed. The runt did catch on to some things. "I guess I—I don't know. She's helping me train you, isn't she? She needs a real name if she's going to help me."

"Right," He-Dong said, sounding happy with this explanation.

I wished I could be so easily pleased. I wished Myung-Ja was actually helping me. I'd been ready to come back and reassure Mother that Father was fine. *Keep your mother and brother safe,* the print-shop lady had said. I was incapable of such a thing. My head hurt. Another day was coming to an end, and I was no closer to helping our family than when I'd wiped drool from my face this morning.

The Greater East Asia Co-prosperity Sphere will not be isolated from other parts of the world but, on the contrary, will be the center of the new World Order.
—Finance Minister Okinobu Kaya, 1942

Wednesday, April 22, 1942—next day

He-Seung

I threw off my comforter. I'd been half-awake all night, drifting in and out of a light haze of sleep, waiting for the sun to rise so I could visit Dr. Lee before he disappeared for the day.

I put away my bedding and grabbed my school uniform. I knew I'd be late for school if I ever made it at all. As I was already on the worst of terms with Watanabe *Sensei,* this would mean just another opportunity for the royal jerk to swat me with his cane. I resisted the urge to wear the long pants of my winter uniform. I picked up my school bag and hopped down the steps, taking them two at a time. Mother met me at the bottom of the staircase.

"You're up early. Thank you." She rubbed her hands together. "I can't remember you ever waking so early, even when you were a baby."

"Yes. Well..." I headed for the kitchen. "The Japs give us chickenfeed. We wake up like starving roosters."

Mother didn't follow, instead staying in the living room. I continued onto the kitchen, curious that Mother didn't rush to serve me. Why had she thanked me for waking up early, and what was she doing in the living room? Getting ready for a sewing circle with that useless housewife In-Young? Making some get-well gift for Mr. Im?

After I finished serving myself breakfast, I went into the living room to see what was so important. Mother kneeled down straightening the string in the middle of the living room floor, as if Father were in his chair waiting for parishioners to show up for his Wednesday prayer meeting. She had laid out cushions on the women's side. Father's Bible rested on the rocking chair.

I remembered a widow Kim whose husband died of pneumonia one winter. Even after he was long dead and buried, she walked the streets turning and talking to the air as if he were right next to her. I felt as if the floor had dropped from beneath me. "Mother?"

"I've been praying all night." She kneaded her hands together, blushing.

Did she think that if she prayed all night and set up the room for Father's mid-week sermon that the Japs would release Father from prison to conduct his sermon?

"You must be tired." I kneeled to help her straighten the string which served as a row divider. My heart beat hard. "People might not come today, you know."

"It's best to be ready," she said, her voice small.

"They might think, well…" I pushed at the string on the floor. "Even if Father came home, he'd need a rest."

"You're right." Mother grabbed onto my hand. She closed her eyes and shook her head. "It's just…it's nice to have a moment to worship."

The grandfather clock ticked. A sore on my leg itched. He-Dong ran the water in the upstairs bathroom.

"Did you hear that?" Mother asked.

"What?" I cocked my head. "He-Dong running the water as if there's no end?"

"Someone's coming." Mother stood.

She ran to the door and I followed close behind, now hearing the sound of footsteps on the front porch. They were soft steps, though, not the sound of Father's black leather shoes.

Mother opened the door. Old Mrs. Im stood on the front porch, a bowl of small dried fish in her hands.

"Good morning." Mother stepped forward. "How good to see you. Is your husband better?"

"Yes, yes. The silly old man, jumping on ladders like a little boy." She handed Mother the treat. "I just thought." She looked at her feet. "Well, today is Wednesday."

Mother gave me a look. Then she opened the door wider. "Yes, it is."

Why would they bother gathering, if Father wasn't here to tell them what God expected? What would they do? Just stare at the rocking chair and hope for some divine inspiration?

I leaned down to grab my shoes. "I've got to—"

"Look." Mother clasped her hands together. "There's In-Young and Deacon Nam."

In-Young skipped behind Deacon Nam like a child, her head down not out of respect, but as if she were searching for flowers along the path. He had a scowl on his face as if he'd just eaten salty soup and burnt rice. Then again, perhaps he, too, was wondering why everyone was gathering at our house.

I hoped Mother hadn't gone around yesterday telling her friends that Father would be home. I felt a weakness in my legs. I slipped off my shoes.

Mother looked over and smiled. She indicated for me to lead the guests into the living room. He-Dong was already seated with his hands folded, his eyes closed. I wondered if he thought Father would appear. The room felt large and cold.

"Shall we pray?" Mother returned, handing out cups of water to all the seated parishioners. "Deacon Nam?"

"Dear Lord," Deacon Nam bellowed as if he were trying to be Father. "We come to you this morning in thanks. Although we do not always understand why you do the things you do, we know You will take care of us. You will show us the light. You will guide us. You will…"

I found myself wishing Father would step through the door and take over. Father certainly went on and on, but this man was like listening to the noisy chatter of birds in the morning. If God was showing us the light, why the hell didn't we understand what was going on? And if God was taking care of us, why was Father not here? I coughed, louder than Mr. Im ever had, drowning out this man's foolish words and hoping he'd finish soon.

"Amen," everyone called centuries later, me the loudest.

"I need to be off to school." I stood, putting my hand up to cover a yawn.

"I remember when I was your age," Deacon Nam leaned forward, as if he were some wise old man rather than just a little older than my brother, He-Chul. "I always went to school early. I got to read from the textbook at school. I got to help the teacher write things on the board. It was in the early morning, I discovered the most."

I bowed my way out of the room before he could impart more wisdom. I had a brief vision of him as a school kid. He probably was a bean-curd boy worse than He-Dong.

Mother followed me. She handed me my *bento* lunch and opened the front door.

Myung-Ja and her mother were coming up the path. I stared as if perhaps I hadn't slept enough last night and was dreaming. They had stopped coming to these gatherings even before Father was taken away. Why were they here today? Where was Dr. Lee?

"It's such a relief to be here." Myung-Ja *uhmony*'s voice cracked. Her eyes filled with tears. "I feel better already."

"What's the matter?" I blurted.

Mother shook her head at me, her earlier gratitude erased faster than Watanabe *Sensei* could clear the blackboard. She gave my shoulder a push.

"Wait. I forgot something." I slipped off my shoes and tripped my way down the hall to the bathroom. Mother laughed, as if I were five years old.

I closed the door and listened. Last time Myung-Ja *uhmony* had cried at our home, her daughter was leaving for the factories. Had she received some word? Or was she crying about Father?

"I'm so glad you came," Mother's voice carried from the hall.

"I hadn't realized how much I'd been missing this," Myung-Ja *uhmony* replied.

"Why don't you come help me in the kitchen," Mother said. "Myung-Ja, dear, you go on in and get settled with the others."

So the old woman's tears were nothing more important than missing prayer time with friends. I would have to tell Gong-Tae he owed me some tears.

I adjusted my collar in front of the mirror above the sink, the small, round mirror which Myung-Ja had stood in front of to remove her dress when she'd come for a fitting. No, I wasn't thinking about that now. Or her. I buttoned the top button and burst out to go find Dr. Lee. Myung-Ja stood right by the door.

"Ah!" I jumped.

She lifted her hand to my mouth, her small fingers covering my lips. They were soft and warm. I inhaled.

"I didn't think you had to..." She nodded toward the bathroom. She let her hand drop.

I felt heat rise to my face. She understood me, had waited for me despite my anger with her last night. I cleared my throat. "I'm—uh—"

"Sorry for getting so ridiculously impatient last night?" Myung-Ja finished.

"Well, I expected too much from you." I said, the words tasting bad even as I said them. "I mean, you're just a—"

She raised her eyebrows at me, cocking her head to the side. Her lips were pursed as if she were telling me to shut mine.

"I'm sorry." It wasn't as hard to say those two words as I'd thought.

"Can you carry these?" Mother's voice sounded from the kitchen. They were coming back to the living room.

I hurried past Myung-Ja and went to the door, leaning down to slip on my shoes.

"I went through some of Father's papers." Myung-Ja came up behind me. "I know where the prison is."

"Still an oxcart ride away?" I said, the sarcasm thick in my throat.

She pointed her toe out from beneath her long black uniform skirt, pushing at the wooden floor. "It's crazy to go there."

"Please, Myung-Ja." I stood up and looked toward the sound of our mothers.

"It's just you have a tendency to—" She poked at the imaginary spot on the floor. "Your temper is always so red hot."

I looked at her intense brown eyes. I felt heat rip through me like I'd never known. "Trust me."

"I prayed all night about this gathering." Mother's voice grew louder. She would see me still standing in the hall in less than a second.

I quietly opened the door and slipped outside. I turned to implore Myung-Ja one last time, and she was there. In my arms. She seemed as surprised as I, emitting a squeak. But she didn't pull away. Instead, she leaned closer and whispered the directions to the prison in my ear.

The position of the United States and Britain today, which points to their
decline to second-rate or third-rate powers, or even to total disintegration
and collapse, is indeed pitiable, even though it was brought about by
their own folly. It is too late for them to gnash their teeth in remorse.
What better lesson can there be to those
that revel in arrogance and tyranny?
—**The New Order in Greater East Asia (Magazine), April 1942**

Wednesday, April 22, 1942—same day

He-Seung

Gong-Tae walked with me down a narrow deserted street. Since we
didn't have an oxcart handy, we'd been travelling for hours on foot. At
least it felt that way.

"Are you sure Dr. Lee said to go this way?" Gong-Tae kicked at the
dust.

"Well, not exactly."

"That's what I thought." Gong-Tae stopped. "I knew this felt wrong."

"You sound worse than He-Dong." I hit his arm, pushing him onward.
"I meant it wasn't exactly Dr. Lee."

"Myung-Ja *uhmony*?" He raised his eyebrows in such disbelief I had to
laugh.

I wondered yet again if Myung-Ja had given me the correct directions.
She'd said she'd read through her father's papers. But I remembered once
when Father was ill and I'd asked Mother to help me with my social
studies. She attempted to read to me out loud, pronouncing each character
so slow, so mangled that I ended up in tears. First of laughter, then
frustration. Maybe Myung-Ja wasn't able to read well either. I would
forgive her that. She had tried. And the memory of her in my arms still put
a smile on my face.

"Please tell me we are not just wandering aimlessly in hopes of finding
this place." Gong-Tae sighed, looking back the way we'd come.

"Myung-Ja said it was this way," I said, feeling my cheeks burn.

"You trusted Purple Face to give you direct—" He stopped walking. He
pulled at his ear. "What did you call her?"

"She's really very…" I crossed my arms. "Funny, kind, intelligent. She
even knows how to play *bahduk*."

"You played *bahduk* with her?" His eyes grew wide. "Gosh, if I'd
known you were going to lose your head the minute I left you alone."

"If the prison isn't at the end of this road, we'll just turn back," I said,
holding out my *bento* lunchbox as an incentive. It held rice, black beans,

kimchee. I had brought it for Father. But I'd share it with Gong-Tae if we couldn't find the prison. "And, no I didn't play *bahduk* with her."

He fanned his hand in front of his face, as if that was such a relief to hear. "Do we have to bother going all the way to the end of this road? I think we can just stop here and admit that Purple Face sent you on a goose chase."

"She has a name." I shoved his shoulder. "Besides, what's that?"

I pointed over the horizon at a cement roof as I picked up my pace. Gong-Tae matched my pace. I put on a final spurt of speed, reaching the cement building on the corner first.

A guard, wearing a blue uniform and cap, stood by the door leaning against a large rifle. He glanced at us, at the knife on my belt, the box in my hands. He pretended not to care, looking away as if we were gnats buzzing about the air. But he ran his fingers over the top of his rifle, where a pointy bayonet gleamed in the sun.

"Excuse me," Gong-Tae said in his most formal Japanese.

"What do you want?" The guard's Japanese was rough, his uniform wrinkled. He was Korean.

"I'm looking for Yamamoto Hirosaki," I said, matching his rough tone.

"Who?" The guard raised his eyebrows.

"Mr. Yamamoto," Gong-Tae said. "He is—was a pastor."

"There aren't any pastors here." The guard yawned and scratched himself.

My mouth felt dry. "Can you check?"

"Check?" The guard laughed, spittle flying from his mouth. "This isn't a boarding house."

"I'm his son."

"I don't care if you're the Emperor of Japan." The guard rocked back and forth on his feet. "He's here—if he's here—because he's a criminal. I don't need to check on him."

Blood raced through my body, pounding at my temples. I wanted to grab the guard and throw him out of the way. We'd spent forever looking for Father. At least this stupid guard could check to see if Father was here. I felt Gong-Tae's hand on my shoulder.

"Anything else?" The guard touched his bayonet again, as if to remind me that his scrawny ass was more powerful.

"You're Korean." I said the one thing that had irritated me from the start. "Just like me." I gritted my teeth. "Just like my father."

The guard spit on the ground next to me. "You're a smart one."

Gong-Tae pulled on my arm. If I looked at his face, I knew I'd see him begging me to calm down, to keep my mouth shut. I could hear him saying *I'm risking my life with you at the helm.*

Still, this guard held a fellow Korean in prison for some rule those foreign Japs had made. I wanted to kick him down the steps. I gripped onto the *bento* box so tight the lid rattled and flew off.

"Ahhh, *kimchee*," the man said switching to Korean, the words tumbling from his mouth.

"His Mother's specialty," Gong-Tae jumped in, chatting as amiably as if we were at a church social. "He and my mother always make it together. Best in town."

The guard stepped closer to get a better look, a better sniff. "If you leave the *bento* with me, I'll make sure your father gets it."

I put the lid tightly on the box. "You said there weren't any pastors here."

"Only criminals." He licked his lips.

"You don't even know who my father is."

"Maybe I do." He let his rifle sway back and forth. "His God keeps him busier than a jealous mistress. Prays all day and night, thanks God for every grain of rice, tries to convert his fellow cellmates."

Gong-Tae clapped his hands together, as if we'd just scored a goal.

"You could be describing any Christian." I stepped back.

"And his temples pulse when he's angry." The guard lifted his chin in my direction. "Just like yours."

Gong-Tae nudged me. "That's him."

Maybe the guard did know Father. I wanted Father to have some of Mother's cooking, to know that we were out here watching him. Waiting. "His name is Yamamoto Hirosaki."

"I heard you the first time." He grabbed the *bento* from my hands.

"Thank you," Gong-Tae gushed over and over.

"Thank you." I forced the words out. I felt Gong-Tae's hand on my back forcing me to bow down before we left.

We walked down the road and around the corner. The sun was setting, and the sky was filling with colors.

"That was amazing." Gong-Tae was full of energy, jumping up and kicking the walls along the road.

"I know." I followed Gong-Tae's path, my footsteps touching the exact spots where he jumped. "How could that guard be such a traitor?"

"Maybe he has no choice." Gong-Tae stopped, and I rammed into his back. "But I meant that was amazing that we got out of there without being killed. Not only that, you discovered where your father is. Your father will be so surprised to get lunch from you…so pleased."

He would, wouldn't he? I could imagine the smile on his face as the guard rapped on the bars of his cell, holding up my lunchbox. Father would know it was mine from the knife scrapes on the lid. He would know

Mother's *kimchee* anywhere. I nodded. We had done it. Sort of. Although Father would get Mother's delicious food and would know that we were out here thinking of him, I felt disappointed. I realized then I'd been hoping to be the hero to bring him home.

"I wish I knew how to find Myung-Hae as easily." Gong-Tae looked back to the prison.

"We could ask the guard if he knows anything," I suggested. "Next time."

"Next time?" Gong-Tae said.

As he stood there, I could already see his idea as if it were written on his forehead. "Okay, this time."

We turned back. As we neared the cement building, I heard slurping noises. I hurried forward. The guard stood there finishing off Mother's *kimchee*. As soon as he saw us, he dropped the chopsticks and gripped onto his rifle.

"You!" I cried. Anger surged through my limbs, pulsing at my temple like a clapper on a bell. Brutal words filled my head. *Traitor. Liar. Manghal Jarshik!*

"Hello again, esteemed guard." Gong-Tae stepped in front of me.

"What are you doing back here?" The guard barked.

I reached over and pushed Gong-Tae out of the way. Then I remembered Myung-Ja pushing the wooden floor with her toes. *You could get hurt.*

"Are. You. Finished?" I asked the guard, each polite word scraping across my throat like a knife.

"That was the best meal I've had in months," the guard said in Korean.

Low-life scum. Gong-Tae hovered next to me. I swallowed these words, words which felt larger than a boulder in my throat. I forced a smile and put my hands out to take the *bento* box. "You enjoyed."

"Yes. Please come back." The guard said, handing me the empty *bento* box. "And bring your father some more delicious food."

"For Father or you?" The words tumbled out before I could stop them. Like thunder.

"For both of us." The guard stepped forward, thrusting his chest in my face.

"We will." Gong-Tae pushed me toward home.

I felt tired, hungry, defeated. We might have found Father...or maybe just a hungry guard. Gong-Tae, in his fear, had forgotten to ask about the factories. Our miracle of a trip had turned into nothing.

The fruits of victory are tumbling into our mouths too quickly.
**—Emperor Hirohito, the 124th descendent of the Sun Goddess,
on his 41st birthday, April 29, 1942**

Thursday, April 30, 1942—eight days later

Mother (*Uhmony*)

I sat in Min-Kook *uhmony*'s living room next to In-Young. In-Young's arms were laden with shirts and socks, as if she'd been helping Min-Kook *uhmony* clean. Books and papers littered the floor. An old tea cup lay on its side, the brown liquid having dried up on a piece of paper. It always felt as if a big wind had blown through here. Today, the mess mirrored my insides.

I had laundry to bring in off the line, mattresses to beat, marketing to do. But I couldn't bring myself to care about any of these things. All week long my dear's parishioners had come by with food. Widow Rhee brought extra cups of rice. Mrs. Choi brought some *kimchee*. Myung-Ja *uhmony* had asked me to lower the hem on Myung-Ja's dress and then given us another huge envelope of money. I was touched by her kindness. By everyone's. But at the same time, I was scared. I wanted Min-Kook *uhmony* to help me understand this.

"I'm so glad you showed up." Min-Kook *uhmony* pushed some books aside to make more room.

"Have you heard any news?" In-Young asked, turning to me.

I listened for Min-Kook *uhmony* to jump in with statistics or rumors or predictions. She cleared the tea cup from the floor, crumpling up the stained piece of paper so loud my insides hurt.

"Not yet." I reached up to move a stray hair from my face, each movement as difficult as slogging through heavy mud.

I waited for sweet In-Young to say everything would be all right, or this was a good way for my sons to grow into strong men, or this was God's will, or one of the other things people said when they came to the house. She didn't say a word, instead leaning over and grabbing onto my hands. Her small fingers felt warm and comforting.

"Like I said, I'm relieved you're here." Min-Kook *uhmony* bustled around, cleaning the table. "I can't help like you can."

I cocked my head. I looked again at the pile of clothes in In-Young's arms. One of the shirts looked like it belonged to Deacon Nam. Had her husband taken her to task again for her poor sewing skills? "Why didn't you come to see me?"

"That's exactly what I said." Min-Kook *uhmony* laughed.

"I didn't want to trouble you with my petty problems." She hugged the clothing tight to her chest as if she could make the pile disappear. "You have so much on your mind."

"But this woman sews as easily as she breathes." Min-Kook *uhmony* handed me her sewing basket. "Besides, it doesn't help to sit and worry about things you can't do anything about."

"I don't mean to sit and worry." I stared at a cobweb billowing above a pile of papers. "It just happens. If I could do something, anything to help my dear." My voice sounded like a question.

"I heard an American pilot firebombed Tokyo. But the Japs—the Japanese are all over the world, like ants on leftovers." Min-Kook *uhmony* looked at me. "All you can do is wait."

That's all I'd been doing. How long would I have to wait? Through my cloudy eyes, I noticed Min-Kook *uhmony* shuffle off to the kitchen, mentioning something about getting us water.

In-Young reached out and held my hand again. I closed my eyes. *Dear God, give me strength to wait.*

"You showed me how to mend a shirt." I heard In-Young's small voice. "But I'm at a loss when it comes to my husband's socks."

I opened my eyes. I couldn't help myself. I smiled.

"I'm a dolt, aren't I?" Her frame crumpled like a flower wilting in the harsh sunlight.

"No. No." Is that what her husband had said? I picked up one of the socks, now noticing stringy attempts at covering the hole. "You can't be expected to know things you haven't been taught."

Min-Kook *uhmony* had a few pieces of wool in her basket, some needles, and an old light bulb. I picked out a piece of wool which looked about the same beige as In-Young's husband's socks. Then I grabbed the old light bulb.

"What's that for?" In-Young leaned toward me.

The light bulb in my sewing basket at home had come from the lamp in my dear's office. I remembered him bringing it to me. I stared at this old bulb as if I could see his strong fingers wrapped around the glass.

"Perhaps Min-Kook *uhmony* forgot to dispose of it." In-Young looked around the room at all the other items that needed disposing.

"I heard that." Min-Kook *uhmony* rushed in the room, depositing two cups of water on the table. "That's one piece of garbage, dear girl, that I intended to keep. The shape of the bulb is almost like a heel."

I stuck the light bulb inside the sock.

"See?" Min-Kook *uhmony* crossed her arms.

In-Young blushed. "You're both so intelligent."

"You're just easy to impress," Min-Kook *uhmony* patted her arm, then returned to the kitchen. In fact, she kept wandering in and out of the kitchen. I assumed she was washing dishes or doing laundry. Or perhaps the kitchen was a place of refuge for her. Each time she surfaced she remembered more tidbits about the war. The Japanese were attacking the Philippines. The Japanese were headed to some Alaskan islands. The Emperor had handed out oranges in celebration of his birthday. In-Young and I nodded and then returned to her sock dilemma.

"Your needle looks bigger than the one I have." In-Young leaned forward.

"This one is for heavier yarns." I showed the thick silver needle to her, passing her the yarn so she could thread the needle for me. I showed her how to catch the sides of a hole, the way to close up even the largest gap.

"You're better than Sim's Tailor," In-Young looked up at me, her eyes wide.

I paused in my sewing. Nobody would compare a minister's wife to a simple peddler at the market. Then I remembered this was In-Young. She often spoke before she thought.

"I'm sorry." She blushed. "It's just that God gave you so much talent. And I have none."

"Nonsense." I reached out and touched her knee. Her self-criticism made my heart hurt. She wasn't good at cooking or sewing or observing rules of etiquette. About that she was right. What was she good at? I concentrated on the needle going in and out of each stitch and the ease with which this problem got solved. I closed the gaping hole in the sock. "You make people happy."

"Do I?" She looked at me, her eyes shining.

"Yes." I looked to the mended socks in my lap. "This makes me happy."

"I'll bring more," she said.

I reached out and patted her arm. Surely she filled the air with sweet noises, for how could she have so much mending? I watched the needle in my hands. In and out. Problem. Solution. In and out. Problem. Solution. There was something soothing about the motion. I had not learned anything new about my dear. But the clamp which had gripped my heart all week had loosened a tiny bit.

Dear friends! Folks at home! You probably sincerely believe that you are
defending democracy from the aggressors, but nothing could be farther
from the truth. The present fighting has been caused by America's greed
to place Asia under its control.
—Japanese propaganda leaflet dropped on Philippines, May 1942

Japan gains control of Philippine Islands—May 6, 1942

Sunday, May 24, 1942—twenty-four days later

He-Seung

Myung-Ja and I stood behind the tall *kimchee* and soy sauce jars in her yard, out of sight of the house. We met there at dusk every day for the ten minutes it took her to get the *kimchee* for the evening meal. For the amount of time it took He-Dong to run around the nearby park five times. It was the part of day I looked forward to the most. To see her smile, to listen to her soft voice, to inhale her flowery scent. Besides, she was the one person, other than Gong Tae, who I could talk to about the prison.

Yesterday, the guard had said he'd told Father of my visits, and Father had been so happy, he'd wept. I didn't think Father had ever wept over anything I'd done. At least not out of happiness.

"You'll never guess what the guard said." I tapped her arm.

She looked agitated. She put her finger to her cheek as if in thought. "That your Father was so happy to have you visit, he wept."

I blushed. Had the guard said this before? Had I?

"You can't keep going back there." Myung-Ja kept her eyes focused on the empty metal bowl and chopsticks in her hands. "Like the guard said the first time, it's not a boarding house. You're lucky you've gotten back safely so many times."

"The guard sounds like he's helping Father." I'd probably said this a lot of times, too.

She cocked her head to the side, her mouth pinched together, her brow furrowed. "I still think he's just after your Mother's *kimchee*." She pointed to my stomach. "Something you could use a little more of."

I shrugged. Mother had also mentioned me looking as thin as a branch. She'd even started giving me some of her rice. "But I can't just do nothing."

She tapped the side of the bowl with her chopsticks. "You're not doing nothing. You're supporting your Mother with her Wednesday prayer sessions."

"And to think I thought she was going crazy." I smiled, remembering that first prayer session when I'd worried she was becoming as nutty as widow Kim.

"You're helping He-Dong get stronger."

I smiled. "He's up to running five times around the park without stopping, fifteen push-ups, a hundred jumping jacks."

"You're keeping the family together." She closed her eyes. "Like it should be."

"We still need Father back." I shook my head. I might have been able to help with little things, but it was like there was this giant cloud over our house all the time. Besides, if it weren't for the kindness of Father's worshippers, especially that silly In-Young who brought us *extra food* each week, we would have starved long ago. "One day the guard might help us get Father released."

"It's so risky." She pulled the top off the *kimchee* jar, the ceramic lid scraping loudly. The chili-spice from the marinated cabbage filled the air, making my mouth water.

I couldn't stop visiting the prison. At least by making the trip, I felt like I was helping in some way, even if it was just to make one guard happy. One guard who might be a bit nicer to Father. I crossed my arms. "I guess it's a risk I have to take."

"Why? Why does everyone I care about have to take unnecessary risks?" She dropped the chopsticks in the bowl and put her hand over her mouth.

I felt a shiver down my spine. "What are you talking about?"

"We got a letter from Myung-Hae."

"That's wonderful." The sadness in her face made me ache. I reached out and brushed a strand of hair from her face. "Isn't it?"

She stood so close to me the cotton of her pink dress grazed my arms. "Most of what she wrote was blacked out by censors."

"Maybe she was giving away information." I ran my fingers against the soft skin of her arm. "That some idiot thought was sensitive."

"Like what?" She gripped onto my hand.

"I don't know." I felt such safety in the warmth of her hand, it was a stretch for me to think of anything. "Her whereabouts?"

She nodded. Resting her head on my shoulder. Then she looked up. "The only words left were, *They're recruiting people for their factories all over. All my love, Myung-Hae.*"

"Your sister's a smart one." I looked at Myung-Ja's furrowed brow. I wanted to see this letter. I wondered if brainy He-Dong would know how to eradicate censor's ink. "She'll figure out what she can and can't write. She'll write you another letter soon."

"If I could just see a guard each week who promised me she was okay, that she was inside, alive and breathing, I'd be happy." She sighed.

It wasn't that Myung-Ja didn't understand me going to the prison. She just worried for me. The same way she always had. My mouth watered again. And not just from the smell of *kimchee*.

"You've got that look in your eyes." She smiled despite her own teary eyes.

"What look?" Could she tell I was curious about Myung-Hae's letter. Or could she sense I'd been thinking of her in my arms?

"Like you'd like a bite of *kimchee*." She leaned down into the jar and brought out a huge chunk of *kimchee* with her chopsticks, the garlic juice dripping to the ground. She lifted the treat to my lips.

I smiled. I felt happy to stand here and watch her. With her near, all the badness of the world disappeared.

Our citizens can now rejoice that a momentous victory is in the making.
Perhaps we will be forgiven if we claim we are about
midway to our objective.
—**Admiral Chester Nimitz after Allied victory on strategic island of**
Midway prevents Japan from invading Hawaii, June 7, 1942

Saturday afternoon, July 18, 1942—about eight weeks later

Baby He-Dong

I put the new red rubber ball in my book bag. Japan hadn't brought any more countries into the Empire in the past month. But it was the last day of school and this present was the Emperor's way of celebrating the victories thus far. I would have the whole month of August as a break. Perhaps even Father would get a vacation from prison. I picked up my burlap rucksack and followed my classmates out to the courtyard.

"Bean-curd," a voice called. Kee-Wok.

He couldn't be talking to me. Thanks to He-Seung, I wasn't such a Bean-curd anymore. Every day of the week, except for Saturdays during which He-Seung disappeared for hours, we went for training. He-Seung called it "seeing the puppy," but we always ended up somewhere else first. The forest. The pond. The cement playground.

I'd stopped being afraid of the dark. Instead of my own heart pounding, I heard the wind talking, frogs singing, and lately the shrill of the summer cicada. Ih-Duk told me the male cicada—of which he had collected several—was the loudest insect on earth. I slung my book bag over my other shoulder, wondering who Kee-Wok was bullying this time.

"I have to hurry home to help my mother." Ih-Duk walked up next to me. "But wanna meet at the park in two hours to catch water bugs?"

I pulled my ball from my rucksack. "Or we could play catch?"

"That, too," he said, although his face said he probably wouldn't want to do that for long.

"I'll be there." I tossed my ball up in the air as he hurried off. I put my hand up to catch the ball, but the red toy dribbled from my fingers. My arms must still be tired from all my trainings. I had done thirty push-ups last night, fifteen laps around the park.

I fumbled around on the ground for the ball. When I stood, Kee-Wok was there in front of me, a smirk on his face. He clipped my shoulder as he walked by. "We're meeting at the wall."

I looked to the wall where Kee-Wok's *sergeants* were gathered throwing their red balls at one another. One of the boys, Jong-Jin, got hit in the chest. His face puffed up. He bent and grabbed a rock to retaliate.

Long ago I would have been thrilled by the offer to join his group. But now I didn't care. Surely he could tell I was getting tougher, and now he wanted me in his army. But all he and his friends did was stand around and make fun of other boys, throw rocks, kick up dust. Ih-Duk said they even stole candy from the uncle who came by each day with a cart of treats for sale.

I turned away from them and walked down the road toward our house, over the electric trolley tracks, past the public bath, past the row of cherry blossom trees.

The boots of dozens of soldiers marched toward me. The soldiers in front wore brown uniforms, had long swords at their side, and marched with their legs out straight. They looked so perfect. Behind them were a group of men wearing black uniforms—like students from a high school. Was this some kind of school outing? The high school students weren't as good at marching. They couldn't kick their legs up as high. They kept bumping into one another. Their eyes wandered. And they didn't get to wear any of the weapons.

I tried kicking my legs out. One, two, three. I kicked one foot out so straight and perfect, I forgot to put it back on the ground. I stumbled to the side. I would have to practice.

As the soldiers came closer, the ground vibrated beneath my feet. Where were they going? Wherever it was, there were so many of them, surely they would win. The Emperor would send us more congratulatory presents. I imagined our living room filled to the ceiling with red rubber balls.

I knew God would want me to wish them a safe journey. But before I did that I wanted to ask them about Father. He-Seung told me not to worry, that Father was fine. But why didn't he come home?

"*Arigato Gozaimasu.*" I held up my ball, waving it back and forth. "Thank you for this."

I waited for one of them to look my way, so I could ask about Father. But they kept moving. Dust shot up in my face as they passed me faster than a cold breeze.

"What are you doing here?" A voice called out in Korean.

I flinched, dropping my ball. Behind me stood Kee-Wok. A drop of sweat fell from his bony forehead. His red cheeks sucked air in and out. "I told you we were meeting at the wall."

"I'm planning to go to the park," I said.

"So the dear ex- Class Monitor thinks I care what he's planning?" He stepped forward.

Last night He-Seung had me run so many times around our missionary compound, I thought my lungs would burst. I didn't dare stop, though.

And, after what seemed like forever, I got used to the burning in my lungs. When I finally slowed, I had this strange feeling of peace I hadn't known since Father was taken to prison. I had this feeling that I could overcome anything. Even Kee-Wok.

"I don't expect you to care." I reached down to retrieve my ball, my hand shaking. "I just thought it would be a kindness to tell you."

"*Arigato Gozaimasu.*" He mimicked the way I'd called out to the soldiers. He thrust out his hand, his eyes on my red rubber ball. He wanted my gift. "Thank you for this."

I looked at the treasure in my sweaty palm. The gift Ih-Duk and I planned to play with. It would be easier to just let Kee-Wok have it. Besides, Ih-Duk wanted to look for bugs more than practice playing catch. But He-Seung would be disgusted with me. I could hear him saying *You runt. I thought you said you were ready to take care of a puppy. You can't even take care of yourself.*

"This is mine." My voice wobbled.

Kee-Wok shoved me so hard I almost fell face-first in the dirt. But I was stronger now. I caught myself from falling at the last minute. Then, without even looking back, I took off running.

"Hey!" Kee-Wok's footsteps pounded after me.

His legs were longer. But I imagined He-Seung chanting at me. *You can do it.* I was stronger now. *You can do anything.* I would outrun him.

I believe that in the future, whoever holds Alaska will hold the world.
—Congressman Billy Mitchell, 1935

Japan occupies Attu and Kiska Islands, Alaska. June 11, 1942

Saturday, July 18, 1942—same day

He-Seung

Summer monsoon clouds dotted the late-afternoon sky. The heat suffocated us. Still, Gong-Tae and I hurried toward Serdamoon Prison for the twelvth time.

Gong-Tae had recently received a letter from Myung-Hae, every line censored. Instead of following He-Dong's *scientific* suggestion to wipe a bar of soap over the black markings and clear them away, we'd brought the letter to Guard Nozaki. He'd promised last week that he would find out where she was, what was behind all the black lines.

"Oy," a voice called as we neared the prison.

We were still far enough away that I couldn't see the features of the man standing in front of the prison door. He obviously could see us, though. His voice sounded different than Guard Nozaki.

"Who's that?" Gong-Tae nudged me.

As we neared, I spotted a tall, thin man with a patch over one eye. His other eye looked blank, almost like that of a dead fish.

"You two are back." A toothpick dangled from his lips. "Again."

We had never seen this guard. How did he know us?

"Where is esteemed Guard Nozaki?" Gong-Tae asked.

"The definition of a guard is one who keeps pests away." He pulled the toothpick from his mouth, slowly. So slowly. Then he stared at the sharp end. "That fool Nozaki couldn't even do that."

I saw that toothpick no longer as an instrument to dislodge food particles, but as a weapon. I imagined it under my fingernails—and on other body parts—jabbing away. I gritted my teeth.

"Well, why are you still standing here?" The guard moved toward us.

I looked up at the dark sky. "Just enjoying a stroll."

"Well, stroll your stupid-child butts the other way." The guard stabbed the toothpick at the air. "And don't let me catch you or your Mother's special *kimchee* back here again."

My heart beat hard. For the past three months, Guard Nozaki had been our communication line to Father. Guard Nozaki had told me when Father had slept well or walked around his cell or soothed a fever-ridden prisoner.

I'd found ways to tell Mother, mentioning that Dr. Lee had told me. This guard would put an end to all of that.

"Esteemed guard," Gong-Tae began.

I'm sure he wanted to ask about Myung-Hae. We'd walked all this way in the heat. We were exhausted and would surely be rained on before reaching home. But the guard poked at the air again, pointing us away from the prison.

We walked back down the road. The cement walls of the prison shimmered. The red dirt beneath our feet looked like the hot coals of hell. I wiped a band of sweat from my forehead.

"Now what do we do?" Gong-Tae asked, kicking a pebble on the road.

The pride I'd held from achieving these weekly visits seeped out of me. I kicked the pebble back to him. "I don't know."

"Psst." A man called to us from around the corner.

Guard Nozaki sat on his haunches, smoking a cigarette, his bayoneted rifle on the ground next to him. We ran over. "What are you doing out here?"

"Waiting for you." He picked up his rifle and stood.

"Did Fish Eye take your job?" I asked.

"I took his." He smiled, dropping his cigarette and stubbing the embers with his boot. "I got a promotion."

I thought of the guard poking the air with his toothpick. *That fool Nozaki couldn't even keep the pests away.* Which of these men was telling the truth?

"Congratulations," Gong-Tae said.

How did Gong-Tae do that? I was still irritated we'd lost our one and only link to Father. Gong-Tae seemed to have forgotten.

The silence grew, with my lack of participation in the well-wishing increasingly obvious. "Yeah, congratulations." I pushed the words out. Feeling Gong-Tae nudge my side, I handed Guard Nozaki my *bento* box. "For old time's sake."

"Thank you." He leaned the rifle in the crook of his elbow and opened the box, sniffing the contents with appreciation. He took a bite of *kimchee*. "Actually, I have something for you men, too."

Men. He'd called us men. I felt an involuntary shiver.

"You found out where Myung-Hae is?" Gong-Tae looked so hopeful, my heart ached.

"I did better than that." Guard Nozaki reached into his coat pocket with his free hand, removing a folded piece of paper. "I got permission for you to be stationed right near her."

My insides froze. "Stationed?"

"Amazing, isn't it?" He lifted the lunchbox and shoveled rice in his mouth.

I snorted. *I'd rather burn in hell than work for the Japs.* My voice banged across my head as I remembered sitting, hot and sweaty, on the borrowed church bench with Gong-Tae while we worried about the voluntary draft. "There's no way either of us—"

"What do I have to do?" Gong-Tae pushed me aside. His eyes stared at the paper in Guard Nozaki's hands. He tapped his foot up and down, as if waiting to be passed his soccer ball.

Guard Nozaki handed the paper to Gong-Tae. The words at the top read *Japanese Youth Corps.* This was the group which had been grabbing students from our school all year.

"But, no." Guard Nozaki slapped his forehead. "Maybe you can't do this. How old are you?"

"Old enough," Gong-Tae answered.

"Not really." I flicked at the paper as if it were fire. Who would ever be old enough to help the enemy? "All he knows how to do is play soccer."

"I'm sixteen." Gong-Tae puffed out his chest. Then he pointed to me. "It's this guy here who's still a child."

"Well, in your case." He looked at me, considering. "We can fudge the dates a bit. Especially after all your efforts, coming to visit me each week."

I hadn't come to visit him. It was Father I was coming to check on. How was he making it seem like he was doing me—us—a favor? We needed to leave. I grabbed Gong-Tae's arm.

"I visited the head recruiter about your situation yesterday." Guard Nozaki nodded in my direction. "When he heard about your father, and that we were friends... well, he promised that if you join, your father will be immediately released."

"What?" Gong-Tae and I asked in unison. I spoke out of disbelief. Gong-Tae looked as excited as He-Dong when I finally let him use my slingshot.

"Just what I said. All you have to do is sign on the X." Guard Nozaki stuffed his mouth with more rice. "You can sign your names, right?"

"Of course." Gong-Tae grabbed the pen.

"Wait a second." I pulled on his arm. Although I'd come to trust Guard Nozaki a bit over the past three months, we weren't *friends.* And I didn't believe him enough to join the Youth Corps. I put my hand over the paper to stop Gong-Tae from stupidity. I looked at Guard Nozaki, "What's in it for you?"

Guard Nozaki shook his head. "Never give me an inch, do you?"

I raised my eyebrows. The paper beneath my palm felt hot. Gong-Tae shifted from one foot to the other, still eager to sign his name.

"The warden has to deliver a quota of young men to the Youth Corps each month." Guard Nozaki shrugged his shoulders.

I knew the bastard had his own interests in mind. "And perhaps you are rewarded for helping fill that quota."

"I can see the extra rice on my table already." He lifted the *bento* box to shovel more rice in his mouth.

I grabbed the box from him. He'd had his last mouthful of Mother's cooking from me. I pushed Gong-Tae's sweaty elbow. "Let's get out of here."

"Oh, but don't think I'm just a selfish old man." Guard Nozaki held up his rifle, cradling it in his arms. "Most recruits just, well, *volunteer*. However the two of you are special. If you two volunteer, you get your father back, and you..." Guard Nozaki looked at Gong-Tae. "Get to be near your girl."

Gong-Tae elbowed me out of the way, and before I could put my hand over the paper again, he signed the contract. Then he handed me the paper and pen. I stared, my mouth dropping as if he'd punched me. I wanted to strangle him. Better yet, I would just cross off his name. I poised the pen over his name. "This is crazy—"

"I understand if you don't want to do this." Guard Nozaki stuck the bayonet through the contract, pulling the paper toward him. "You're still young."

"But you can't have him either." I reached to grab the damn paper, but he held the bayonet high in the air. If Guard Nozaki was such a *friend*, he'd return the contract.

He waggled his fingers for us to follow him. "One more thing, though." He led us to the back of the prison and tapped twice on the door. "I understand he goes back into interrogation next week."

An officer opened the door and motioned for us to come in. The hall was dark, the smell of urine and sweat so strong, my nose burned. He led us to the first cell and pointed. "Look. Don't speak."

Three men sat hunched against the cement wall, their eyes closed. One sat in the corner, his hands folded in prayer. He wore the same clothes he'd had on the day he was arrested. They were wrinkled and dirty. His face was unshaven, his hair greasy, his eyes sunken with fatigue. I gulped, blinking fast. Father.

I stared at the metal bars separating us, wishing I could tear them down and we could run home together, although he didn't look in shape to be running anywhere. *He goes into interrogation next week.*

"That's enough." The officer pushed us back down the hall toward the exit.

I felt as if all the air had been sucked from me. My dear father. My eyes burned.

The officer pushed us outside, and lifted his hand to pull the door shut. He paused, looking at Guard Nozaki. "Can I tell the traitor he can go home?"

So this officer knew of the deal to release Father? Maybe Guard Nozaki had truly arranged something for us.

"Naw." Guard Nozaki looked at the paper dangling off the end of his bayonet which only held Gong-Tae's signature. He shook his head. "This one's still a child. We'll forget that for—"

"Would I be stationed in the same place as Gong-Tae?" I asked.

The officer barked with laughter. "Hell, who—"

"You ask for a lot, *Smart Boy.*" Guard Nozaki patted me on the shoulder. "But, I guess we could do that, too."

"I'm not sure I want him with me," Gong-Tae said, smiling so broadly I thought his face would crack.

If Guard Nozaki kept his promise, Gong-Tae and I would get to be together, he'd be near Myung-Hae, and most importantly, Father would get to come home. Of the three promises, I only really cared that Guard Nozaki make good on the last. Of the three promises, surely he would keep one. Wouldn't he?

"What's it going to be, *Smart Boy*?" Guard Nozaki asked. "I've got other things to do."

I thought of Mother needing firewood chopped and stacked for the kitchen stove, of He-Dong at home waiting to do training, of Myung-Ja expecting me for our nightly rendezvous. "So do I."

"Come on, He-Seung." Gong-Tae frowned at me. "We'll get to be together."

"Yeah, listen to your buddy," Guard Nozaki said. "It's not as if you won't have to *volunteer* anyway, sooner or later."

"Probably sooner." The officer slammed the back door of the prison, the clanging sound reverberating through my whole being.

I rubbed my palm across my face. Gong-Tae joked around as if this was some overnight outing to the countryside. He cajoled me as if begging for an extra game of soccer. Still, this was a huge decision. I felt sick to my stomach as I stared at the contract sticking to the end of the bayonet. Was there no other way?

I feel sure that America, Britain, Chungking and other enemy countries now realize the folly of further resistance, now that they have seen a sample of what the Imperial forces can do.
—General Hatto, over radio, June 9, 1942

Saturday, July 18, 1942—same day

Mother (*Uhmony*)

He-Dong and I sat in the living room. I guided my darning needle in and out of one of In-Young's hole-ridden socks. She had a never-ending pile which needed mending. He-Dong read his comic book. He-Seung's dinner remained cold and untouched in the kitchen. If my dear were home, he wouldn't allow this kind of wandering about at all hours of the night.

I sighed. Every thought I had these days started with *If my dear were home*.

A stifling hot breeze blew through the window screen, slapping my face with the threat of heavy rain. The cicadas called out, a piercing cry. I wondered if my dear could hear them.

"Did you know only the male cicada makes all that noise?" He-Dong flipped the pages of the comic. "And the cicada is the loudest insect on earth?"

"Did you learn this at school?" I looked up from my sewing.

"No." He frowned. "Ito *Sensei* never teaches us about bugs or science. Today she talked about how the Japanese are conquering islands in the western United States. Ih-Duk told me."

"I see." I looked toward the sound of the cicadas.

"Ih-Duk said the Chinese consider the cicada a symbol of re-carnation."

"Reincarnation?" I smiled at him.

"Yes. That." He nodded. "Because the bug constantly sheds its shell."

"Hmm." I pulled at a loose thread. Where was He-Seung? I got up and went to the door.

"Maybe he's out playing with Gong-Tae." He-Dong came up behind me.

I put my arm around him, squeezing him tight. I breathed in the air one last time, gulping down the hot air.

"Why don't you go to bed?" I shut the door. "It's late."

"But there's no school tomorrow." He frowned. "It's vacation."

"Yes, I know." I brushed at the stubble on his head. I needed to shave his head. Again. He was my constant reminder that time hadn't stopped the day my dear was arrested.

A key sounded in the lock. We both jumped at the sound. I opened the door.

"Mother, He-Dong." He-Seung bowed his head, then looked up at me through his lashes, giving me a smile. "I'm back. Sorry it's late."

"Dear child." I could not muster anger when here he was in front of me, safe. "Where have you been?"

He stepped inside, his eyes darting from me to He-Dong. He rubbed his hands together. "I went to get Father."

"Father's home?" He-Dong raced outside, not bothering to put on his shoes.

I, too, peered outside. The sky was dark. The pathway leading to our house empty. The only sounds I heard were the shrill cries of the cicadas and my thumping heart. "What's this all about?"

"He's coming on an oxcart, isn't he?" He-Dong came rushing back inside, leaned over and put on his shoes. "I remember Myung-Ja saying he was an oxcart ride away. When's he coming?"

"Stop talking nonsense." My voice sounded sharp. He-Dong flinched and dropped his shoe.

"He's not out there." He-Seung watched his little brother. His eyes shone. "Not yet." He turned to me. "I saw him, though, at Serdamoon Prison."

"What?" I frowned, silently thanking the Lord for saving my son from arrest, too.

"Why didn't you take me with you?" He-Dong put his shoes back. "We could have brought him home together."

"Next time." He-Seung patted his brother on the shoulder.

"No," I said. "No next times. You must be hungry. Go wash up."

He-Seung went into the living room, and I brought him his dinner. In between bites, he talked of visiting the prison once a week with food for my dear. About befriending one of the Korean guards. About being led through the prison to see my dear. I felt as if I'd fallen inside He-Dong's comic magazine. Visiting prisons? Talking to guards? Making deals. This sounded like the fiction of comic book characters. Not activities for a teenage boy whose face was still as smooth as a peach.

"When is Father coming home?" He-Dong sat anxious by his brother's side, ready to hop up at any moment and race back to the door.

"Probably not tonight." He-Seung finished up the last of his rice. "Guard Nozaki promised it would be soon."

"Really?" I asked, rubbing one hand over the other. Thunder boomed across the sky. "How...how did you do this?"

He looked at me, then he closed his eyes. "Gong Tae and I agreed to join the Youth Corps."

"What?" I grabbed onto him, willing him to look at me with those dark brown eyes which could brighten the room or fill it with fury. Willing his face to break into a huge smile as he said he was joking, that he'd really stayed out playing soccer all night long and was sorry for being so disrespectful.

"I leave on Monday." He opened his eyes.

I held my hands to my heart which ached as though I were being stabbed by my darning needle. "No."

"Father should be home by then." He-Seung nodded.

"He will?" He-Dong peered out the window. Rain pattered on the roof, first gently than with increasing force. "Brother, you're a genius. Thank you for making my prayers come true."

"Oh, God. My dear, dear son." I had a sudden memory of when He-Seung was little, and we were walking in the park. I saw a bush of roses and stopped to smell one. "This smells like heaven," I'd told him.

"How do you know?" He stared at the pokey thorns on the stems.

"Just smell." I took another deep whiff.

He stuck his face into a blossom, wrinkling his nose. Then he reached for the stem. "We should take this to Father."

I grabbed his hand before he could start plucking. "Let's leave them for everyone to enjoy."

He wriggled from my grasp, and cupped his hands over the top of the rose, as though catching a butterfly. Then he ran ahead of me all the way home. When he entered the house, rather than taking off his shoes, he hurried into the living room and put his chubby hands beneath my dear's nose.

"Mother and I found Heaven." He opened his cupped hands. "Can you smell it?"

"Mother." He-Dong now grabbed my arm. "You're shaking."

I covered my face with trembling hands. I felt as helpless as a child trying to capture a scent. How could I hold onto my son?

As soon as the darkness of the night gave way to another hot morning, I would see what I could do. Perhaps Gong-Tae *uhmony* or Min-Kook *uhmony* would have some idea of how we could save our boys.

I stared at the door, listening to the rain beat down, listening to the cicadas cry out. How was it that my son, who had always caused nothing but storms in the house, was now putting his life on the line for his father? I thought of the cicada shedding its skin. Their call screamed so loud in my ears, I thought my head would burst.

Devote yourself to your most important obligation of loyalty to the Emperor, and realize that the obligation is heavier than the mountains but death is lighter than a feather.
—Imperial Rescript to Soldiers used to train Kamikaze Pilots.

Sunday, July 19, 1942—next day

He-Seung

I stood next to the *kimchee* jar at Myung-Ja's house. The light had long since left the sky, replaced by storm clouds. The rain beat down with a vengeance.

If He-Dong had been with me, it would have been easy to rap on the door as visitors seeking shelter from the rain. It would have been easy— even jovial—to explain my leaving for the Youth Corps. I couldn't do that to Myung-Ja, though. I'd left He-Dong at home on the front porch waiting for Father.

How would I ever get Myung-Ja's attention without alerting the rest of her family? She would never hear the soft ping of a pebble on her window through all this noise. I squeezed the front of my wet shirt, like Mother rinsing our laundry.

Mother had been gone all day, probably visiting Min-Kook *uhmony,* Gong-Tae *uhmony*, the local police, the Youth Corps office. When she came home this evening, exhausted, she said, "You're a man and must do what you've set out to do. But my heart aches."

Her heart would feel better when Father came home. I ran my hand over my head, a stream of water flowing off my scalp. I felt like a rat drowning in the sewer. I should just go home.

The rough warmth of a towel ran up against my arm. Myung-Ja pulled me to the shelter of the front porch. The porch light cast a soft glow on her hair, her long neck, her slender arms.

"How did you know I was here?" I asked, my words drowned out by the beating of the rain.

"What?" she shouted.

"How?" I indicated the towel, her presence.

She shrugged her shoulders, watching me. She must have been waiting, hoping to see me. I felt such warmth, warmer than any towel. We stood there, side by side, listening to the rain until it stopped just as abruptly as it had started. *Like God turning off the water faucet*, Mother always said.

I didn't want the quiet. I'd been happy standing near Myung-Ja in the rain. I'd been happy not to have to fill the space with words I didn't want to say. I wrung out the towel and handed it back to her.

When she reached for it, I noticed a blood-red tint surrounding her nails. I grabbed her hand. My heart pounded.

"It's just dye." She giggled, a soft sound like a hug. The wind blew rain across the roof, tinkling an echo.

"Really?" I examined her fingers, the feel of her soft skin sending warmth through my body.

"Flowers," she whispered into my ear, her breath sending shivers down my spine. "If you crush the petals of the *Bongsoonghwa* flower, and keep the paste on your nails all night, you'll get this color. The petals are harder and harder to find these days, though, what with all the cherry trees we have instead."

I nodded, reluctant to let her hand go, to have her mouth move from my ear. I wondered why I'd never seen such a thing before. Perhaps I'd just never thought to look.

"Every girl knows how to do this." She put her other hand out to show me. "Myung-Hae and I always did this together."

She stood so close to me her arms grazed against my stomach. She looked up at me, that watchful gaze again. "You're trembling."

"I'm fine." I rubbed my arms, looking down into her eyes.

She hung the towel on the front railing, and we naturally moved to our spot by the *kimchee* jar. I wanted to be with her like this every day. I would when I got back. I was sure Dr. Lee wanted a doctor's son for his daughter. Perhaps a Reverend's son would be good enough, though. For once I was happy to be a Reverend's son.

She came over to me and used the front of her dress to continue dabbing off the rain from my arms. Her soft arms brushed against my skin. I cleared my throat. "I—Gong-Tae and I—we—"

She stopped dabbing, her watchful eyes burning. "So, it's true."

Had Mother stopped here as well? I took a deep breath. "The Youth Corps has offered to station us near your sister."

"Where?"

"I—" Myung-Ja had a tiny freckle on her wrist. I ran my finger around and around the small dot. "We'll know tomorrow."

She brought her hand to her mouth, shaking her head. She closed her eyes tight. "Tomorrow?" she repeated, her voice cracking.

"Guard Nozaki promised that Father would be released, too." I stepped closer. I wanted to say something but was unable to think of even a noise that would be comforting. I rubbed her shoulders.

Her small voice asked, "Until when?"

"Soon." I held her tight to me, feeling the warmth of her body against mine, kissing the top of her head. "When the war ends."

"Myung-Hae's letter said they were in need of more women." She stepped back. "Maybe I should join up—"

"No." I shouted as if to be heard over the rain. "No, no, no."

"Why not?" Myung-Ja crossed her arms and paced back and forth. "We could all be in the same area."

"Let Gong-Tae and I find out what it's like first. Besides, your parents need you here." I gestured to the house. I cleared my throat. "I need you here."

She paused in front of me, her arms still crossed, her eyes still full of fire. "What for?"

I coughed. "To look after Mother and He-Dong."

She frowned. "I thought Guard Nozaki said your father was being released."

"I'm not sure exactly when, though." I pulled her close. Even though her body was rigid with anger, I wished I could hold onto her forever.

"Is that you, He-Seung?" A deep voice cut through me like a razor. "What's going on out here?"

Myung-Ja and I jumped away from one another. She ran her hands over her dress, pushed back a stray hair. We had not heard her father approach.

"Dr. Lee." I bowed. "I was just coming to say goodbye."

Dr. Lee's jaw clenched. Surely he didn't care what I'd come to say. His eyes roamed his daughter's figure, as if looking for damage.

"Father, he's leaving. He and Gong-Tae." Myung-Ja stepped toward her father. "They're leaving to find Myung-Hae. They've joined the Youth Corps."

Dr. Lee tore his stern gaze from his daughter. "Did you sign the papers already?"

"Yes, sir." I felt relieved, actually proud, that I'd signed the contract. "And they've promised to release Father, in return."

He nodded. Slowly. Reluctantly. "Well, you be careful out there. We'll keep you in our prayers." He rocked back and forth on the balls of his feet, his hands behind his back. "If the two of you have further goodbyes, let's get them over with. Now."

I looked at Myung-Ja, wanting to wrap her in another embrace, wanting to feel her cheek against my heart. I closed my eyes, taking a deep breath, remembering the faint smell of flowers. I felt a teardrop on my arm.

"The puppy." Myung-Ja jumped, her hand grasping onto my arm. "Father. You remember. I told you. He-Seung delivered those puppies."

I hadn't really. Not all of them, probably not even one. But if that raised Dr. Lee's level of esteem for me, I wouldn't deny the honor.

"He can't leave without saying goodbye to them." She pushed me toward the back. "Especially the runt. He would be devastated."

She pushed me off before Dr. Lee could protest. As we moved toward the backyard, she gave me one last hug. When we got to the dog pen, she thrust the runt into my arms.

The air was crisp and clean from the rain. My heart beat hard with dear Myung-Ja next to me. The soft puppy squirmed against my chest. This moment was precious. I must have said as much.

"Yes, *Kwidong*—precious." Myung-Ja petted the puppy, her fingers brushing against my arm. "That's the perfect name for that little guy."

I smiled, letting her misunderstand.

A mother, at least with the face she wore in public, was obliged to appear happy and grateful to the Emperor and country for giving her son such a fine way to die.
–Hideo Suzuki, former Japanese naval aviator, WWII

Monday, July 20, 1942—next day

Baby He-Dong

I sat outside on the front steps, my new puppy, Kwidong, in my lap. Everything was happening so fast, I couldn't make sense of it. Father was no longer a bad man and would get to come home. He-Seung, who was always angry at the Japanese, was now going off to help them. And I now had my new puppy, Precious.

He licked my face and neck. I rubbed his soft ears while I waited for Father to come home. My bottom ached from sitting so long. He must be riding a very slow oxcart from far away.

I mentally practiced what I'd do the moment I spotted Father. I would jump off the steps and bow low, apologizing a hundred times for letting those mean policemen in the house. I'd take off his shoes and offer to massage his feet. I'd lead him to his rocking chair where I'd already laid out his Bible and reading glasses.

I spotted a lone figure in the distance hurrying toward our house. I repositioned Kwidong in my arms and stood up.

As the figure got closer, I noted he was too short to be Father, and he held a pole with a net attached to the end. His eyes scouted the bushes for movement, as he scooped the air with his net. Ih-Duk.

I sat back down.

Ih-Duk saw me watching and held up the pole. "Do you want to help me catch—" He spotted Kwidong and raced forward. "You got a puppy!"

"He's sleeping." I put a hand up to stop Ih-Duk from disturbing him. Then I whispered, "And my father's coming home."

"That's great." He squinted, looking down the path. Then he put his pole down and sat next to me, nudging close so Kwidong's paw touched his knee.

The front door opened and He-Seung came out. He was dressed in a uniform like I'd seen the soldiers wearing who marched in the street. He had a bulging rucksack on his back. He held a brown cap in his hands.

Ih-Duk gave me a quizzical look.

"He has to join the Youth Corps for Father to come back," I whispered.

Kwidong squirmed in my lap, opening his eyes. He lifted his head, sniffing the air.

"He knows when you're near," I told He-Seung.

"Or something else." He-Seung reached down and grabbed Kwidong by the skin of his neck. He held the puppy off to the side of the porch. The little fella peed in the grass.

"How did you know?" Ih-Duk's mouth dropped.

"Any dog that sits in someone's lap for four hours will need to pee." He-Seung laughed, offering the dog to Ih-Duk's outstretched arms.

I intercepted, grabbing my puppy. "He needs time to get used to you. I'll hold him."

Mother hurried out to us, carrying a *bento* box. Her eyes were dark and puffy. She'd been gone a lot since He-Seung said Father was coming home. I didn't know where. I didn't know why she wasn't waiting for him like I was. Why she was now holding so tight to that *bento* box that her fingers shook.

"Looks like we're ready then." He-Seung gave my shoulder a pat. He continued down the steps.

"You're not leaving, are you? Not now?" I looked down the road. Nobody was in sight. "Father's not home."

He turned and squeezed my shoulder. "I've got to be at the station by noon."

I jumped down from the steps, fitting Kwidong under my right arm. "Can't you wait a little while longer?"

"I wish." He adjusted the heavy pack on his back.

If I left my post, Father might come home to an empty house and have to wait for us to return. That would not be a welcome. On the other hand, how could I not see my brother off? He said he might be gone for many weeks.

"We'll go with you." Ih-Duk jumped down from the steps, grabbing his butterfly net.

"Actually, Ih-Duk, can you just stay here for an hour?" I asked. "In case my father comes home?"

Ih-Duk looked around. "Can the puppy stay with me?"

The puppy was warm and soft against my skin. He licked my arm. "I'll let you hold Kwidong when I get back."

"If he stays here with me, he'll have a chance to get used to me."

"When I get back, he'll be used to you." I held Kwidong tighter. "He'll have seen you twice."

"Well, all right." Ih-Duk rested his pole against the porch.

He-Seung and I started down the path toward town. Mother followed us. Her footsteps stumbled every once in a while. She whispered along the way. She was praying.

"You're going to have to be in charge until Father gets back." He-Seung took the slingshot from his pocket.

I couldn't imagine having to be in charge even for a minute. "What do I do?"

"It's no different than being Class Monitor." His eyes scanned the ground for a pebble. He pointed. "Just help Mother whenever she needs something."

"What if I don't know how?" I picked up the pebble for him.

"Your friend takes care of his mother." He nodded back to the house where Ih-Duk was probably already hunting about our garden looking for butterflies while waiting for Father. "He'll have advice for you."

"Ih-Duk's father is at home," I said.

"Don't worry so much." He wrapped the leather of the slingshot around the pebble, took aim at a cherry blossom tree. And missed.

"I forgot to tell you." I switched Kwidong from one arm to the other, a sheen of sweat rolling down my arm. "That bully Kee-Wok tried to get me to join his group the last day of school and I ran away—I was faster than him."

"See? There you go." He-Seung patted me on the shoulder. "You'll be fine. And take Kwidong to visit Myung-Ja every once in a while."

I reached down and got him another pebble. He aimed at another tree trunk. He missed again. He would get irritated soon. I thought he said all he needed was a clear enemy. Did this mean that he didn't have one anymore?

"San toki, toki-ya urdero kanunya." Mother sang softly in Korean behind us. Little Mountain rabbit, where are you going?

He-Seung and I turned to look back at Mother. She always sang that song with us when we were little. I hugged tight to Kwidong. My insides felt wobbly.

"I remember on our last school outing," He-Seung whispered to me. "Our class monitor got angry when I changed the words of that song to *Little mountain samurai, when are you going?*"

Why would he sing that? Wasn't he going to help the samurai? Again, I was confused with what was good or bad, right or wrong. "Brother, if you still don't like them, why are you going?"

"Good question." He laughed. But he did not answer.

We entered the station. Clusters of families stood around. I'd never seen so many people. Lots of ladies were crying.

I pulled at his sleeve. "Maybe they won't notice if you stay back."

"Don't be silly." He barked with laughter. My insides shriveled. "Besides, you've got Kwidong with you now."

"There's Gong-Tae," Mother said.

Gong-Tae stood with his mother. She held onto both his arms as if she couldn't let go. I wanted to do the same with He-Seung.

The train whistle blew. Black smoke filled the air. The circle of families broke up, the men pushing toward the train.

"Take —" Mother started, but her voice broke. She shook her head unable to continue.

"I'll be fine," He-Seung said to Mother. "And so will you. Father will be home soon. Please, don't forget to ask him to arrange with Dr. Lee for Myung-Ja to join our family."

Mother nodded, pushing her face into a false happy look. "I won't forget."

Then he turned to me. He stroked Kwidong. "Train this little guy well."

My eyes stung. My heart ached. Before I could respond, though, he went to join the crowd of uniformed men. I rubbed Kwidong's fur over and over and over as I watched He-Seung disappear into the black arms of the train.

To Die for the Emperor is to Live Forever.
—**Japanese Army Slogan, WWII**

Tuesday July 22, 1942—next day

He-Seung

Gong-Tae and I spent so long on the crowded train, standing, kneeling on our haunches, leaning against each other, I didn't think we'd ever get off the moving beast. I never realized a train could travel so far. Finally, the train squealed to a stop. We'd reached the end of the line, Pusan.

I'm not sure what I'd expected. Perhaps that Myung-Hae would meet us at the station. Or that an officer would approach us and lead us away from the raucous group of new soldiers who had spent the night passing around bottle after bottle of rice wine.

Gong-Tae sniffed his uniform. Yesterday he had looked all starched and clean and ready to greet his girl. A day of travel had left him wrinkled and sweaty. He looked around. "Where do we go?"

"This way," another Korean recruit directed for us to follow him.

"We're not with everyone else," I said.

Old ladies sold food from baskets hanging around their neck. Young boys watched us, then marched around, sticks over their shoulders. The recruits stumbled down the road.

"There's only one place to go." The fella pointed in the direction of the bedraggled recruits.

Gong-Tae and I went with him. His name was Dae-Hyung. It turned out that he went to our high school, was a grade ahead of us. He had seen Gong-Tae playing soccer.

"I'm the oldest." Dae-Hyung chattered away worse than Baby He-Dong. "My parents have five more to keep them company, although you wouldn't have guessed it the way Mother carried on at the train station."

I barely contained a sigh listening to this windbag. I wondered how Mother and He-Dong were doing back home. Perhaps that little puppy Kwidong was keeping them busy. Perhaps Father was already back.

"I got a girl, too." Dae-Hyung pointed for us to move forward, but to avoid stepping in a puddle of fresh vomit. "Her family even brought her to see me off."

I felt a sudden rush of regret. Although I knew it was impossible, I'd still thought I'd see Myung-Ja this morning. I could still see her eyes full of fire, her arms crossed in anger, telling me she was going to join the factories, too. I hoped that she would listen to me and stay safe at home.

Gong-Tae, Dae-Hyung and I had formed our own little party by the time we'd walked to the port and joined the line to check in. Together we walked up to the officer sitting at the table.

I stepped forward. I pointed to Gong-Tae, feeling a bit bad about leaving our new buddy out of things. "Guard Nozaki from Serdamoon told us to check in together."

The officer gave me a blank look. He gave Gong-Tae a once-over and pointed left. He nodded at Dae-Hyung and me and pointed to the right. I felt a finger of fear traveling up my spine.

"Wait." I put my hand up, again pointing to Gong-Tae. "I meant the two of us. We're together."

"You don't look joined at the hip to me." The officer lifted his arm to signal for the next recruit to come forward. "Besides we need strong men to work in Siam now."

Panic rose in my chest. Gong-Tae had bigger muscles, but I flexed mine just the same. "I'm strong, too. Besides Guard Nozaki from Serdamoon prison said we would be together."

"Kid, I don't know this Guard Nozaki you're gummin' away about—"

"Well, is there someone else we can speak to who might know him?" I asked.

"Yes." He tapped his forefinger on his chin, furrowing his brow as if in deep thought. "When you get on the boat, ask to speak to Mr. Yamamoto."

He was lying. And not as well as Guard Nozaki had. I pulled Gong-Tae next to me. "We can wait here for him."

"We're probably all headed in the same general direction." Gong-Tae gave me his look, the one that said *Keep cool.*

I shook my head at him. "We should just go on the same boat then."

"And if you were making assignments, you could decide." The officer looked at Gong-Tae and I like we were noisy children.

"At least I'll be near Myung-Hae," he said to me. But his voice trembled. "I will be near Myung-Hae Lee, right?"

"Who?" The officer stared.

"Kimiko." Gong-Tae corrected himself, remembering her Japanese name. "Kimiko Li. She was recruited to help with one of the factories."

The officer stared at him as if he were speaking Russian. Then he stood up, knocking over his wooden chair with a clatter. Another officer hurried over, picking up the chair for him. Then he pushed Gong-Tae away from us.

"Don't." I shouted at Gong-Tae. "Don't get on the boat. Don't!"

The officer guided him all the way down to the water's edge. To a boat that was not the same as mine, to a place that was not the same as mine.

"I've never been near the water before." Dae-Hyung said. "Look at all that water. As far as the eye can see. I hope our boat doesn't get stuck out there. What if it gets stuck?"

Guard Nozaki had waited for us to visit the prison on Saturday. He had acted so conspiratorial. He had promised Gong-Tae and I we'd be together. *I think we could arrange that.* He had promised Gong-Tae he'd be stationed near his girl. The officer didn't know about any of this. My heart raced, my head pounded.

"I'm not normally afraid of things." Dae-Hyung was still at my side. "Although I don't like heights much. Never have. If there are bunk beds, will you take the top? I brought some dried cuttlefish from home. I'll share with you."

"This was a trick." I looked around for someone else I could talk to. I wasn't getting on any boat.

"Maybe it'll be okay." Dae-Hyung patted my arm.

"No, it won't." I pushed his arm away, my hand trembling.

I looked around. Women were waving handkerchiefs and crying. Young boys, tired of marching back and forth, pushed and shoved one another. I thought of Myung-Ja, Mother and He-Dong, and I wanted to be home.

"*Oy*," a voice called to us. A short Japanese soldier stood nearby, a cigarette dangling from his lips. Two green duffel bags lay at his feet.

"Yes?" I turned toward the soldier.

"See?" Dae-Hyung said, continuing toward the boat. "Somebody's here to help you already."

"Boy," the soldier called louder. He took a drag from his cigarette. He indicated the duffel bags at his feet. "Carry these to the officer's galley."

Helper or not, who did this bastard think I was? "Carry your own damned bags."

His scrawny neck turned red. His eyes bulged. "How dare you talk to me like that!"

"You've got no stripes." I moved closer, pointing to his shoulders. The name on his lapel said *Tanaka*. "You've got no medals. You look just like me, soldier."

"You're nowhere close to being a Japanese soldier," Tanaka said. "You're just Korean Youth Corps, which means—if you're lucky—I'll let you lick my boots."

"You bastard." I stepped forward to punch him. Arms locked me from behind.

"What's going on here?" A stern voice barked in my ear.

"Sir," Scumbag Tanaka said in a voice as oily as his face. "This idiot refused to carry my bags to the galley."

"I'm supposed to be with my friend—"

"Shut up." The owner of the stern voice kneed me from behind. I fell to the ground. He kicked me in the back.

I pushed up to my knees. Wham. A boot slammed me in the stomach, over and over and over, as if I were a soccer ball. I thought my guts would spill out of my ears.

"Take the bags to the officer's galley." The voice spat. "And next time, Cockroach, do as you're told."

I had been lied to, tricked, separated from my best friend. The Japs had sunk lower than even I had expected. I laughed at my stupid self. Then I leaned over and vomited on oily Tanaka's bags.

We are a nation of 90 million never once in battle defeated, ruled over by a dynasty seated upon the throne since before the beginning of the memory of men
—Japanese schoolbook during WWII.

Friday morning, August 7, 1942—fifteen days later

Baby He-Dong

I sat in front of Kwidong's dog house, his furry head on my lap. My legs were wet with perspiration. I was tempted to get up. But for once, Kwidong was not chewing on something. Not on the steps, not on the comforters hanging from the laundry line, not on my shoes.

The branches of the cherry tree swayed, even though I never actually felt the breeze. I remembered how He-Seung used to hold me up on his shoulders so I could touch the lowest branch. He'd been gone fifteen days now, and still Father wasn't home.

A mosquito landed on my thigh. Ih-Duk said only female mosquitos bit you, taking proteins from your blood to produce eggs. I slapped at the bug, just as the needle poked my skin. Kwidong raised his head, growling at the noise.

"It's okay." I rubbed at the welt.

He barked, a shy "woof, woof, woof."

"Silly dog." I rubbed Kwidong's smooth shoulders. Mother gave him a raw egg each Sunday, a treat which made his coat glisten. "Go back to sleep."

Footsteps sounded on the front porch. Voices.

"Well, aren't you a smart one?" I patted Kwidong's small head. "You heard someone coming to the door. Didn't ya, boy?"

Father. Finally. I jumped up, my legs tingling as if a thousand of Mother's needles poked at me.

Mother came out back. Instead of having Father with her, she held a letter in her hands. I took the letter, opening it. Words were typed out on thick yellow paper. Surely this wasn't from He-Seung or He-Chul or Father. An official stamp decorated the top of the page. I remembered Ito *Sensei* telling us how people were sent letters saying, *The Cherry Blossom has fallen*, whenever a soldier died. My hands shook.

Since Father, He-Chul and He-Seung were gone, I was the man of the family. In my new position, I could have moved into He-Seung's room on the men's floor. But I was afraid to sleep upstairs alone at night. In my new position, I should have taken on additional chores, breaking the soil in our vegetable garden, chopping the wood, bringing in kindling to the kitchen stove. But Mother never asked. *I'm going to need you to be in charge while I'm gone,* He-Seung had said. So far I hadn't been able to do much. But now she looked at me waiting for me to read.

"That's our last name there." I pointed to the third character. "I think that's Father's name." Was the letter addressed to him or about him?

"Can you read it?" Mother stood behind me, looking over my shoulder.

I brought the letter into the living room and took out our character dictionary. Although Mother spoke some Japanese, she couldn't read well. I didn't read well either. This year our class had only learned the basic *katakana* and *hiragana* characters. None of the *kanji* that were used on typewriters.

I started with the first character. He-Seung told me there were all kinds of different parts to a *kanji* character, that the left side was the sound and the right side was the meaning. That if I wanted to look up a character in the dictionary, I needed to count the number of strokes.

"Does that help?" Mother sat next to me.

I searched through the dictionary. There were so many characters, I was drowning in a sea of black. My heart ached.

"Well?" Mother touched the letter.

I wished I were back outside sitting in front of the dog house with Kwidong, my biggest worry a female mosquito stealing my blood to produce eggs. He-Seung said being in charge of the family was just like being Class Monitor. But that wasn't quite right. A Class Monitor got to go home, and when he was confused, he could turn to the teacher for help.

Who could help us? I didn't want to take our mail to a stranger and have him read it. What if it said something horrible? Besides, to visit the Letter Reader in town would cost money. If only one of Mother's friends read Japanese. I put the dictionary down. There was that noisy friend of Mother's, the one Mother prayed would learn some sensitivity. She was pretty smart. "What about asking Min-Kook *uhmony*?"

"My little man of the house." Mother grabbed my hand and pulled me toward the door. "Of course. You're a genius."

Her words took some of the ache in my chest away. I might not be able to do as much as He-Chul or He-Seung, but I could help a bit. Maybe we would survive until Father came home.

The United States makes its first amphibious landing in the Pacific, invading Tulagi and Guadalcanal in the Solomon Islands, and capturing the airfield on Guadalcanal.
—August 8, 1942

Friday, August 7, 1942—same day

Mother (*Uhmony*)

He-Dong and I hurried down the road. My stomach felt as if it were hanging on the outside of my body, being scraped empty with a knife. What was in the letter? I hoped my boys and my dear were safe.

As we rushed up the path to Min-Kook *uhmony's*, the sound of the printing press nearby clanged over and over. Her dog jumped up from his pen in the side of the yard, barking and growling at us. All the noises didn't block out the pounding of my heart.

I pulled He-Dong close.

"That's a real watchdog, Mother." He-Dong withdrew. "Kwidong will be like that someday."

"Do you think so?" I knocked on the door.

Min-Kook *uhmony* opened the door a crack, her face flushed. Strands of hair had fallen loose from her bun and lay pasted to her cheek. "Dear Lady, what brings you out this morning?"

Normally, I would have asked if she needed anything from the market, as we were on our way there. I would have listened while she complained that the price of rice had risen again, that food got scarcer every day. I would have asked after Deacon Mah and tried to soothe her irritation with him. I smiled, but my lips trembled. "The mailman brought this."

She looked behind us to the street. Then she opened the door wider and pulled the letter from my hands, squinting at the return address.

"I fear." I swallowed. "I fear it's bad news. I—we—wondered if maybe someone in your house could read it."

"I can read the thing." Again, she looked out to the street, her eyes shifting back and forth. "Come inside."

We took off our shoes and followed her. As usual, books and papers littered the living room floor. She pushed a pile of papers into the corner, making room for us.

"Please sit." She dropped the letter on the table next to a mountain of loose papers, tea cups, pencils. "I'll get some water."

"No, no." I pulled a piece of paper from beneath my backside and added it to the pile in the corner. "Please don't trouble yourself."

She rushed out of the room anyway. He-Dong and I waited, listening to the constant thwack of the press from the print shop which bordered Min-Kook *uhmony*'s back yard. The sound gave me a headache, made the wait feel longer.

"Mother." He-Dong stood, pacing back and forth. "Where did she disappear to?"

At that moment, Min-Kook *uhmony* rushed into the room. She had large sweat stains under her arms and her forehead glistened. She had no water. "Oh, wonder of wonders," her voice sang with joy "The Japs lost control of Guadalcanal."

"What?" She not only used an un-Godly epithet, but spoke words I'd never heard. "What is that?"

"Not what. Where? It's an island in the Pacific." She sat down and wiped sweat from her forehead with the back of her hand. "A tiny place, but very strategic. Whoever is in charge of that island has control of all the land, sea and air in the Pacific."

"Who's in charge of—of that place you said—now?" He-Dong sat back down.

"The Japs have had control since May." She took out a pencil and made some notations on a paper. Then she stuck the paper in the middle of one of her books. "But the Allies just flew in—undetected because of rain clouds—and had a huge battle. Now they're in charge."

"The Allies?" He-Dong cocked his head.

"America, Britain, Australia." She named several far-away countries on her fingers.

"Min-Kook *uhmony*, how do you know all this?" He-Dong asked the question I'd been wondering.

She cocked her head and smiled. "Storybag."

"Who?" He-Dong looked toward the kitchen as if expecting someone to come out.

She laughed. "Don't you know the tale of the Storybag?"

He-Dong looked to me. I smiled. Of course my child didn't know those silly old stories. We only shared the important stories from the Bible. David and Goliath. Joshua and the Battle of Jericho.

"*Aigo.*" Min-Kook *uhmony* brought a hand to her chest. "You poor child."

He-Dong blushed. But, before he could ask, before she could continue, I put out my hand, my eyes focused on the letter.

"It's addressed to your husband." Min-Kook *uhmony* blew a strand of hair from her face and picked up the letter we'd brought. She didn't bother reading to me in Japanese but translated directly into Korean. "*Dear Mr. Yamamoto.*"

"He-Dong recognized those characters as his father's name," I said. I held my breath.

"We've decided." Min-Kook *uhmony* shook her head as she continued reading. *"to requisition your house as police headquarters. We offer you—* yes it really says that—*we offer you two weeks to vacate. Signed, Yamaguchi Hideko, Chief of Police, Seoul Headquarters."*

"Are you sure?" I gripped onto He-Dong. Perhaps she'd read it wrong. Maybe I should pay to have the note read at the market.

"What does 'vacate' mean?" He-Dong asked.

"If I'm wrong." Min-Kook *uhmony* pointed out the horrible character to me, as if I might recognize it. "You can have all my rice rations. You can string me up by my toes. You can—"

"It's fine." I should be grateful the letter contained no news of death. I folded my hands together in my lap. "I believe you."

"I'm glad you believe me, but it's the farthest I can think of from fine." She blew out a heavy sigh. "Now what?"

Min-Kook *uhmony* always cut to the heart of the matter. How could the Japanese kick us from our own home? Where would we go? We had long ago been thrown out of my dear's family. My older brother lived in the countryside, and he might have enough room for us. But then what about He-Dong's education?

"Offer you." Min-Kook *uhmony* repeated, her words dripping with scorn. She underlined the characters with her fingers. "The dogs."

I shook my head. My insides trembled. "We're all God's child—"

"Don't tell me that." She tossed the letter down on the table, her eyes fierce. "Those Japs are dogs. Always digging, digging, digging. They don't care what they have to do to get control over the world." She paused, glancing over at He-Dong. "We don't have much room. But you are welcome."

"Oh, Min-Kook *uhmony,* you're too generous." I grabbed her hands. There was barely room for her and Deacon Mah, and all their books and papers. Besides, how would it look for the minister's wife to be living squished into another parishioner's house? "I feel we should wait for my dear. He will know best what we should do."

"We're in a different world now." She shook her head, handing me the letter. "You, my friend, need to decide what to do."

"Do the police want to live with us?" He-Dong tilted his head to one side.

Outside that guard dog of hers started barking. Min-Kook *uhmony* went to the door and glanced outside. She gasped and shut the door.

"What is it?" I got up, beckoning He-Dong to follow. I put on my worn rubber sandals. My dear always said he'd buy me a new pair when we had some extra money. I needed him now more than ever. I reached up to open the door.

She put her arm up. "I need a favor." Her eyes darted about. She looked me up and down. Then her eyes focused on He-Dong. "Will you go to the market for me?"

"Actually…" I was eager to get home. I prayed my dear would be waiting for us, would look at the letter and tell us not to worry, that he would take care of everything. Even if this was not the case, I needed the quiet to pray about our new situation.

"Please." Her hands trembled as she went over to a book she'd shoved in the corner, opening it to the middle and removing the piece of paper she'd written on earlier. "I know you have so many other worries. But I need your help."

The dog continued barking, his chain rattling against the wooden pen. Who was outside that made Min-Kook *uhmony* so nervous? "What are you doing?"

"I'll tell you some other time." Her eyes locked onto mine as she shuffled into her shoes.

I didn't know what Min-Kook *uhmony* was involved in, but I trusted her. I could still remember her grabbing hold of my hands four months ago, saying, *Now is the time to feign interest in their bean sprouts.* She had warned me of trouble, and I hadn't listened. I often wondered what would have happened if I had. "What do you need from the market?"

Min-Kook *uhmony* let out a deep sigh, as she reached down to help He-Dong tie his shoes. "I just need this note delivered to the jar seller."

I put my hand out to accept the note, but she pulled He-Dong close and dropped it down the top of his shirt. "Make sure no one is watching, then drop it in the jar with the long scrape across the middle."

I nodded and grabbed onto He-Dong's hand. What information was he holding close to his chest? Was it about this battle she'd mentioned? And who was she sending the news to? I had a million questions. But I turned to leave.

"No." She picked up a shopping basket, stuffed some newspapers inside, and opened the door. She touched my arm. "Let me go first."

She walked down the path and turned away from the market. She looked over each shoulder before sneaking a peek in her basket of newspapers. At that moment, a police officer stepped out from behind the tree to follow her.

"Look, Mother." He-Dong pointed. "Is that one of the men who will live with us?"

"Come along." I grabbed his hand.

I closed her door behind us. The dog barked, the printing press banged, my heart pounded, and my stomach was now filled with a different anxiety.

*A victory of the democracies can only be complete with the utter defeat
of the war machines of Germany and Japan.*
—**General George. C. Marshall, WWII**

Friday, August 7, 1942—same day

Baby He-Dong

I walked next to Mother, or rather she walked on top of me. She was so close that her sweaty arm nudged my cheek. The paper Min-Kook *uhmony* had stuffed in my shirt tickled my stomach. I just wanted to be home with Kwidong.

"Mother." I pushed away from her. "What if we don't want to leave our house? Can we live with the police?"

She hugged me tight, making the paper on my stomach itch more. "Let's not worry about that now."

What else would we worry about? What if the police were already at our home scaring Kwidong? Besides, Min-Kook *uhmony* seemed to think it was something to worry about, ranting on and on about the horrible Japanese. I reached up to adjust my shirt. "Can we go home now?"

"We will." She pushed my hands away from my shirt. "After we do this one favor for—"

"Why would God let the police take our home?" My voice trembled, and my eyes burned.

"The Japanese must be making their base of operations larger," Mother said in her too-cheery voice, as if I were a baby. "That must mean they're winning and He-Seung will be home soon."

I felt a bit of relief, but not as much as I wanted. Where would we go? Why wasn't Father home yet? What was this note in my shirt? "Mother, what was Min-Kook *uhmony* talking about? The Storybag?"

"That's just a silly old story." Mother wiped drops of sweat from her forehead. "It's been a long time since my grandmother told me."

"Then you better tell me quick." I pulled at my shirt. "Before you forget any more of it."

Mother grabbed onto my hands to still them. "It's about a boy who loved stories." She tucked my shirt back in. "Each time he heard a story, he stuffed it in a small bag he carried at his belt."

"Like you're stuffing my shirt in." I pushed her hand away.

Mother patted my shoulder. "This boy tied a string around the neck of the bag to make sure none of his stories escaped."

"Do you think we could stuff that official letter from Police Headquarters into a bag and forget about it?" I looked back in the direction of our house. I stopped walking.

"No, Dear One." Mother urged me onward. "The boy in the story eventually grew into a handsome man."

"Like He-Seung?" He-Seung would know what to do about this *vacate* business.

"Yes." Mother smiled. "And a bride was chosen for him."

"I choose Myung-Ja." I fanned my shirt.

Mother batted my hands away from my shirt. "The morning of their wedding, though, the man's faithful servant heard whispering coming from the story bag."

"What did the voices say?" I asked.

"Something like." Mother looked up to the sky. "'Listen, everyone. That man has made us suffer long enough stuffed in this bag. It's time to take revenge.'"

Mother didn't do angry voices well. Besides, how could a bunch of stories take revenge on a man? Again I looked back toward home.

"The poor man had a long journey ahead of him to meet his bride." Mother urged me forward again. "The stories could turn into anything. So they made plans to turn into different things to try to—"

"Get rid of him?"

"Actually, yes." Mother raised her eyebrows. "One story planned to turn into beautiful poisonous berries ripening by the roadside. One planned to turn into a poisonous bubbling brook. And another would change into snakes."

We were already at the edge of the marketplace. In front of me, a little boy stopped to pee in the road. An ox thrashed its tail at buzzing flies. An old woman readjusted her empty shopping basket.

"The loyal servant insisted on accompanying his master on his journey to the bride's home. And sure enough, along the way, bright berries grew by the side the road. The man wanted to stop."

"So, he ate the berries and died?" I guessed.

"The loyal servant pretended not to hear." Mother shook her head at me. "She did not let the man stop for berries."

"That was smart," I said.

"Further down the path," Mother said, "they came across a bubbling brook. There was even a ladle floating on top. The master shouted for the servant to stop."

Now, an old man spit on the ground. A farmer pulled a cartload of potatoes. A girl pulled on her mother, asking if they could get a treat from the candy-seller. I wondered if they all would have to do this *vacate* thing. "So the man drank the water and died?"

"No." Mother shook her head again. "The servant again pretended not to hear anything."

I liked this servant guy. He was smart. He saw the problem and came up with a solution. "Ah, but what about the snake?"

"You don't forget a thing." Mother smiled. "Late that night, as soon as the bride and groom retired, the servant leapt inside their room."

"The servant went into their marriage room?" I didn't really know what that meant, but I knew everyone giggled about the bride and groom being alone together in the room on their marriage night.

Mother nodded. "The man shouted at the servant, telling him to leave."

I jumped ahead of Mother. The paper beneath my shirt rustled. "The snakes bit the man...and he died a painful death... and his wife ended up letting all the stories go."

Mother kept walking. She looked over at me, inclining her head like she did when she wanted me to think again.

"The servant didn't leave the marriage room?" I asked.

"Not until he'd checked to make sure everything was safe."

"And he found the snake?" I asked.

She nodded. "Hundreds of them, slithering back and forth under his Master's mattress."

"Wow." This story was almost as good as He-Seung's comics. "How could he kill hundreds of snakes?"

"He was good with his sword," she raised her eyebrows. "From that day on, the man always trusted his servant, and never kept his stories tied up in a bag. In fact, he shared them with as many people as possible, so others could learn from the tales."

"You ended up remembering that story pretty well."

"I did, didn't I?" She blew at a hair that had fallen in her face.

We were in the middle of the marketplace. The bean seller tossed a few rotten beans to the ground. The tofu lady shooed away a fly. And right nearby was the jar lady.

I thought of Min-Kook *uhmony* all excited by news of a battle in some strange place. "What does the Storybag have to do with Min-Kook *uhmony*? And Guadal—what was that place name?"

"Shhhh." Mother's eyes went wide. She whispered, "I don't know, but I don't think we should talk about it to anyone. Anyone at all."

Mrs. Hong rushed over to tell us about her wonderful new jars. Solid, large, crack-proof. Mother nodded, as if she'd never heard Mrs. Hong do this before, as if we really needed one. I felt the note wanting to get out of my shirt, though. Like the stories. Perhaps in all Mrs. Hong's talking,

Mother had forgotten the instructions Min-Kook *uhmony* had given us. But I remembered.

I spotted the jar with the long scratch. "Over there," I shouted.

Another shopper paused to look. Mother blushed scarlet, wrapping her arms around me so tight I couldn't breathe.

I whispered, "I found the—"

"I know." Mother put her finger up to my mouth.

Mrs. Hong gave Mother a quick nod, then hurried away to help the shopper who had come to take a closer look. Mother took the note from my shirt and dropped it in the jar. Then she grabbed onto my hand and pulled me away faster than I thought she could move.

I thought of the fairytale. All those horrible things could have happened to the handsome man , yet the servant stopped all of them. I hoped a servant like this was looking after He-Seung.

**US Pres. Roosevelt forms *Manhattan Project*,
a research project to develop the atomic bomb.
—August 13, 1942**

Monday, August 17, 1942—ten days later

Baby He-Dong

I stood in the backyard. A fly buzzed nearby, and Kwidong snapped at it. I yanked on his leash, attempting to get his attention.

Since we'd gotten the police letter, our church friends had come to visit. Gong-Tae *uhmony* had come to say there was always room at her house, but then she went on to talk about how her sister and two baby nieces were staying with her already, as her brother-in-law had joined the army. In-Young had come by with more pickles and a cup of precious white rice. She had said that her mean husband was leaving for the army, and that it would have been fine for Mother and I to stay with her, but her in-laws were against it. She cried so much you would have thought the Japanese had asked her to vacate. Mr. Im's wife had hobbled over, bringing a white radish and saying that she feared with all of Mr. Im's illnesses, we would get ill, too. Even Myung-Ja *uhmony* came over. But given that Dr. Lee had just accepted a job working for the Japanese in the prison, it didn't seem appropriate to take us in.

Mother had even stopped by the church, thinking we could pry open a window and stay in there for a while. But while the church was no longer padlocked, it was occupied. The pews had been pushed to the walls. Desks replaced them. Officers rushed back and forth, waving papers and shouting orders. I'd prayed so often that the church would re-open. I guess I forgot to ask God that it re-open for Father, not some army people.

In between lots of praying, Mother had organized our clothes and bedding, Father's books, her pots. There were so many things. How would we take all of them? Where would we go? Would Kwidong get to come along? My brain felt tired by these questions. The Japanese would be moving into our house in four days.

"Kwidong, heel." I held tight to his leash as I walked around the yard.

He would get confused too, if we switched homes. He needed to learn to follow me always. When I stopped he did, too. Well, sort of. I had stopped near the old rooster pen, and he sat down to chew on the wood.

Good boy." I untied his rope. "Now let's try without the leash."

He shot off running to the front yard. I ran after him. "Stop!"

At the end of the path out front, he stopped and barked.

"Good boy." I ran over and grabbed his collar. I would have to tell He-Seung about his good behavior next time I wrote.

Last week, we'd had our first letter from him. A thin blue airmail note written all in hiragana. The way he wrote in such big handwriting, such baby Japanese that even I could read, I could tell he knew that Father wasn't home yet.

He said that he was in Japan in a place called Okinawa. He said that the weather was so hot he always felt as if he were in the public bath house. He spent every day digging holes to shelter the soldiers in case of bombing. He said Gong-Tae had been sent elsewhere. I kept wondering if he was teasing us. I kept waiting for the punch line.

I grabbed onto Kwidong and returned to our back yard. Mother had come outside and was now kneeling next to the rooster cage. She held up a piece of wood with her right hand, a nail in her left. "He-Dong, can you help me?"

Kwidong bounded over as if she were giving instructions to him. He pushed his snout in to grab at the wood. I pushed him away. "Down, boy."

Although I planned to tell He-Seung that Kwidong was such a good boy, that wasn't always true. Our *Precious* still chewed on everything, and I had to keep him tied to a rope all the time or he'd run off. I leaned over and grabbed a branch from the ground. I tossed it close enough that he could reach it despite the rope attached to his collar. "Go fetch."

"That was smart." Mother's face was red with heat, a drop of sweat rolled down the side of her cheek. "Now. Here. Hammer here."

Why did we have to fix the rooster house? Perhaps she didn't want the Japanese to think we were so low class we didn't care about our things. But I'd never hammered anything before. He-Chul or He-Seung did the hammering.

I tried to remember how they'd done it. Pulling the hammer way back and smashing the head on the nail. I thought of what poor aim I'd had with He-Seung's slingshot. How he'd told me to look at my target with anger. Then again, what if, in my anger, I missed and hit Mother's thin fingers?

Kwidong returned with the branch. He didn't drop it at my feet, though, to have me throw it again. Instead he wrestled it to the ground as if it were a squirrel. He looked funny. I'd write that to He-Seung as well.

"Mother." I watched Kwidong with his imaginary enemy. "Remember the time He-Seung hid the shovel?"

Mother's shoulders sagged. "Are you still thinking about his letter?"

I was. And now, if I looked off toward the garden, I could imagine him pretending not to know where the shovel had disappeared to. We had all stopped what we were doing to search. When was the last time it had been used? Who might have borrowed it? Could it have been stolen? "How could he be digging ditches big enough for twelve men when he didn't even want to weed our garden?"

Mother laughed. "Oh, your father. I've never seen him so angry with He-Seung's games."

We both looked at each other. I could almost hear her thinking that it would be nice to have that unhappy noise in our house again.

I tapped the hammer on the ground. "What are we going to do?"

"We're just fixing the—"

"I mean, where are we going to do our vacating?"

"Don't worry." Mother put her hot hand on my arm. "An answer will come."

"What if it's doesn't?"

"We have to trust that it will. We have to prepare for that." Mother positioned the nail against the wood. "Now enough procrastinating."

"What is procast—procast—"

"Procrastinating," she said. "Putting off something that you don't want to do."

A truck engine sounded out on our road. Kwidong stopped wrestling the branch to the ground and perked his ears. He strained to the end of his leash to see what was going on. Trucks didn't often come near our road, but perhaps it was police officials looking for another home to take.

"Here." A drop of perspiration fell from Mother's brow. "You'll do fine. Hit right here."

I pulled my arm back as far as I could, aimed and let the hammer fall toward the wood. Kwidong barked. My hand jerked.

"*Aigo*," Mother cried. She dropped the wood. She wrapped her thumb in her skirt.

"Oh, Mother." I threw the hammer to the ground. "I'm sorry. Are you hurt?"

Kwidong continued barking. He strained at his leash, jumping up on his short hind legs, as he tried to get to the front of the house.

"Is there somebody at the door?" She hunched over and squeezed her finger.

Bam. Bam. Bam.

Mother prayed so much for guidance and help, and I couldn't even hammer a nail for her. "What about your hand?"

"Go answer the door." She blew a wisp of hair from her forehead. She smiled. "Go on."

I hurried inside. Were the police coming to move in early? To check on our vacating?

Bam. Bam. Bam.

I rushed to the door. A uniformed policeman stood on the porch, a wooden baton dangling at his side. Behind him, two more men dressed in simple yellow clothes stood holding a stretcher. The stretcher was covered with a brown, ink-splattered blanket.

My underarms itched just looking at that hot blanket. The police had come to make us *vacate*. They were going to move their things and people in already.

"Is your mother home?" the policeman asked, speaking Korean. "I'm from *Serdamoon* prison."

Behind me, Mother gasped. Her fingers dug into my arms, the nails piercing my flesh. She made a horrible sobbing sound.

"Lady," the policeman said. Not *Dear Lady*. Just *Lady*. "Stop all your noise. Your husband fell down. We don't have any place to care for him."

Your husband f*ell down? Care for him?* That was Father on the stretcher.

We both rushed forward. Mother put her shaky hands out toward the blanket. Her thumb, where I'd accidentally hit her with the hammer, was red and black at the nail. It was then I realized the black splotches on Father's blanket were not ink, but blood. My stomach flip-flopped.

Mother lifted the blanket. Father lay on his back, his eyes shut, his face pale and thin. I grabbed onto his hand. His warm, live hand.

"Lady," the policeman said. "Where's his bedroom?"

"He-Dong." Mother stood back. "Go. Show them the way."

I led the police helpers up the stairway, looking back each step, worrying that Father might slide off the stretcher and fall down the steps. Fortunately, the helper in the back lifted the stretcher higher so Father stayed straight. Mother followed behind. When we got upstairs, I opened the door to Father's room. Mother rushed in and pulled back the bedspread, something she hadn't done for forever.

The helpers set the stretcher on the bed. One of them put his arms under Father's shoulders. The other held Father's legs. They lifted him up.

"Boy," barked the one who held his shoulders. "Pull the stretcher out from under your Father. Now."

Mother and I both pulled the stretcher out. The helpers plopped Father on the bed. He didn't shout or complain. He didn't even move. His face looked like stone.

"Father." I touched his hand. Then I shook it a little. "It's me, He-Dong. And Mother. You're home now. And guess what? We have a new dog— Kwidong. He-Seung named him. Don't you like that name?" My throat ached from talking. My eyes burned.

"Come." Mother pulled me away. "Let your father rest."

We led the helpers back down to the front door where the policeman stood outside waiting. He fingered his baton, his jaw set, his black eyes fierce.

"Lady," the policeman said, using that horrible word again. "You've got your traitor back. Hopefully, he's learned his lesson."

"Thank you," Mother bowed to the policeman, as if he were someone great.

From the backyard I heard Kwidong still barking, his voice hoarse with anger. My insides felt hoarse, too. I thought of how He-Seung used to pretend he was exercising. I thought of him so far away. I bent at the waist. One, two, three, four.

"We'll be watching you." The policeman tapped his baton on his hand. "If we find any suspicious activity, we'll take him back to prison for good."

"Thank you." Mother bowed again. "Thank you for bringing my husband home."

The policeman walked away with the helpers. One helper carried the stretcher on his shoulder like a white flag on a long pole.

"Go now." Mother turned, heading back inside. "Go get Dr. Lee. Hurry."

I started down the path. My limbs shook. Tears streamed down my cheeks. He-Seung had left. The Japanese were taking our house. Father was hurt. Why were only bad things happening to us? I felt a tickling sensation on my right leg. I turned. Kwidong had broken loose. He was following me. I picked him up, hugging him tight, as the two of us ran to get help for Father.

What kind of people do they (the Japanese) think we are?
Is it possible they do not realize that we shall never cease to persevere
against them until they have been taught a lesson which they and the
world will never forget?
—**Winston Churchill, 1942**

Monday, August 17, 1942—same day

Mother (*Uhmony*)

The policeman had said my dear had fallen. Had he tripped? Had he been so weak from a lack of food and water that his legs gave way? I rushed into the kitchen to get him a cup of water. When he woke up, he would be in need of something to drink. I raced up the stairs, taking the steps two at a time, water sloshing over the side of his tin cup. His cup. After 122 days, he was going to use his cup.

"*Yubo?*" I called to him. "Dear?"

His eyes were still closed, the left side of his face slanting downward. I adjusted the pillow under his head, but his face still looked lopsided. If he had merely fallen, why would his face look so? "I brought you some water."

I set the cup on the nightstand and grabbed hold of his hand. His fingers were limp in mine, waxy like chili peppers which had fallen from the vine. I looked closely at his strong hands. The spots where his nails used to be were black and green. The pinky finger of his right hand was oozing with an ugly, yellow pus.

I quickly put his hands beneath his comforter, bile filling my throat. Then again, perhaps putting his mangled fingers beneath a heavy blanket hurt. I pulled them back out into the fresh air. Hadn't Myung-Ja *uhmony* said her husband was always called to the prison when there was torture? Yet, why hadn't Dr. Lee been called? What was taking him so long now?

"*Yubo.*" I leaned down and whispered. "Dear." His neck smelled of sweat and urine, as if he hadn't bathed in months. "Do you want to wake up yet? Are you in pain? So much has happened since you've been gone. It feels like years have gone by."

I didn't think now was the time to mention He-Seung having left for the army. I patted my dear's chest. "The Lee's gave He-Dong one of their puppies. I know now's not the best time to take on another mouth to feed, but you should see He-Dong. He treats that dog as if it were his baby brother. He talks to it, naps next to it. He'll do anything for his Kwidong. It's such fun to watch him with the puppy, I don't mind when I see teeth marks all over the front porch or have to build a new rooster pen. In fact,

He-Dong and I have been doing the work all by ourselves. Just the two of us. Can you imagine that?"

My dear made a sound in his throat. I was so relieved. I put my head on his arm. I patted him some more. Laughing with him. Surely he couldn't imagine his wife with a hammer and nails. He would be proud of the way we'd kept the house together, I hoped.

"There is one immediate problem." I looked up. His lips were cracked. Surely he was thirsty. "We have to leave here in four days. The Japanese want to use our home as a police headquarters."

His lashes fluttered. I'd always loved his long lashes, how they fluttered before he opened his deep brown eyes and looked at me.

"We tried the church, but it's now..." I patted his arm. "Well, it's now being used. Min-Kook *uhmony* offered to make space for us. But I didn't think we could all fit, and that was before you got home. At the worst, we can go live with my brother in the countryside. What do you think we should do?"

His lashes fluttered again. He breathed in, making a snorting sound in his nose. Then he sighed.

"*Yubo?*" I patted him. "Dear, would you like a drink of water first?" I patted him some more. "Dear?" The sound of a thwop-thwop-thwop filled the air. Then a groan. I looked down to realize I was doing more than patting.

"Oh, God." My dear had taken a bad fall, worse than Mr. Im who fell from his ladder, and here I was hitting him, demanding attention. "Forgive me."

I took the water from the nightstand. I dipped the skirt of my *cheemar* into the cup, squeezing out the excess. I stood up, using the wet cloth to wipe his face, still hoping each time I rubbed the cloth over his eyes that they would open.

Before we're through with them, the Japanese language
will be spoken only in hell.
—**Admiral Halsey, 1942**

Wednesday, August 19, 1942—two days later

Mother (*Uhmony*)

I sat next to my dear's bed. Dr. Lee had said my dear had an old man's falling sickness that most didn't survive. That it was a miracle he was home with us.

He-Dong was downstairs in the living room, packing up his *bahduk* set, his comic, his readers. I knew I should get moving, too. But my heart was even more tied in knots than ever. I feared leaving my dear's side. What if he woke up with words of advice when I was away from his side? I wiped a thread of drool from his chin.

On the morning of my wedding, Mother had brushed my hair, saying, *Marriage is the relation between heaven and earth, between solid and soft, between sovereign and subject. It begins with a distinction between the two. The distinction should be kept between man and woman, as it is proper and will lead to the stability of the world.*

What would she say now? The other half of me had returned home, but my world still shook. Outside, Kwidong barked.

"Mother?" He-Dong called. "Min-Kook *uhmony* brought ice cream."

"We have a visitor." I leaned down and whispered to my dear. "I won't be gone long."

When I finally pulled myself away from my dear and went downstairs, Min-Kook *uhmony* was already seated on a cushion in the living room. He-Dong had not only made her comfortable, but had even brought out some bowls and spoons. He sat next to her holding onto the lacquer bowl of ice cream—a treat he'd tasted but a few times.

Surely she had brought the sweet in celebration that my dear was home. She looked up when I entered, glancing behind me as if she might spot him. She would be surprised to hear that he was still sleeping, that all of our boxes were not yet packed to vacate.

"Min-Kook *uhmony*." I sat on the floor next to He-Dong. "It's so good of you to come. Let us pray."

He-Dong looked at the contents of the lacquer bowl. Min-Kook *uhmony* smiled at him, folding her hands. With reluctance, he set the bowl on the table and put his hands together. I bowed my head, the whole time thinking of my dear upstairs. Was he still sleeping? Had his eyelashes fluttered?

"Dear Father," I said. "Our hearts are filled with gratitude for the many blessings you've bestowed upon us. You've blessed us with wonderful friends who support and console us as we welcome home He-Dong's father. We know under Your care, he will soon be strong again. We also pray for He-Seung in the Japanese Youth Corps, for He-Chul as he studies so far away from home. Please protect them and let them know that You are always there."

A pain stabbed my leg, like a bedbug or mosquito. I swatted at the interruption. My hand hit another hand. He-Dong. He-Dong pinching me.

"Thank you again for blessing us with such kind friends." I inwardly smiled at my impatient child. "Amen."

"Amen," He-Dong said with such emphasis that Min-Kook *uhmony* laughed. He pointed to the lacquer bowl. The frozen red bean ice cream had melted into milky red pools with little dots of red beans here and there. "You thanked the Lord for ice cream, but this isn't anymore."

"Never mind." Min-Kook *uhmony* poured the ice cream into the three bowls. "It's soup."

He-Dong picked up his bowl, slurping loud to show his appreciation. A thread of red-bean liquid dribbled down his chin. Again, I wondered how my dear was faring all alone upstairs.

"What's wrong?" Min-Kook *uhmony* asked.

"Perhaps He-Dong's father would enjoy a taste," I said. "Perhaps I should go—"

"I hear he's very tired." Min-Kook *uhmony* set her bowl down. "He may not need ice cream now."

"Besides," He-Dong added. "I don't think he'd be happy about this soup stuff."

I lifted the bowl to my lips. It was kind of her to bring this treat. The mixture tasted salty as it swirled with the worries in my heart.

"Have you found a place to 'vacate' to?" Min-Kook *uhmony* tapped the table.

I had spoken to God. I had asked my dear dozens of times. *Min-Kook uhmony's* words pounded in my head. *It's time for you to decide.*

"No." The word came out so loudly, it took me a second to realize that He-Dong had spoken along with me.

"Perfect." Min-Kook patted my arm. "I wonder if you'd do me a favor. My father-in-law is ill."

"I'm sorry." My eyes filled.

"Never mind." Min-Kook *uhmony* batted her hand back and forth. "He's an old goat. He'll be fine."

"Kwidong and I could go fetch Dr. Lee," He-Dong offered, licking the side of his mouth.

She smiled at him. "Actually, Deacon Mah and I, we just need to go take care of him for a while."

"Go?" He-Dong lifted his head.

"He lives in the middle of nowhere." She shrugged.

I'd forgotten. My mind was in such a fog. Her in-laws lived further away than my younger brother.

"I don't know how long we'll be gone." She scratched at a mosquito bite on her arm. "A few months, maybe more."

Surely my mind wasn't just in a fog, but I was hearing things. I was used to people bowing to me. To calling me *Dear Lady*. To honoring my every move. He-Dong reached over and pinched my leg again. I realized, as I swatted his hand away, that I wasn't a Dear Lady, but an impoverished mother with a small boy and ill husband who needed a place to live. And my friend was offering us the use of her entire home.

"Oh, Min-Kook *uhmony*." I scooted over in front of her and bowed my head to the floor. "God bless you."

I heard He-Dong rustling on the floor, felt him bowing next to me.

"If there are any blessings to be had." She pulled me up. She pulled He-Dong up. "They should go to you. You and your brave boy."

I thought of my mother's words of advice when I married, her wisdom on how to maintain the stability of the world. With God's grace, two women and one small boy had figured out how to keep the earth from shaking. At least for today.

The leaders of America are truly running their nation in a laughable manner. They may be high in producing capacity, but without the more essential qualities, such as lofty war ideals, America cannot win over us.
—**Masayuki Tani, Foreign Minister, 1942**

Saturday, August 22, 1942—three days later

Baby He-Dong

We had been living at Min-Kook *uhmony's* house for a day. While Father rested in Deacon Mah's bed—one that was narrower than his own—Mother was in the kitchen, organizing shelves. I was in charge of mopping out Min-Kook *uhmony's* bedding closet which smelled of rat pee. I wondered if Min-Kook *uhmony* had missed Father's sermon on practicing cleanliness before approaching the Lord.

Mother's prayers had grown even longer over the last few days—for the friends who had helped us move, even In-Young who was waiting for a baby to come, for the friends who had let us use their space, for the light of the Lord, and on and on. But all I kept thinking was that the Japanese were moving into my yard, my house, my room. Today.

I wedged the mop inside the closet and let it sit in the darkness for a while. Then I brushed out the contents. There were a few dead brown bedbugs, some black specs which turned out to be ants, a cockroach which lay on its back, its wiry legs still flailing. Ih-Duk would be fascinated. I just felt tired. I wanted to be back home.

I dropped the mop. The wood hitting the floor made a loud thwack. I waited for Father to shout in anger. I hoped that he would.

"Mother," I called, as I went to the front door and put my shoes on. "I'm going outside."

"Are you finished so soon?" Mother called back.

"I—I just need to check on Kwidong."

There was a silence. I knew that meant Mother didn't really think that kind of checking was necessary. At the same time, she didn't stop me. So I hurried out the door to the side of the house where Kwidong waited in his small pen. I don't know how Min-Kook *uhmony's* big dog had ever survived in such a small spot. Maybe that's what made him bark so much. I opened the door of the wooden pen and Kwidong jumped up on me, licking my face.

"Okay, okay." He jumped up again. I picked up the Emperor's red ball and threw it on the small patch of lawn along the side of the house. "Fetch, boy."

He ran and grabbed the ball.

"Come on, Kwidong," I shouted over the thwack-thwack-thwack of the print shop. "Bring it back."

When he ignored me, I went over and grabbed the ball. Then I threw the toy so far it went into a small space near the back of the house.

Kwidong chased after the ball, but he didn't return. I called to him, but perhaps he couldn't hear me over the noise of the printing press. I jammed my fists in my pockets. If we'd been home, I wouldn't have to pack up my desk to be stored. I wouldn't have to spend my vacation cleaning out someone else's closets. I wouldn't have to squeeze into small spaces to retrieve Kwidong's toy.

"Kwidong?" I went behind, which backed up against the print shop. The air was stifling. The printer had even stopped its clang-clang-clang.

Kwidong sniffed at a vent at the back of the shop. I reached down to grab the ball on the ground beneath him. "You're supposed to bring this back to me."

"Stupid Japs," a soft male voice said in Korean.

I turned around. Behind me, there was Kwidong's pen and the rooster cage. Min-Kook *uhmony's* small cherry tree stood bare. I didn't see anyone. I reached down again to grab the ball.

"Savo's as bad as the Solomons," the voice said. "They just don't want people to know."

I looked at the print shop's vent. The voices were coming from there. I'd heard of King Solomon in the Bible, but not Savo. Were these men in the print shop studying Christianity in secret?

I looked up at Min-Kook *uhmony's* house. If Mother were in the kitchen, she would see me with my head at the vent. She would come to the back door and ask exactly what was I doing. She would want me to return to cleaning out the bugs in the closet.

"Come on, Kwidong." I picked up the ball, the sound of the voices calling out *stupid Japs* bouncing in my head. "Let's get out of here."

We walked to our real home. Out in front, I spotted a truck, its back filled high with chairs and desks. A police officer in full uniform stepped down from the truck. Kwidong barked, jumping up and down.

"Shh." I felt an aching in my throat as I knelt down next to him. "They're just borrowing our house."

The officer had a short mustache which looked as if he'd dipped his upper lip in soy sauce. He wore a sword at his side. Three helpers in yellow clothing jumped down from the back of the truck, stood before the officer, and bowed. The officer strolled inside my house as if it were his. I stared at his back, feeling a burning in my eyes.

Both of the workers pulled out long cotton straps. One of them put his strap around two chairs, pulled the chairs onto his back, and hurried up my porch steps. The other put his strap around a huge desk and pulled it on his back. Sweat glistened off his bald head.

"Mother says it's temporary," I said.

Kwidong licked my cheek.

I took Kwidong's ball from my pocket and untied his leash. "Here." I threw the ball down the path. "Fetch."

Kwidong chased after his toy. I looked at the porch. I could spot notches in the bottom step where He-Seung had secretly tested the sharpness of his pocketknife. I could envision my broom resting by the rail, waiting for me to pick it up and sweep away the dust.

A wet nose on my knee made me look down. Kwidong had returned with the ball, dropping it at my feet. As usual the ball glistened with slobber.

I reached down to retrieve the toy, when I heard a loud thumping noise followed by angry shouts. Perhaps the worker had dropped the desk. I wondered where they were putting it. I could imagine He-Chul inside sitting at his desk, Father working upstairs in his office, Mother sewing next to the window in the living room. It was our house.

I threw the toy for Kwidong again, but he was no longer with me. He had wandered over to the truck. He sniffed around it, as if confused that it was here in front of our home. He found a rope dangling off the back.

"No, Kwidong," I said automatically, as I knew what he would do.

He looked over at me, but then he grabbed onto the rope and chewed.

I watched him yanking at the rope. These people had pushed us from our home. Why should I care so much about the rope on their truck?

I leaned down to the ground to wipe off Kwidong- slobber from my hands. I rubbed and rubbed. Then I grabbed a fistful of dirt and moved closer to the truck which was full of furniture, and a picture of the Emperor, some fancy Japanese scrolls. I looked up at the door of my house to see that no one was coming. I tossed the fistful of dirt into the truck, letting it rain on their fancy wooden chairs.

Do unto others as you would have them do unto you, Father always said. However, they'd already done such meanness unto us, what was a little dirt for them to sit on, in comparison?

I leaned down and picked up another fistful of dirt and threw it on a lamp. I threw more on a picture of their Emperor, their God— the One responsible for closing our church, arresting Father, taking He-Seung away, and now taking our home. I leaned down to grab another handful. Boots scraped on the steps. I stood up, glancing over toward the porch. The soy-sauce-mustache officer was coming back.

I stepped away from the truck. My legs were so full of fire I wanted to run. But Kwidong was still busy chewing.

I reached in my pocket, realizing I didn't have his ball to attract him. "Kwidong? Boy. Come."

"What are you doing here?" The soy- sauce-mustache officer hurried over, his hand on his sword. "Who are you calling 'boy?'"

I returned to the truck and pulled on Kwidong's collar. "M-my-my dog."

What if the officer saw the mess I'd made on his truck? The rain of dirt across the Emperor's face? Maybe I'd be put in prison like Father, and come home asleep.

The officer batted his hand at Kwidong. "Get. Both of you."

Kwidong let the truck's rope drop from his mouth. He looked at the officer, a growl rumbling from his throat.

"Shhhh." If we could get away from here, back to the safety of Min-Kook *uhmony's,* I wouldn't care about the bugs in the bedroom. Or the smell of rat pee in my closet. I'd be happy to just be under a roof with people who loved me. I picked up Kwidong and ran down the path, the officer's laughter vibrating in my ears.

And when he gets to Heaven
To Saint Peter he will tell:
'One more Marine reporting, Sir!
I've done my time in Hell.'
**—Marines' Epitaph re campaign in Guadalcanal which lasted August
'42-Feb '43**

Monday, August 24, 1942—two days later

Baby He-Dong

I stumbled into the kitchen wearing my school uniform. The second half of the year began today. Normally I would be excited. But, this morning my head ached as if cotton were stuffed in my brains. I had eight bug bites on my legs. Five on my stomach. Three on my right arm.

"Mother." I thought we had cleaned the house pretty well. But obviously it needed more work. "I don't think I should go to school today."

Mother wiped her hand on her *cheemar* and came over to feel my forehead. "Are you ill?"

"No, but we have a bug problem that needs attention." I scratched my leg.

"The best person to help us with that is your friend, Ih-Duk." She handed me a bowl of rice. "And he'll be waiting for you at school."

I shoveled some rice in my mouth. Still, Kwidong would miss me. And how could I leave Mother at home all day with Father still being so tired? "I shouldn't be wasting time at school."

"Don't be silly." Mother smiled. "Besides, what would your brothers say if I allowed such a thing?"

I put my bowl on the counter. "Well, He-Chul might not like it. He would use lots of big words to tell me that I should go. But He-Seung, He-Seung would say I should protect my family."

"I think both your brothers are right. The best way for a young boy to protect himself and his family is to go to school." She added a few pickles to the top of my *bento* box before closing the top and handing it to me. "Now, hurry up or you'll be late."

She followed me to the front door. I bent down to tie my shoes when I heard a creaking sound, the wobbling of a nightstand. A clearing of the throat. Mother and I exchanged a look.

"Father?" I raced up from the entryway, kicking my shoes off as I ran to Father's room. He had pushed himself to a sitting position. He looked around the room, the left side of his face was still drooping.

I wondered if he was confused being in Min-Kook *uhmony*'s tiny bedroom, if he smelled rat pee, if he wanted to play *bahduk* after staying in bed for so long, if he'd like to go outside and see Kwidong, if he wanted to see how I could read He-Seung's letter all by myself.

"Good morning, *Yubo*." Mother came up behind me, her voice shaky. "You're awake. Are you hungry? Can I get you some rice soup?"

He turned his head toward her. I was sure he'd say she was talking too much, like a blackbird chattering on the treetops. He opened his mouth and moved it up and down. A gargling noise came out.

"Mother?" I pulled at her *cheemar*. "What's wrong with his voice?"

She rubbed one hand over the other. "Maybe he's still tired."

"But he's been sleeping for days."

"Come, you need to go." She turned me toward the door. "Why don't you stop at Dr. Lee's on your way to school and ask him to visit Father?"

"Don't you think Father would want to go visit Dr. Lee and get some fresh air?" I pushed her hands away. "We could walk together."

"Not today." She patted my shoulder. "*Yubo*," she called to Father. "He-Dong is on his way to school. Do you wish to wish say something to him?"

Father looked at Mother. A sliver of saliva ran down his mouth.

I was late. Ito *Sensei* pushed me to the back of the class with her bamboo cane. I sat in an empty desk near Ih-Duk, dropping my knapsack, and standing at attention with the rest of the class.

In the corner of the classroom an old fan hung from the ceiling, whirring around and around, generating more noise than cool air. The room was as hot as a charcoal fire. My cheeks felt even hotter.

"Don't worry." Ih-Duk whispered, giving me a sympathetic glance. "Class hasn't started."

I shook my head at him. I remembered what had happened to me at the beginning of the year when I'd tried to help him. I would hate to see Ih-Duk up in front of the class with his hands outstretched forever. My own shoulders ached at the thought.

"You missed Kee-Wok." Ih-Duk nudged me.

I glanced down the row to where Kee-Wok stood taller than his lieutenants. Up until this moment I hadn't given too much thought to Kee-Wok. All summer my mind had been too busy with other things. Would he still try to take my lunch? Would I have to fight him? Perhaps Ih-Duk thought I was late on purpose to avoid the bully.

"Father sat up," I whispered. "Dr. Lee is with him now."

"I caught a beetle." He smiled. "My biggest yet."

"You should see all the bugs in our house." I started to explain, but then spotted Ito *Sensei* looking my way, tapping her cane against her leg. I dropped my gaze, mumbling. "It's an Ih-Duk paradise."

"Before we start the morning pledge..." Ito *Sensei* wandered down our row of desks, pausing before me.

Had the *Sensei* heard us talking? I closed my eyes, listening to my heart thumping.

"I just wanted you to know that our country is fighting hard," *Sensei* continued. "We should be proud of our sacrifices—I know most of you have siblings supporting the Imperial Cause."

I'd never told anyone—not even Ih-Duk—that my brother was just digging ditches. I still didn't really believe it. If *Sensei* knew, she might not be making this big speech. Still, it felt good to hear these words. I let out a deep breath, exchanging glances with Ih-Duk.

"Their efforts—all of our efforts—will soon be victorious." She gave me a slight nod. "With that in our hearts..." She returned to the front of the room and pointed to the Class Monitor, Bon-Hwa. "Let's give our praises to the Emperor."

"*Tenno Heika.*" He lifted his arms to the ceiling, leading us in the pledge to the Emperor. "*Banzai.*"

"I'd forgotten about this," I moaned.

"Stop." Ito *Sensei* thwapped her cane against her desk.

I froze. Sweat rolled down my cheek.

Ito *Sensei* pointed with her cane, thankfully not at me. "Kee-Wok, why aren't you doing the pledge?"

He bowed. "I can't."

It was then I spotted a sling wrapped around his right shoulder. I nudged Ih-Duk. "What happened?"

"Fell or something." Ih-Duk shrugged. "You're safe for a while."

I rolled my eyes. I had a brother in the army who'd taught me to be strong. I had run faster than that bully who had longer legs than me. I had delivered a note in secret to somebody from the Storybag. I'd even thrown dirt in the Emperor's face—well, a picture of the Emperor. Ih-Duk shouldn't talk like I was still a bean-curd boy.

Ito *Sensei* inspected Kee-Wok's arm, attempting to lift it. He moaned. I felt a twinge of sympathy. Just a twinge.

"Never mind then." She let his arm down. "But just because you can't lift your arm, doesn't mean you can't shout out your praises. Now, shall we begin again?"

"*Tenno Heika, Banzai.*" Bon-Hwa started again. Imperial Emperor, live 10,000 years.

I felt a buzzing in my brain as if a fly were trying to get out. I couldn't understand why people kept wishing long life to this horrible Emperor. We should give a cheer for more important things, like Father waking up, the war about to end....and that bully Kee-Wok not being able to lift his right arm.

"*Tenno Heika*," the class said for the third and final time. "*Banzai.*"

"Father," I whispered instead. "Get better fast and live 10,000 years."

**US invades Japanese positions in Alaska
—August 30, 1942**

Monday, September 7, 1942—two weeks later

Baby He-Dong

The bell rang for lunch. I snapped awake, although my mind was still floating on the clouds of this morning's achievement. Father, after awakening us with grunting sounds three times during the night, finally spoke.

Now, I sat up, my neck aching where I'd held it upright the whole morning. Just last year I was Class Monitor, and now here I was sleeping through lessons. I was a delinquent.

Instead of comparing bed-bug remedies with Ih-Duk during lunch, I'd have to ask him to tell me what had happened while I slept. Sweat made my thighs stick to the chair. I peeled one, than another off the wooden seat.

The sun beat down hard, the rays pounding into my brain. Kee-Wok, despite his broken arm, still thought he was King of the class. What was stranger was that so many people still followed him even though he'd lost a lot of his bullying ability. He didn't steal my lunch, because he couldn't. But he did bump into me on purpose with his good shoulder whenever I passed. Perhaps he thought by just scaring me this way, I would offer up my rice. I wouldn't.

He went out into the yard and established his territory, the shade of the one cherry tree. He put his back up against the thin trunk, one leg up behind him. His lieutenants surrounded him, offering food and water. I spotted Ih-Duk, sitting at one of the tables and went over to join him.

I stepped over the bench to sit down next to him. Jong-Jin and Kyu-Chang had already started an eye-crossing game. My eyes hurt just watching.

"Did you take notes this morning?" I pulled my eyes away from the competition.

"No, it was all I could do to get out of the house without a smack." Ih-Duk squinted at me, putting his hand up to shield the rays of the sun. "My mother's tired of me experimenting. Besides, I didn't have any good results. In fact, I've got five new bites."

"Not those notes." I coughed, heat traveling up my neck. He was sure he'd find the remedy to those pesky bedbugs."I mean, during class."

"Of course I took notes." He pulled his head back. "Didn't you?"

"It's just." I hated telling him that I'd slept through everything. I hated saying that the minister's son—*brightness in the east*—had turned into darkness in the west.

"I agree." He opened his lunch, the smell of soy sauce filling the air between us. "I don't know why the Japanese are always fighting in these small, unknown places. I had to pinch myself to pay attention."

"I couldn't—" I focused on the metal catch of my lunch box. "I couldn't stay awake."

"Really?" He looked up from his rice. Then he leaned over and confided. "There were a lot of names. In fact, while I was writing all of them down, I was thinking maybe the Japanese just make up new names to make it seem as if they're conquering more places. Savo island?" He put both hands in the air, shrugging his shoulders. "What kind of name is that? Or the Solomons?"

Savo? The Solomons? Someone else had mentioned those names recently. I opened my *bento* box. "Ito *Sensei* said there were really such islands? That the Japanese are fighting there?"

"Not just fighting." He raised his eyebrows. "Gloriously defeating."

I took a bite of my rice. I tried to search my memory for where I'd heard those names, but I was too tired. "I'll have to write and ask my brother."

My brother. That was what had gotten Father talking this morning in the wee hours. The thing about Father having slept so many days, Mother explained, was that now he didn't understand sleeping time and waking time. He woke up at all hours of the night. Mother would hear him moving or making that gargling noise as if he were protecting himself from sickness with Mother's vinegar gargle.

This morning, when Mother hurried to his side and I followed, he didn't want any of the usual things—his bedbug bites scratched, porridge, a prayer. With each question Mother asked, he moved his head to one side of the pillow, rested, then moved to the other.

"No. He's saying, 'no.'" I had looked at his soft pillow, hoping we could return to bed soon. I felt the weight of the dull grey morning pulling me down, and it was all I could do not to flop down on the end of Father's bed.

"Are you thirsty?" Mother tried some more. Her hair was tangled at the back, like a bird's nest Ih-Duk had once found laying on the ground by the school.

Father pointed to me.

"He-Dong, go on." Mother kept a pot of boiled water on the stove. "Just a half cup should be enough."

I turned to leave, wondering if He-Seung ever felt this tired. The kitchen seemed days away. Father grabbed my arm. It wasn't a grab like the time when I climbed up to the top of our ladder all by myself and then couldn't get down or the time I tried to fix the lights like I'd seen He-Seung do. It was more a soft pressure, like a leaf falling from a tree.

"A full cup?" I looked to his head on that soft pillow, waiting to see a movement.

He pointed at me then with a big effort, he lifted his hand higher.

"Two cups?" I asked. He must be really thirsty. I licked my lips. I would take a sip of water myself while I was doing all this work.

"No." Mother looked at Father who shook his head from side to side. "That's not it. I know. He's saying how much taller you've gotten." She tried not to sigh, but I heard a rush of air come out of her mouth before she stopped. "He just wants to talk."

I waited for Mother to tell him it was sleeping time now and we could talk about my growing when the sun woke up. Besides, I hadn't really grown. I still wore the same uniform I had at the beginning of the year. The seams weren't stretching like they did on the Class Monitor's shirt.

"Son."

Mother and I looked at one another. Father had said a word, a real word.

"That's right," Mother smiled, her eyes bright.

"Son." Father pushed the word out again. But he pointed above my head.

"He's your son. Yes. Very good."

Father closed his eyes. I longed to close mine, too. But then I could see his forehead all scrunched up. He wasn't going back to sleep.

"That's not what he's saying." I pushed myself away from the bed and stumbled over to the dresser, picking up a piece of paper and pencil. He wasn't good at writing yet, as his hands were still bandaged. But maybe he could try.

"Son." Father pushed the pencil away. He pointed even higher.

"Perhaps he means the Son of Heaven." Mother folded her hands in prayer. "Yes, you're right. We should give thanks to the Lord."

Now, Ih-Duk nudged me, bringing me back to the schoolyard. "He-Dong?"

I was still in a fog, recalling how I felt when I realized Father had been talking about He-Seung, where was He-Seung? How his eyes had closed when I read the letters from Okinawa, and tears dripped down his cheeks.

"He-Dong," Ih-Duk spoke more urgently.

I looked up to see Kee-Wok coming forward. "Hey, bean-curd."

I secretly hoped—God forgive me—that his arm would take a long time to heal. I hunched over my rice, gobbling it down as fast as I could shovel it into my mouth. Even with his arm in a sling, he still managed to look menacing.

"Hey!" Kee-Wok put his foot up on the bench, blocking my exit. "Aren't you saving some for me?"

I looked down at the scoops of rice left in the box, the salted pickles. My stomach rumbled. I wouldn't give this to Kee-Wok today.

"No." I pushed at his foot. My hand flopped back. His leg remained there like a giant blockade.

"What did you say?" He frowned, looking over at his sergeants.

"No." I stood up. I must have still been tired, because I felt dizzy. I reached out and grabbed at the closest thing to me. Kee-Wok's bad arm.

"Ow! You idiot," Kee-Wok cried, his voice higher than a girl's. Tears sprung to his eyes and he quickly looked away. He grabbed onto his arm and hurried off into the corner of the yard, away from his sergeants, away from everyone.

"Wow." Ih-Duk sat back down, heaving a sigh. "I think you found something more effective than bugs."

"I didn't mean to do that." Although Father would have been disappointed in me for hurting someone, I couldn't help but smile. It felt good to watch the bully run away like an injured dog.

Japanese floatplane flies two missions dropping incendiary bombs on U.S. forests in the state of Oregon, the only bombings of the continental U.S. Newspapers in the U.S. voluntarily withhold this information.
—September 9, 1942

Monday, September 7, 1942—same day

Mother (*Uhmony*)

I sat in my dear's bedroom, listening to his soft breathing, a pair of pants across my lap. The damp heat of the afternoon hung on me, sucking air from my lungs. I wiped the sweat from my forehead with the bottom of my *cheemar*.

I still needed to bring in the laundry, clear up the breakfast dishes. But I didn't want to move from my dear, in case he said another word. I knew his words would be harsh. How could I have let our son leave for the military? Why hadn't I trusted that God would take care of His flock? I had seen the sadness in my dear's eyes as He-Dong read his brother's letter.

I talked all morning until my throat was dry. I told him how He-Seung had secretly done this all on his own. How I had tried to find a way to keep him home. How I had prayed. That I still trusted the Lord. What more could I have done? His eyes remained closed.

I pulled my needle and thread across the hole in the worn pair of pants In-Young had asked me to sew. These pants looked a bit small for anyone in her family. The waist was tiny. I would need to have a talk with In-Young. Months ago when she'd come to the house asking for help, I'd been only too happy. But her family seemed to have a never-ending supply of clothing in need of repair. Socks, pants, jackets. I rarely saw the same piece of clothing twice. And while In-Young was always very generous— she gave us a delicious jar of pickles yesterday—she no longer stayed to learn how to do the sewing herself. I knew with her baby coming, she was often tired and nauseated. But I wanted her to know how to help her family, so she wouldn't have to rely on me. I also was curious to know why she was sewing clothes that her family surely no longer wore. Were her in-laws as ill-tempered as her husband, insisting she do useless jobs?

Kwidong barked, signaling a visitor. I glanced at my dear whose eyes were still closed. I let out a deep breath, put the pants down at the end of the bed and got up to answer the door.

Dr. Lee stood on the front step, Myung-Ja *uhmony* right behind him. "He-Dong stopped by this morning and mentioned the Reverend is up and talking "

Up and talking. I looked toward the bedroom door. He-Dong and I had certainly prayed for that. I had a momentary hope that my dear would walk out of his bedroom door and offer salutations, sit in his rocker, and discuss issues as if no time had passed. Perhaps he would even bring up the issue of marriage between He-Seung and Myung-Ja, as He-Seung had requested of me before he left for the Youth Corps.

"Please." I stood back. "Come in."

Dr. Lee stepped forward and stood impatiently while Myung-Ja *uhmony* removed his shoes.

She lined up the shoes next to one another, straightening and re-straightening them. In the past few months, her hair had grown white. Her dress hung from her like a giant potato sack.

"Have a seat." I put out some cushions on the living room floor. "Let me get you a drink."

"I'll just go in and check on Reverend Chai." Dr. Lee moved toward my dear's bedroom.

I started for the kitchen. Myung-Ja *uhmony* came with me. "Let me help you with something."

"It's easy," I said. "I'm just going to get some boiled water—"

"It's better if I don't sit." She had dark bags under her eyes.

Surely she was frantic. Every letter she had received from Myung-Hae had been censored so much that she couldn't read anything more than the salutation. I patted her arm. "If you don't mind, I haven't yet brought in the laundry."

"I'd love to do that." She gave me a weak smile as I took her out back.

The printing press sounded. I watched as Myung-Ja *uhmony* removed the white rags from the line. She automatically dropped them in the bamboo basket. I let the noise of the press and the heat of the morning envelop us.

"Have you heard anything from He-Seung?" Myung-Ja *uhmony* shouted as she ran her wrinkled fingers over a sock.

We obviously were thinking of the same issues. "We just got a second letter."

"Could—could you read it?" She gripped tight to that sock as if it were a rope that would pull her up from her well of worries.

"He-Dong could." I took the sock from her hands. Gently. "The censors must have let his letter slip through."

She leaned forward closer to my ear. "What did he say?"

I had heard He-Dong talking to his friend, Ih-Duk, using fancy words like, "he's helping the war effort" or "he's working so hard he can barely think enough to write." I too had an urge to make him seem like a hero, especially in the eyes of Myung-Ja's mother. Then again, it seemed cruel when she didn't even know where Myung-Hae was. "He's digging ditches."

"What?" She grabbed for another sock off the line.

I mimed digging. "Digging ditches."

"Don't they know he's the minister's son?"

I was tired of competing with the noise. I put my arm around her and led her inside the kitchen. "Maybe in Japan digging ditches is an important job." The words sounded ridiculous as soon as they popped from my mouth. "They also have him carrying bags for the Japanese officers."

She put her hand to her mouth, shaking her head. "That's just criminal."

"That's what I thought at first." I nodded, ashamed I'd said so much. He-Seung wrote his letters to us. I'm sure he didn't want us sharing the news with anyone who asked. Although, really, this wasn't just anyone. "But while digging ditches isn't as honorable as doing, well, whatever soldiers do, he is one person I don't need to worry about."

She nodded. Slowly, at first. Then with more vigor.

"Maybe that's it." She let her hand drop. Her eyes shone bright. "That's it. Myung-Hae must be doing manual labor too. That's what she's been describing in her letters and the censors have taken offense. I'm sure of it. After all, what if my dear got so upset he refused to help at the prison?"

"Of course." A drop of sweat ran down my neck. "That's it."

"Do you really think so?" She pleaded.

"A mother knows." I patted her arm. "A mother knows when her child is safe."

Myung-Ja *uhmony's* eyebrows furrowed. Then, she covered her face with her hands. "But, I have nothing but nightmares of her calling out to me, begging me to find her."

"No, no." I remembered Min-Kook *uhmony* once saying how the Japanese kept digging, digging, digging. I hadn't understood her then. But now I did—and with each shovel of dirt they tossed away someone I loved. My dear, my son, my friend, our peaceful life. Thank heavens, God stood by me in this pit. "That's your imagination."

"He-Dong *uhmony*." Dr. Lee's voice rang throughout the house.

"Be strong. The Lord is watching out for her...and you." I gave Myung-Ja *uhmony's* arm a squeeze. Then I hurried to my dear's room. He sat propped against a pillow, his eyes attentive.

"He's doing much better." Dr. Lee put his stethoscope back in the leather satchel. "I hadn't expected him to be speaking so soon."

Can he speak? I wanted to ask. *More than one word?*

But I looked at my dear, his shoulders slouched to one side, his hands still wrapped in gauze, his mouth drooping.

"Can he—Will he be talking a lot again soon?" I asked.

"I look forward to him giving us the sunrise Christmas service." Dr. Lee nodded to my dear as he snapped his bag shut.

I felt my heart beat hard. My dear gave a heartwarming service last year, his voice booming across the pews about the beautiful baby Jesus who was born to save us all. Still, while Dr. Lee made it sound like this was a fast recovery, I felt like we were watching my dear struggle through winter honey. Christmas was four months away.

Four months. A lot happened in four months. Our church had been closed. My dear had been arrested. Our children had gone off to fight. We had been kicked out of our home. Four months was an eternity.

"Keep adding ginseng to his porridge." Dr. Lee moved toward the bedroom door. "Massage his feet morning and night, especially in between his toes."

"There's one more thing." I felt a tingling sensation in my head.

"Yes?" Dr. Lee turned, expectant.

"It's." I closed my eyes. "Well—"

"Life will be back to normal soon," He assured.

Everyone said the war was about to end. I could hardly wait. When the war ended, He-Seung would be home, and he and my recovered dear could work out the marriage issue. But what if He-Seung came home before my dear recovered?

"Before you leave…I know it's inappropriate." I looked toward my dear. "But I—I promised He-Seung before he went off to join the Youth Corps. And since my husband is feeling better and you're here, Dr. Lee , it seems only fitting to bring it up."

"Are we discussing Myung-Ja and He-Seung?" Dr. Lee shook his head.

Perhaps I'd offended him by bringing up a topic reserved for men. Perhaps he didn't think He-Seung, the son of an ill and currently shunned figure of society, to be a suitable match for the daughter of a respected doctor.

"I think it would be a grand union." He looked over, speaking to my dear. "And we can discuss it more after the Sunrise Service."

I had built up the issue to be bigger than Mt. Nam San. It hadn't been that difficult. I smiled, already eager for He-Dong to come home to write He-Seung a letter.

The British-Americans want obstinately to continue their counter-attacks, but making use of our great material resources, we are ready to annihilate them at any moment at any point on the globe. —Premier **Hideki Tojo before War Ministry, Dec 8, 1942**

Friday, December 25, 1942—four months later

Mother (*Uhmony*)

For today a miracle came to us in the form of an infant, the baby Jesus. My dear's voice boomed across all our heads, his breath visible in the freezing church. *He absolved us all of our sins.* My d stepped from behind his podium. *All of them.* He wore his long black robe. His black leather shoes which He-Dong had polished til late in the night shone like a mirror. *He asked in return only that we follow His teachings of love, peace and salvation. We are blessed.*

Amen, the congregation chorused.

"He-Dong *uhmony?*" A woman's voice broke through my fantastical imaginings. "In need of a new *kimchee* jar?"

"No," I assured, letting my mind return to the present where I stood near Mrs. Hong's display at the market.

A large kerosene lamp hissed in the center of the congregation of jars. Short ones, fat ones, old ones, large ones. In fact, lots of large ones. People probably didn't need to buy large ones anymore. With the war dragging on and on, there wasn't much food to fill them with.

"You're out awfully early." She pulled up the collar of her old wool coat. A button was missing on the sleeve. "Is everything all right?"

"Oh, yes." I nodded. All last night He-Dong had imagined the taste of marinated beef, our usual Christmas meal. He said he could taste it on his tongue already. I didn't have the heart to tell him that there wasn't money for that kind of meal. "I was just out to get a block of tofu, a piece of fish. Today's a special day."

"Is your boy home?" Her eyes widened. "So soon? I'll bet he's wanting lots of *kimchee*. You probably need an extra jar. I could offer you—"

"No, no. He's not back yet. But thank you, anyway." She wasn't a Christian. She wouldn't understand Christmas.

She frowned, disappointed at being wrong. Certainly more disappointed that I didn't need a new jar.

"But we just heard from him," I added. "He says the weather in Okinawa is still as hot as summer."

"What a funny boy." Mrs. Hong rubbed her arms, shaking her head. "He always did have a sense of humor."

It was interesting how people thought of my children differently than I. But I didn't think he'd been joking. I tried to remember the exact line He-Dong had read. *Every day is the same. Hotter than the blistering fires Father saves sinners from.* I blushed at his word choice. I couldn't repeat that to Mrs. Hong. I hurried away, taking a shortcut to the fish seller. I had our sunrise breakfast to prepare.

At the end of the alley, I saw a familiar figure sitting on a piece of cardboard on the ground. The sky was still dark, but a lantern illuminated her small figure, her worried face. A young woman in a slightly torn *cheemar* approached my dear friend and handed her a pair of pants. When the woman left, I stepped forward.

"In-Young?" A small basket of clothing sat by her side, the pants, which had a large rip in the knee, were folded neatly on top.

She stood and bowed again and again. "Dear Lady."

Dear Lady. Was I? I remembered the many times In-Young had suggested I open a tailoring shop and how I'd chastised her for suggesting such a low-class idea. She'd gone ahead anyhow. No wonder she brought me clothes which I couldn't imagine belonging to her. No wonder she always had food for us to eat. "You sit here every morning?"

"No, no." She shook her head. "Just, well, sometimes."

"Does Deacon Nam know about this?" It was shameful for the wife of a Deacon in All Holiness Church to be sitting on a piece of cardboard collecting clothes like a beggar. "And today? Of all days."

A cold wind blew. Her lantern hissed. She put her head down.

I knelt down and fingered the stranger's clothing. I thought of my He-Seung far away across the seas, the son of a Minister, doing even more degrading work than this. Of Myung-Hae, the daughter of a doctor, surely doing manual labor as well. "This is so—well it's unbelievable."

"I know." She bowed again and again. "I'm sorry. I thought, well, with Reverend Chai ill and your sons gone—I was only trying to help."

"What I can't understand," I shook my head, grabbing onto both her small bony hands. "Is why you didn't suggest the woman have her own dress fixed as well."

In-Young's face broke into a huge grin.

"Come," I helped her pick up the basket and the cardboard. "It's too cold this morning. Especially in your condition."

I fluffed the rice, taking the pot off the stove. I turned the fish over on the coals. He-Dong was in his father's room adding another coat of petroleum jelly to the legs of the bed.

He and Ih-Duk had been experimenting with different ways to get rid of the bedbugs, putting salt around my mattress one night, chili flakes the next. "The little critters get stuck in the jelly when they try to climb up," He-Dong had explained. I hadn't seen him so excited since he was named Class Monitor so long ago. I didn't want to mention that bedbugs didn't need to climb. I didn't want to mention that they always disappeared with the cold weather.

"Another day of no new bites." He-Dong walked into the kitchen, head held high, shoulders back. A little man in charge. He sniffed the air. "I smell—no beef."

"We have another delicious meal instead." I held up the barbecued fish. The skin was brown and crackled. I spread some chili paste on top. "Where's your father?"

"He's already waiting," He-Dong wrinkled his nose and frowned. "For beef."

I smiled at him. We both knew better. "Let's go join him."

My dear was sitting in his rocking chair, the Bible on his lap. He wore pants and a long-sleeve shirt, buttoned to the top. He'd lost so much weight the chair swallowed him. I put a blanket over his legs. I set out cushions on either side of the floor. Just then Kwidong barked.

"They're here." He-Dong jumped up. "They're here."

In-Young and Deacon Nam came in, In-Young handing me a covered dish of marinated black beans. Gong-Tae *uhmony* and Elder Su followed. They brought a bowl of dried fish. Dr. Lee, Myung-Ja *uhmony* and Myung-Ja brought a dish of marinated sprouts, and some precious pastries with bean paste.

We all gathered in the living room around my dear. He nodded and smiled. He opened his mouth. We all sat forward. In my mind, I could see him standing up and proclaiming in a strong but quiet voice that this was the day of the Lord, the day when we were all washed of our sins, that we should proclaim our joy, couldn't we feel it in our hearts?

"It'ssss—" He closed his eyes, his jaw tightening. He got frustrated when his mouth didn't work as he wanted.

"It's wonderful of all you to come this morning." I put my hands together. "Let's give our praises to the Lord on this glorious day."

Just then Kwidong barked, yanking and pulling at his chain. Footsteps sounded on the porch. Fists banged on the door. Elder Su reached up and grabbed my dear's bible, stuffing it under his coat. I answered the door.

"It's colder than a grave digger's shovel out here." Min-Kook *uhmony* rushed inside. She held a small dish in her hands. The smell of marinated beef filled the air. "Merry Christmas."

The end is near. You're advised to surrender.
—Japanese to Americans, December 1942

Friday, December 25, 1942—same day

Baby He-Dong

Father stayed in his rocking chair, and Mother put a small table in front of him for Dr. Lee, Deacon Nam, and Elder Su. She set out another small table for the women. Although I could officially sit at the men's table, I moved over to be closer to Min-Kook *uhmony* and the beef.

The women started in right away about how nice it was to see Min-Kook *uhmony* and how she looked well and how was her relative, the man she called the 'old goat.' I wondered what she was doing here, and where was Deacon Mah? Would they be coming back home? Would we have to find a new place to live? I grabbed morsels of barbecued marinated beef with my chopsticks, the juice dripping on the table.

"So tell us your news." Mother said to Min-Kook *uhmony*. Perhaps Mother worried like me.

Min-Kook *uhmony* leaned forward. "Well you've heard about The Line?"

"The Line?" Mother glanced out toward the back where she hung our laundry.

"The Japs are building hundreds of bridges through the dense jungle of Siam to make this railway line."

Gong-Tae *uhmony* looked up. Siam was where He-Seung's buddy—her son—had been sent. He had written of hard work, cutting down forest, carrying logs. The sounds of chopsticks ceased.

"It's an estimated five-year project, and they want it done in a year. It's impossible and crazy." Min-Kook *uhmony* glanced around, realizing that everyone stared at her. "I'm the one talking crazy. Listen to my nonsense." She brought her bowl of rice to her mouth, shoveling the grains in fast. She looked over her bowl. "What's new here?"

"There's a huge hole in the road around the corner," In-Young offered when nobody said anything. "I've almost tripped over it twice. It's a menace."

"Any news from your boys?" Min-Kook *uhmony* put her bowl down, looking up at Mother.

"They're working hard in Japan." Gong-Tae *uhmony* stared off in the distance. "And Siam. Oh, God. Do you think Gong-Tae is working on the crazy railroad?"

Min-Kook *uhmony* took a long sip of her soup, as if she was suddenly so thirsty she couldn't speak.

Mother patted Gong-Tae *uhmony's* shoulder. "The Lord will look after him wherever he is."

"We've decided that Myung-Hae is stuck somewhere doing hard work like the boys," Myung-Ja *uhmony* said, her face coloring.

Min-Kook *uhmony* closed her eyes a moment. When she opened them, she stood. "I should leave. I just wanted to stop by and wish you all a…" She leaned forward and whispered, "Merry, merry Christmas."

Well, that answered one question. She wasn't moving back home.

"You can't leave," Mother pulled on her. "You must have travelled for hours. You must be exhausted. Besides, this is your home."

Mother was right. Min-Kook *uhmony* had travelled a long way.

"No, no. I don't want to be sitting here too long." Min-Kook *uhmony* bowed. "Might start noticing the way you put your sewing basket where my books should be."

Mother apologized and insisted she take some food with her, although we only had such a small amount to offer I was embarrassed over the fuss.

I got up and put my shoes and warm jacket on. I was curious as to how Min-Kook *uhmony* knew so much. She knew so many things that nobody else did, not even my intelligent Father. I wondered if it had something to do with the Storybag.

"Where are you going?" Mother said to me. "You've still got time before school."

"Well I'm ready. I might as well go too."

I guided Min-Kook *uhmony* past the corner, pointing out the dip in the ground. "Careful."

"This is nothing." Min-Kook *uhmony* laughed. "You should see the country roads."

I stopped. "Does the Storybag live there?"

"Excuse me?" Her face went pale.

"You—you once told me that you learned things, like stuff about the war, from the Storybag."

"Did I say that?" She laughed, a loud noise.

"Yes, yes." I looked at her. "Where do I find him?"

"What year are you going to be in school?"

"I'm almost in third year," I said.

She let out a deep breath, nodding. She smiled at me. "It's just a silly old fairytale."

"Oh?" I cocked my head to the side, feeling my cheeks flush. "That's all?"

"Yes, yes." She gave that laugh again. She grabbed onto my arm. I could feel her icy fingers even through the thickness of my jacket. I could feel that she wasn't telling me the truth.

Guadalcanal is no longer merely a name of an island in Japanese
military history. It is the name of the graveyard of the Japanese army.
—**Major General Kawaguchi, 35th Infantry Brigade at Guadalcanal**[1]

Saturday, December 26, 1942—next day

Mother (*Uhmony*)

He-Dong and I walked home from the market. I felt at peace for once, my mind, my spirit full of gratitude. Yesterday all of our good friends had visited, my dear had stayed up most of the day. Today we'd had a letter from He-Chul.

This time he'd written in hiragana so He-Dong could read the words, obviously having gotten the letter from us that it was difficult for my dear to talk. The way He-Chul wrote about the equality of everyone, my heart felt soothed. That was something I had sometimes forgotten as the Minister's wife. I had come to expect people to honor me. I had come to expect a grand home. I had come to expect more than God provided others. My son's words reminded me of the Lord's true scripture.

"One thing I'm always grateful for about living here." I pointed up the road to Min-Kook *uhmony's*. "We don't have much further to walk."

He-Dong didn't even look up. He kicked at the dust. "Why did Min-Kook *uhmony* come and go so quickly yesterday?"

I had wondered the same. At first I thought it was because she didn't want to impose. But that wasn't like her. "I don't know."

"And where was Deacon Mah?"

"Maybe he needed to stay with his ill father," I said.

"She didn't even talk about him or ask us to pray for him." He-Dong frowned. "Mother, Min-Kook *uhmony* lives in the countryside and knows so much more than us." He fingered the bamboo handle of our shopping basket. "Why don't we hear this news?"

"I don't know," I said again.

"Well, I want to know." He kicked a pebble across the path. "Don't you?"

I wasn't sure I did. I had my hands full worrying about my dear's health, how to get enough food on the table, and where my boys were. We turned up the path to the house.

"Let's get inside and have a glass of hot water." I gave his shoulder a squeeze.

"Omori-*san*," a voice called. "Mrs. Omori?"

That was Min-Kook *uhmony*'s Japanese last name. I turned. An officer stood beneath a tree on the opposite side of the road. He tossed his cigarette down, grinding the sparks out with his steel-toed boot. He walked towards us.

"You? Mrs. Omori?" the officer asked in Japanese, a silly smile on his face. He wore a blue cap, but it didn't cover the acne dotting his forehead.

"No," I replied in halting Japanese. "She away."

"Where?"

I stared at this boy officer. I remembered an officer once following Min-Kook *uhmony* so many months ago. I remembered her hurry to leave yesterday. While I still said a prayer for her father-in-law, I no longer believed that he was the only reason for her being gone. A sense of dread filled my being. I looked to the house as though hoping my dear would come to the door and protect us. I tried to form an explanation.

"She went to care her—" I wasn't sure how to say *Father-in-Law* in Japanese.

"Tell me." I smelled the tobacco on his breath. "Where is Omori-*san?*"

The Japanese had lied to our family, stealing my son for their Youth Corps, torturing my dear and not releasing him until he could no longer function, and taking away our home. Even if I did know where my friend was, I wouldn't tell this angry teenager, God forgive me. "I don't know."

"Yes, you do." He stepped closer, his rough uniform brushing against my arm.

"Mother." He-Dong stepped in between us, grabbing onto my waist.

"*Baka-yaro,*" the officer yelled. Idiot.

He pushed He-Dong out of the way, as if my boy were some pesky rat. He-Dong fell backwards. The contents of our shopping basket—two radishes, a jar of soy sauce, a cup of rice—spilled to the ground.

"How dare you," I shouted in Korean. "How dare you treat someone like that!"

The officer slapped me.

"Mother!" He-Dong called.

"I feel sorry for your mother," I continued yelling. "Having a son like you."

The brat pushed me. I tumbled, tripping over He-Dong and falling to the ground.

"Where is Omori-*san?*" he growled, kicking me in the shin with his steel-toed boot. "Tell me—"

"We not know Mrs. Omori," He-Dong said in Japanese, his voice trembling. He stood up and bowed up and down, up and down. "Why not ask neighbors? We live here little while only. Police live in our house."

The officer stared at He-Dong. Then he gave me one more kick before turning and stalking off.

"Mother." He-Dong leaned down, his eyes welling with tears. "Are you hurt?"

My shins burned as if I'd kneeled in fire. My backside felt numb where I'd fallen. My hand throbbed where I'd scraped the skin.

"Remember during the summer when Min-Kook *uhmony* brought us ice cream?" I carefully sat up.

"Yes?" He held onto my arm.

"Remember how you pinched me while I prayed?" I squeezed his hand. "It's not much worse than that."

"Oh, Mother." He helped me to my feet. "You're just saying that."

I hobbled up the path to the house, leaning on He-Dong for support. Warm liquid trickled down my ankle. Despite the pain, I felt a renewed sense of purpose. For the first time, I wanted to know what Min-Kook uhmony was involved in. "It would be nice if we found the Storybag."

They died like flies.
--Cyril Gilbert, OAM, 27th Brigade, Australian Army Services Corps,
Survivor of the Death Railway, a military railway constructed by the
Japanese between 1942 and October of '43. The rail spanned the
Siam-Burma border and required the forced labor of approximately
60,000 Allied POWS and 180,000 conscripted Asian laborers.
Approximately one in four workers died during construction.

Saturday, June 5, 1943—six months later

Baby He-Dong

Mother didn't find our Storybag. I did. Months had gone by, during which a new school year had started, He-Seung was still off being a soldier in Japan, He-Chul away learning new things in Manchukuo, Mother sewing for people at the market and Father not better.

Mother said Father was improving. In fact she gave thanks for his being better every day. But I always remembered the Father who smiled at me as he sat thumbing through his Bible and making notes.

He could now walk to his chair in the living room, but he didn't smile, and Mother had to help him turn the pages. He often stared at the same page for hours and then fell asleep.

Yesterday when I got home from school with my best friend, Ih-Duk, Father and Mother stood on the porch. Mother held onto Father's elbow, her grip so tight her hand shook.

"You didn't tell me your Father was out and about." Ih-Duk whispered.

The only thing which would have gotten Father up so far would be the police. Had they come?

"Mother?" I hurried up the path.

Sweat glistened on her forehead. "Your Father wanted to get some fresh air."

The air wasn't really fresh. It was hot, hard to breathe even. But if Father was outside, perhaps all Mother's thanking God had worked. Perhaps he'd finally recovered.

"Here." Mother indicated with her shoulder, a drop of perspiration falling from her chin. You can walk on one side."

"Where are we going?" Father would want to go past his church. But Ih-Duk would prefer the park. I would, too. Perhaps Ih-Duk and I could even sit in the shade by the pond and dangle our feet in the water.

"There." Mother held up her arm, pointing to the end of the path.

That was all? I looked over at Ih-Duk. He sat on the front stoop, waiting.

Mother, Father and I walked down the path. Father shuffled forward in fits and starts. Mother and I did our best not to go too fast or too slow or to trip over each other. Kwidong must have thought it was a game, for he watched us, racing back and forth in his pen. When we reached the end of the path, Father stumbled. We grabbed onto him. We did not fall.

"There," Mother said. "You did it. Now, let's go get a cold drink of water."

"Sounds good to me," I said.

Ih-Duk was already standing, looking toward the house.

Father lifted his stubby fingers—the nails had never grown back right-- and pointed to the porch. "A-gain."

"We can try again tomorrow." Mother's eyebrows crinkled. "In the morning before He-Dong goes to school. It won't be so hot then."

"A-gain," Father insisted.

So, we shuffled back and started over. Each time he stumbled, he insisted we return to the front stoop and start over. He stumbled every time. I started praying for God to please let us get to the end of the path without one stumble. Ih-Duk decided he better get home for dinner. Even Kwidong gave up and flopped to the ground.

Today, Ih-Duck and I went directly from school to my backyard. I feared if we went inside—even for a cool drink of water— Mother might remember that Father hadn't awakened early to walk, that we should try again now.

Out by the back door, wet laundry hung on the line. Mother must have only just gotten around to washing it. These days Father kept her busy helping him.

"It's so hot." Ih-Duk moved to the back step and knelt below the laundry hanging from the line, drops of water dripping on his head. "Here's a good spot."

"I hope that's just water." I snickered, pointing to a pair of my underwear he sat beneath.

Ih-Duk stood up and put his face directly into a towel next to my undies. He moaned with happiness. "Who cares?"

I grabbed the towel. "You can't do that."

"Say that again. Louder." He pulled the wet towel in front of my face. "Right there."

"You can't do that to my—my mother's washing," I shouted.

He put the towel up in front of his own face. "You can't do that to my mother's washing! Feel it?"

"Feel what?"

He let the towel down, dabbing the damp cloth on his arms. "You'd feel something if the wind was stronger. We need a fan, before the clothes dry."

Ever since experimenting to get rid of bed bugs, he'd decided that it was our destiny to become great inventors—although perhaps not great bed-bug-control inventors. I wasn't sure what he was thinking. Still, when he got an idea, he couldn't get rid of it.

"Hurry up." He pushed me off the step.

"Just don't go touching all Mother's laundry while I'm gone." I headed toward the front door. I would get the fan that already had a tear in the corner, just in case he got carried away. Besides it was in the basket closest to the door.

I put my key in the lock. I had my own key now. I turned it slowly, and gently pushed at the door. I leaned inside and reached toward the small basket in the entryway, pulling out the folding fan.

"He-Dong?" Mother called out from the living room.

I'd made too much noise. Surely they had been waiting for me to come home so we could walk the path together. I cringed.

"He-Dong?" Mother called again. "Is that you?"

I slipped off my shoes, went into the living room, and bowed. Father had the Bible in his lap. Mother had a pile of sewing on the floor, but was up helping him turn pages.

"Ready for another walk?" I asked.

He closed his eyes.

"Not today," Mother said.

I felt a rush of relief. I could go back outside. Then I felt bad for thinking such things. "Are you sure?"

"If he changes his mind, I'll call you." Mother smiled at me.

I hurried back outside and around the corner of the house. Ih-Duk paced back and forth, staring at our laundry as if each piece was part of some huge science problem.

"What took so long?" Ih-Duk grabbed the fan from me. "I thought you were never coming back. Now, stand in front of the wet towel."

I went to the other side of the laundry line and stood. I had to stand in a small space between Min-Kook *uhmony*'s house and the print shop. I wiped sweat from my forehead.

Ih-Duk stood in front of me, the wet towel between us. He used the fan, as though he were trying to cool off the towel. "Do you feel that breeze?"

This had to be his dumbest idea yet. Dumber than putting petroleum jelly around my futon to keep the bed bugs away. "No."

"No kidding." He sounded surprised. "Here, you try doing it for me." He held out the fan. "Come on—"

I accidentally knocked the fan from his fingers. I wasn't eager to retrieve it. There was no way this was going to work.

"Did you know that the fan is the only invention the Japanese can claim credit for?" he said.

I sighed. When Ih-Duk's inventions didn't work, he always talked a lot about other things.

He pointed to the fan, indicating for me to pick it up. "Just that little thing. Apparently, a monk was ill and a devout young woman sat over him with a piece of paper, trying to fan his fever away."

I leaned down. "Why?" a deep voice sounded in my ear.

I stood up fast, pulling the towel back to look at Ih-Duk. "Did you say, 'Why?'"

He scrunched his eyebrows. "I was thinking about it—I mean why would a country be around for so long and only invent one thing?"

I stared at the ground. The print shop vent. I had definitely heard a voice.

I had a memory. *Japs, Solomons, Savo*. The words floated up at me. I'd been out here when I had heard those words. Those words which I'd thought were people studying Christianity, but which must have been people discussing what had turned out to be a bitter battle.

I was reminded of the time Mother and I came to ask Min-Kook *uhmony* for help reading He-Seung's letter. How Min-Kook *uhmony* had hurried us inside and disappeared into the kitchen to get us water. How she'd rushed back with no water for us, but with news about the war. She must have been out here listening. I felt a tingle of joy better than any cold splash of water from the pond. I leaned down again, staring at the vent as if it might be alive, or suddenly open up and reveal marching ladles, poison berries, a hundred snakes.

"The Japs are done with the Alaskan islands." A voice came though the vent. "They're all committing mass suicide."

"What are you doing?" Ih-Duk kneeled down, took the fan and waved it back and forth in front of my face.

"Shh." I put my hand up, sweat rolling down my face. It was wrong to tell my friend to be quiet so that I could eavesdrop on someone else. But this sounded important. "I'm listening."

Ih-Duk cocked his head. "I don't hear anything."

"Just be quiet." I leaned closer to the vent to listen.

"Those little islands were just stepping stones across the Pacific to bigger places. Like America," the voice said, making a sucking sound. A pipe? "In fact, that's all we Koreans ever were. A stepping stone. I wonder when they'll be done with us. "

"Hey, if you don't want to play, all you have to do is say so." Ih-Duk stood to leave.

I didn't want to miss a word of what was being said through the vent, but I didn't want to lose my best friend. I grabbed the back of his shirt and pulled him back down right next to me. I fanned us both without the interference of the stupid towel. After months of wondering who he was, I had found him. Or them. "Shhh! It's the Storybag."

The decisive moment has come when one hundred million of us take up battle positions and overcome the hardships confronting our Fatherland.
—**Prime Minister Tojo to 35,000 drafted students, October 21, 1943**

Tuesday, April 17, 1945—approximately two years later

Baby He-Dong

Over the past two years, the Storybag men had talked of how the Japanese killed millions. How the Emperor was willing to let every last person in Japan die rather than surrender. How the Imperial army was sending boys up in planes and telling them to crash like human bombs. These Storybag men made the Japanese seem meaner than our strictest teachers, than the policeman who beat up Mother, than the police who took Father, than any humans I'd ever met.

The Allies didn't sound much better. Last summer, they'd invented something called Napalm which stuck to people like honey, burning them up. They'd dropped firebombs in the center of Tokyo. They'd made this amazing promise around Christmas of 1943 that if they won, Korea would be an independent nation—free just like brother He-Seung had always wanted. Then this February, they'd changed their minds, offering up half our country to Russia in exchange for help with the fighting. *As if Korea were an extra piece of fish at the dinner table,* Ih-Duk had said.

Every day, Ih-Duk and I listened to make sure Russia didn't join the war against Japan. Well, mostly I listened. Ih-Duk wasn't as excited about locating the different battles, instead burying his nose in his latest reader or working on a new invention: I often had to bribe him into listening with me, as if he were no bigger than baby Jae-Won. Today, I promised that if he sat with me, I'd quiz him for our upcoming test and give him a cup of honey water.

We sat out back, close to the vent. Ih-Duk pulled out his notes from school. "Did you know that a girl invented the first novel?"

"We're not starting that." All term we'd been busy studying about Japan's historical periods, a country which was older than Korea, *Sensei* always reminded us. We learned about the bronze-making period and the weaving period and the spread of warring kingdoms. We learned about the present war. Leave it to Ih-Duk to focus on the inventions. I took the map from my pocket. "Not yet."

When we first found the Storybag men two years ago, we kept track of battles in the dirt. The rains ruined those, and I traced a map from Father's atlas. It wasn't a world map, but had four locations: Western America where Father's colleague lived, Siam where Gong-Tae was, Okinawa where He-Seung was, and Korea. After years of comparing the map to Father's atlas, I knew where the small islands and other countries were, and could figure out the direction the armies were advancing or retreating.

Japan had gone from being an adventurous octopus, grabbing as many countries as possible, to a turtle just protecting itself. I leaned down ready to hear about more of Japan retreating.

"—Allies landed for an April Fool's Day Battle."

I pressed so close to the vent that I felt the metal grate making marks on my ear. "Another battle," I whispered. "An April-Fool's-Day battle."

"What is April Fool's?" Ih-Duk asked. "Is that another weapon?"

"No." I turned my head to explain, remembering the Thomas family. He-Seung's friend Jim had come over saying he found gold. Only when He-Seung raced to go outside and follow, Jim had said, *April Fool's.* "It's a holiday on the first of April in America when you play tricks."

"I thought Easter was a holiday on the first of April in America." Ih-Duk said.

"No. Just this year." I pulled out my pencil to draw airplanes over whatever area the armies were fighting. "It's complicated."

"Sound like the Allies like to have holidays." Ih-Duk sighed.

"Shhh." I leaned back down to listen.

"Thousands landed on the beaches of Okinawa," the voice said. "The Japs would be fools not to surrender."

A numbness descended on me. I dropped my pencil.

"What is it?" Ih-Duk set his notebook down. "Did Russia join the war?"

I shook my head. I didn't want to repeat the words. I couldn't.

Ih-Duk pushed me out of the way. He stuck his head down, listening, his eyes growing wide. "Maybe the Allies are playing this April Fool's trick."

"Is that what they're saying," I asked, the words so quiet, I wasn't sure he'd heard them.

He listened some more. Then he sat up, pulling me with him off the back step. "Or maybe, maybe the Storybag men got it wrong. Remember the time they said there was an oxcart loaded with beef spilled on the road outside of town? Remember the time—" he paused.

He couldn't think of another time. Aside from the false alarm about meat, the Storybag men had been accurate about everything.

"Besides, He-Seung's not a bean-curd." Ih-Duk shook my arm. "Remember the first time he came to the school and poked at my shoulder, thinking I was the school bully? He's a fighter."

What kind of fighting was happening? If the Allies just had guns, He-Seung could hide somewhere. But if they had airplanes dropping bombs or that fire honey, then... I looked back toward the vent. "Did you hear what kinds of weapons the Allies had?"

"No." Ih-Duk turned me back around, his voice sounding like it was coming through a tunnel. "Just that there are a lot of soldiers on the island. He-Seung's smart, though. He's probably hiding in one of the air-raid ditches."

"Yeah." I felt my head moving up and down.

Ih-Duk pulled me inside my own house. He took off my shoes and guided me to the living room, pushing me down on the floor.

"Now." He opened his notebook. "Let's get down to the stuff that's really happening. The inventor of the world's first novel: tell me, if not the date than the—"

"Do you think *Sensei* would know more about the fighting?" I tapped my fingers on the table. "Where it is in relation to He-Seung?"

"Definitely no." He stopped my nervous fingers. "He always predicts our *honorable soldiers will soon be victorious*. Besides, we're not supposed to know about this stuff. We can't mention any of this to anyone—you know that."

I had already calculated that it took two weeks for a letter to arrive from He-Seung. Two weeks of not knowing where He-Seung was, more time if he was too busy to write us. That was a long time to wait. "This is my brother."

"I thought I heard you boys." Mother came into the living room with two cups of honey water.

I took the cup, my fingers clasping tight to the metal. I loved honey water, but I wouldn't drink another sip, if God would just let He-Seung come home. *Please, God, hear me and don't mix up my messages.*

"He-Dong, you look pale." Mother paused. "Are you feeling all right?"

"We're just both nervous about the test tomorrow," Ih-Duk answered. "Our *sensei* can make tricky questions."

"He-Dong?" Mother put her hand on my arm.

I put my cup down. She would know how best to talk to God. "Mother—"

Just then Kwidong barked. In the last two years, Father had grown so strong he walked everywhere by himself to visit his parishioners. Perhaps he was home early. We could all pray together.

I looked out the window. Gong-Tae *uhmony* was coming up the path. Kwidong raced back and forth in his pen, jumping up and down. I watched him, remembering the day He-Seung had brought him home.

Mother walked over and opened the door. "Good afternoon."

Gong-Tae *uhmony* looked inside. She smiled when she saw Ih-Duk and me sitting in the living room. "I was on my way to market." Gong-Tae *uhmony* patted her basket. "My sister's youngest child has a toothache," she explained, although Mother hadn't asked. "The boy has been crying all day."

"You must be exhausted." Mother shook her head.

"This is the day that the Lord has made," she said, sounding like Father reading the Bible. *"Let us be glad and rejoice in it."*

How could we rejoice in a day when the Allies had landed on Okinawa and were chasing down my brother to kill him?

"Come in," Mother suggested. "My dear's teeth suffered from the poor food he got in prison. He often has aches which a cup of chrysanthemum tea soothes. I might have some buds in the cabinet."

She smiled, slipping off her shoes. "I also brought this."

Gong-Tae *uhmony* waved a blue aerogramme back and forth. I noted that the flaps were still glued shut. Although it was ridiculous of me to hope, I stared at the writing on the front to see if it was from He-Seung and had been delivered to her by mistake. That he was writing to say his group had been moved to a different island.

"You heard from Gong-Tae?" Mother indicated the letter. "What did he say?"

"It just came." She held the letter in her lap like a jewel. "I thought." She looked at Ih-Duk and me out of the corner of her eye. "I—well, my husband is at work."

"The boys might not be able to read all of it," Mother said. "They're only in fifth grade."

"It's just there's so much uncertainty these days," Gong-Tae *uhmony* explained, using the sharp edge of Mother's scissors to open the note. "Anything...any words would be lovely."

I felt the same. Anything would be great. I wanted to read the words *I'm safe. Don't worry.* The last thing I wanted to do was read about someone other than my brother.

Mother thrust the letter in my hands. "He-Dong would be happy to read what he can."

My hands trembled as I unfolded the note. *Dear Father and Mother...* I looked at the words about how hot it was in Siam, the work was hard, and there were mosquitoes everywhere. He wrote that he itched himself more than He-Seung ever had. My eyes stared at the characters for *He-Seung.* I read them over and over, like a prayer.

"Well?" Mother nudged me.

Gong-Tae *uhmony* looked up at me, her eyes stopping at my unbuttoned collar. Mother had let the hem out of my uniform three times this past year. Still, my collar was tight and my shorts rode up so high my underwear almost showed. Mother had promised me she'd take in He-

Seung's old uniform for me. He-Seung. Please be hiding in one of your air-raid ditches.

I handed the letter back. "It says he's safe."

Mother turned to Ih-Duk. He shrugged. "He-Dong is the best reader."

Mother looked back at me. "Is that all you can—"

"You can't expect everyone to be as intelligent as your He-Chul." Gong-Tae uhmony fingered the letter.

Normally I'd be worried to be considered not as smart as my eldest brother. Today, I left my full cup of honey water and got up to return to the Storybag, unable to sit still a moment longer. Ih-Duk followed.

"What's the matter?" Mother joined us at the door. She leaned close to me, whispering, "Was there bad news in that letter?"

I glanced back at Gong-Tae *uhmony*. "No, no."

"Then why are you acting like this?" Her voice sounded angry. "You can read. Both of you can."

"It's just." I looked up at her disappointed face, suddenly blurting, "Well the Storybag men—"

"Minkook *uhmony's* Storybagmen?" Mother looked as if I'd said I'd flown in an airplane. "You found them?"

I wanted to tell her we'd not only found them but had been following the war, making sure everyone stayed safe. I wanted to tell her that now I was scared. But I felt Ih-Duk digging his fingers into my side. I glanced over at him. He gave a quick shake of his head. I could hear him saying, *We can't tell anyone.*

"I was just thinking about them." I slipped on my shoes. "I need to take Kwidong on a walk."

"So Gong-Tae's safe?" Mother put her hand on my arm.

"He's fine." Ih-Duk assured, pushing me out the door.

When we started listening to the Storybag, it had been more fun than reading comics—the secrecy, the unbelievable battles, the strange weapons. Then, I'd prayed that Japan would be victorious and He-Seung would come home a decorated hero.

Last year, when the Allies said Korea could be a free country, I rooted for them.

When the Allies changed their mind and offered up our country as a prize to the Russians if they joined the war, I prayed the Soviets would stay home.

Now I just wanted the fighting to end—no matter what— and He-Seung to be home.

We must express our deep regret over the death of President Roosevelt.
The 'American Tragedy' is now raised here at Okinawa with his death.
You must have seen 70% of your CVs and 73% of your B's sink or be
damaged causing 150,000 casualties. Not only the late President but
anyone else would die in the excess of worry to hear such an annihilative
damage. The dreadful loss that led your late leader to death will make
you orphans on this island. The Japanese special attack corps will sink
your vessels to the last destroyer.
—Propaganda Poster following death of Roosevelt, April 12, 1945

Wednesday April 18, 1945—next day

Baby He-Dong

When someone is ignorant or uninformed, we say the person is like a frog trapped at the bottom of a well. I felt like I was drowning in that well, as I listened to *Sensei* talk on and on of old, exaggerated news about Japan's superior fighting ability. I wanted to get home and hear what was happening in Okinawa.

Finally, the school bell rang signaling the end of the day. I pushed my reader into my rucksack and looked over at Ih-Duk. He nodded at me. Today he wouldn't suggest catching butterflies or looking for spiders in the park, like he normally did. Instead, we'd huddle together by the vent and listen to the latest news.

"Yamamoto-kun," Endo *Sensei* called out. "Ohata-kun. Stay behind."

Kee-Wok snickered as he slapped my desk. "Chalkboard duty."

Had that bully volunteered us? He'd stopped stealing my lunch and being tough guy on the field, preferring to bother a new student who was really a bean-curd. Still, he often did sneaky things, like telling *Sensei* I liked reading in front of the class or wanted to sweep the floor to build my muscles.

Ih-Duk and I walked to the teacher's desk. I hoped *Sensei* would remember that we'd already helped him once this week. Instead he watched the other students leave before turning to us.

"You're both very intelligent students." Endo *Sensei* took out two rice balls from the drawer of his desk. The scent of seaweed filled the air. "Smarter than me, I think."

"No, no." we both protested. My mouth filled with saliva as I imagined those thick white grains of rice dancing on my tongue. Ih-Duk's stomach growled.

"So, I'm wondering what you can tell me." *Sensei* drummed his fingers on the desk.

"About what, *Sensei*?" Ih-Duk asked.

"Anything you might know." He pushed the rice balls closer to us. "That, say, someone else does not."

I could tell the new student that he needed to practice running around the park if he wanted to escape Kee-Wok. I could tell baby Jae-Won that two plus two equals four. I knew *Sensei* would not care to hear of these things. I waited for Ih-Duk to say something. He stared straight ahead.

"Yamamoto-kun, you live in the Omori family's home, don't you?" Endo *Sensei* looked at me.

"We've lived there a long time."

"The police are using his home as their headquarters," Ih-Duk added.

"Have you seen Mr. Omori lately?" Endo *Sensei* tapped the desk in front of that fat rice ball. "Or his wife?"

So he was looking for Min-Kook *uhmony*. I remembered the policeman waiting for Min-Kook *uhmony* outside, beating up Mother instead. That was over two years ago. We hadn't seen her since. A shiver traveled up my spine. "No."

"Are you sure?" Endo *Sensei* leaned forward so close, I smelled his stale tobacco breath. "Why do you keep pulling on your collar like that?"

"My uniform is too small, *Sensei.*" I pulled again, my fingers trembling. "My mother promised to fix it, but she's always busy."

"What makes your Mother so busy?" Endo *Sensei* asked. "Is she busy meeting Mrs. Omori?"

"No, she's busy taking care of my father and..." This year, Father had given a Christmas sermon so perfect that if I closed my eyes I could almost have imagined him standing behind the pulpit in the church rather than seated in Min-Kook *uhmony's* small living room. But we still didn't have too many parishioners. It was too dangerous. So, Mother was always helping Jae-Won *uhmony* with her sewing business. "And sewing for other people."

Sensei took two exam booklets from his desk. He placed them on his desk. Our Social Studies exams. I could see I'd gotten a 90%. So had Ih-Duk.

I was surprised, as I hadn't studied at all. I'd listened as long as I could to the Storybag, the gnats flying into my eyes and mixing with the water there. Not that the Storybag men had said anything more about Okinawa. In fact, they'd spent a lot of time arguing about the print size for the headlines in the newspaper. I'd listened until Mother called me to come inside. I'd lay on my futon all night praying and wiping away gnats.

Endo *Sensei* pushed his chair back and stood. His boots clacked on the wooden floor as he paced back and forth. He thwacked his cane against his leg. Then he leaned over and opened the last page of my test.

I hazarded a glance. The last question had a red mark. He tapped the tip of his cane on the booklet. "Japan has the ninth largest economy in the world and the third largest navy. That was the right answer."

Surely I'd put that false fact down, although I remembered thinking, after losing battle after battle, they certainly didn't have much of a navy left. I just hoped there was enough of a navy to help He-Seung out on Okinawa.

"Strangely, you put your answer in the past tense." Endo *Sensei* picked up my booklet, shaking his head. "Why would you do that?"

"We can't all be as intelligent as my eldest brother." I repeated what Gong-Tae *uhmony* had said.

"And why would your stupidity affect Ih-Duk?" *Sensei* picked up Ih-Duk's test booklet and shook it open to the last question, the same wrong last question.

I didn't have an answer for that. Why had we both written that Japan's glory was past history? Ih-Duk's foot pressed on the toe of my shoe. I felt a finger of fear touch my spine. I closed my eyes.

"I copied," Ih-Duk said.

I felt myself color. It not only sounded like a lie, it was. He would burn in hell.

"Really?" Endo *Sensei* looked down at him, pointing his stubby, tobacco-stained fingers in Ih-Duk's face. "Really?"

Ih-Duk bowed his head. "I'm sorry."

"Automatic F." *Sensei* ripped Ih-Duk's test in half. Then he ripped up my test. "For both of you."

I probably should have been thinking of how the test would affect my final grade, and if I'd be put into a lower class next year. I should have been worrying about Father's reaction. Instead, I was listening to my heart beat, a loud thud-thud-thud.

Sensei thwacked the desk so hard, his cane broke in half. He took what was left of his cane and hit Ih-Duk across the face. I must have made a noise, for he then turned and hit me, again and again and again. On the leg, the side, the neck. Each blow seared with pain.

Was this really our teacher? *"Sensei?"* I called out.

He stopped. He let the cane drop to his side. He straightened his uniform.

"If either of you are lying." He waved a shaky finger at us. "You'll be sorry. Your families will be sorry. All of Korea will be sorry."

"Yes, *Sensei*," we both chimed between ragged breaths.

"The Japanese Empire will not lose this fight with the barbarian enemy because we Japanese embody unique characteristics no other race has.

Loyalty, strength, bravery." He grabbed the rice balls and returned them to his desk. "Get out."

Ih-Duk bowed again.

I didn't really want to bow to this man who was so desperate he was beating us up worse than Kee-Wok ever had. I forced myself to lean down.

"Out." *Sensei* put his hands up, shooing us away.

We ran as far from the school as possible before pausing. My side ached worse than when there wasn't enough food to eat. I grabbed onto Ih-Duk, making him stand with me while I prayed not only my hourly prayer that He-Seung be safe, but this new one of thanks for getting us away from our crazy *sensei*.

*If we are prepared to sacrifice 20 million Japanese lives
in kamikaze effort, victory will be ours.*
**—Admiral Takejiiro Onishi speaking of his brainchild of turning boys
into human bombs**

Thursday, April 26, 1945—eight days later

Baby He-Dong

I headed home. The cherry trees along the path were in full bloom. Their blossoms were fluffy, pink, and painful to look at. We hadn't gotten our bi-weekly letter from He-Seung.

"Want to come to my house?" Ih-Duk caught up to me.

Since the teacher had beaten us, Ih-Duk hadn't wanted to come over and listen to the Storybag. He hadn't wanted me to listen either. But that was all I could think to do.

He held out a circular object. "I've got this."

In the past week, he'd tried to get me to his house to see his neighbor's kittens, organize his bug collection, and check on his garden to see when the carrots were going to come up this year. Instead I'd gone home to find out that the fighting in Okinawa was so bad, the Japanese were committing suicide instead of surrendering. I knew He-Seung would never do that, though. Suicide was a sin. "Not today, thanks."

"Here." He unrolled part of the object, a thin clear piece. "Touch."

I wondered if the mailman had come today. I kept walking toward home, but I put my hand out to touch the clear piece. One side was sticky. "What is that?"

"Neat, huh?" He rolled part of his torn-up test together and put the sticky piece on it. The paper stayed rolled up.

I stopped walking. "Did you make that?"

"Some Scottish person did." He smiled at this suggestion. "It's called Scotchman's tape."

I nodded, examining the roll. "Pretty uncreative name." I handed it back to him and continued toward home. "When you invent something, I expect it to sound more exciting."

"Funny you should mention that." He kept pace with me. "I have an invention for us to make."

"That's a surprise." I rolled my eyes at him. We had reached my front yard. Kwidong jumped up and down, wagging his tail. I nodded for Ih-Duk to come along with me. "Can we do it at my house?"

First we went inside so I could check for mail. There was none. Mother and Father weren't home. Perhaps they had taken the letter with them.

Then we went into the kitchen to get a cup of boiled water. The water kettle was still hot, so Mother couldn't have been gone long. Perhaps she'd gone to drop off her sewing to In-Young. Since she'd had baby Jae-Won, she was called Jae-Won *uhmony*. But I still thought of her as In-Young.

We headed out back. Ih-Duk put his rolled-up test paper to my ear. "Can you hear me?"

I rubbed my ear. "You're shouting."

"No, no." He tapped the paper cone on his palm. "I was talking normally. But, you see, sounds travel through the air. And if you capture the sound waves in a space, you can hear better. Or something like that." He patted his rucksack. "It's all in my reader. I have a new one on sounds."

I nodded. That would be a useful thing to have if you wanted to hear things better. I looked toward the vent, already saying a prayer that the news about Okinawa would not be bad today.

He hurried over to the vent. He stuffed the cone into one of the slats. He held out his hand, beckoning me to listen.

I put my ear to the cone.

"…pulling women off the streets."

Ih-Duk was right. With the cone against my ear, I could hear much better. I gave him a thumbs up.

"I told you." Ih-Duk nodded his head, satisfied.

I leaned closer to the cone.

"Yeah," the soft-spoken Storybag said. "If I had a teenaged daughter I wouldn't let her out on the streets alone. It's like dangling a bone in front of a dog."

Ih-Duk squatted down next to me. "What's the news?"

"They're talking about kidnapping girls off the streets." I said. "No news about Okinawa."

"That's good." Ih-Duk smiled. "Let's make these Koreanman's Callers then."

I cocked my head, scrunched my face at him. "What did you call them?"

"It's just a name," Ih-Duk said. "We'll think of something better later. Come on. We're only half finished. We need some string."

If Storybag wasn't talking about Okinawa, maybe the fighting there had ended. I took a deep breath, the first one in eight days. Then I stood up. "Okay. Okay."

We went back inside. Again I checked for the mail, as if maybe I'd missed it the first time. But there was still nothing.

"It says here that sounds are vibrations," Ih-Duk read from his tattered book before he'd even removed his shoes. "Like waves traveling through the air. It says here we can make a phone, sit in different parts of the room, and hear each other as if we're standing right next to one another."

"That *sounds* unbelievable, no pun intended." Still, I went to Mother's sewing basket in search of string.

Next to the basket lay a pile of clothes Mother needed to sew for In-Young. Sticking out at the bottom, was He-Seung's old uniform. Mother still hadn't gotten around to hemming it so I could wear. I put the uniform on the top of the pile so she'd fix it first. Then I grabbed a ball of string.

"Here." He tossed me another piece of his old test paper. "Make a cone and put a piece of Scotchman's tape on it."

Mother knew about the test now. She had not told Father. She had not even scolded me. But she had gotten all serious, trembling even, telling me it was important to remember, in everything I did, about the future. I wasn't sure if she meant the future, as in my entrance into a good high school or if she worried of other punishments. I'm sure she'd meant both.

I put the Scotchman's sticky stuff on the ugly paper. At least, I didn't have the piece that had the 'F' written on it.

"Now, put a knot in your end of the string and attach it to the small end of the cone. Hold the big end of the cone to your ear." He took his cone with the string attached and walked backward a few feet. Then he spoke into the cone. "Can you hear me?"

I laughed. Of course I could. He was right in front of me.

"Listen through the cone," he said. "Can you hear me?"

His voice sounded muffled through the cone, but I could hear something. "I can!'

"You're supposed to speak into your cone." His muffled voice bounced up at me from the paper cone.

"I can," I said, enunciating into the cone so that maybe my voice wouldn't sound as muffled as his did.

"Let's try it from farther away." Ih-Duk said, pulling the cone and heading for the kitchen.

This was Ih-Duk's best idea yet. I felt a shiver of excitement. I couldn't wait to show…to show He-Seung.

Just then Kwidong barked his friendly bark. Perhaps it was Father or Mother. Footsteps raced up the steps.

"Someone's at the door" I called to him. "I'll be right back."

I took my cone and hurried into the hall. Surely Father would be impressed with this new invention. Mother might even forget about the 'F.' I opened the door.

Myung-Ja stood on the front stoop, her eyes wide, her hair falling in her face. "Is your…" She leaned over, gasping for breath. "Mother here?"

Was she in need of a fitting? "She's gone out."

"Can I?" Her whole body shook, as if it was the middle of winter. She looked back the way she'd come, her lower lip trembling. "Can I come in?"

I opened the door wider. She rushed inside. She stood in the entryway, her arms crossed over her chest, tears pouring from her eyes.

"What?" She'd heard something about He-Seung. I felt my own eyes tearing. "What is it?"

"Soon-He and I were walking down the street." She sucked in a deep breath, her eyes to the ground. "And we saw these officers smoking cigarettes by the tree across the road."

If I had a teenage daughter, I wouldn't let her out on the streets alone, the Storybag had said. *It's like dangling a bone in front of a dog.* I felt a chill.

Myung-Ja lifted a trembling finger, pointing outside. "Soon-He insisted we go close by. She said they looked so handsome dressed in their uniforms with shiny brown boots and shiny swords. They saw her and..." She put her head in her hands, sobbing.

"The police took Soon-He," I said.

She nodded, looking toward the door as if the police might burst inside at any minute.

I thanked God this had nothing to do with He-Seung, then remembered that it did. This was Myung-Ja...and Myung-Ja's good friend.

"I must get home." She wiped her eyes and turned to leave.

"Wait." I put my arm out to stop her.

I dropped my cone and ran to my bedroom. I opened my closet. Between my futon and pillow, I saw the blue pile of letters from He-Seung. He'd written about trading bunks with a new guy who was afraid of heights, about catching a frog and roasting it for a snack, about how his sores didn't bother him much anymore. But those were old stories. I wished for new ones. On the bottom of the pile was his school uniform hat. I dusted off the rim and took it back to Myung-Ja.

Myung-Ja stood where I'd left her. She had stopped crying. She was leaning down over the cone, fiddling with it. "What's this?"

"It's nothing." I gave her the cap. "Put this on. This way you can slip through a crowd and people might not notice you."

"You're a genius." She twisted her hair up underneath it. She pulled the cap down low. "How do I look?"

She looked like a girl. A girl wearing a boy's hat. I rubbed my hands together, one over the other.

She looked out the window, her expression serious. "How will I get home?"

My eyes scanned the room, stopping at Mother's mountain of sewing. If only she could hide beneath some big sheet until she got home. He-Seung's uniform was on top.

Myung-Ja saw the uniform at the same time as I. "That's the perfect idea."

Would she drape the coat over her shoulders? I went over and got the shorts and jacket for her, wondering if I should just suggest she stay here until Mother got home. She must have thought the same, for she slipped off her shoes. But instead of coming into the living room, she hurried down the hall and into the bathroom.

"He-Dong. Calling He-Dong." The paper cone on the floor made noise, and I cocked my head toward the kitchen so I'd be sure that I could hear what Ih-Duk was saying. "What if we could talk from your house to mine? Wouldn't that be nifty? I thought of a new name: Best Buddies' Buddy."

"Let's keep thinking," I called in the direction of the kitchen.

He paused. He probably could tell I hadn't used the cone. "What are you doing out there?"

"Waiting on a guest," I said picking up the cone and speaking into it. "Who is using the bathroom."

"Oh." Ih-Duk responded, but I could tell he hadn't really heard me.

At that moment, Myung-Ja came out of the bathroom. She was holding her clothes and wearing He-Seung's uniform, the belt tied in a knot, the fabric flapping down. The shorts looked like a loose bag around her waist. She disappeared inside the jacket like a flower in a barrel.

I frowned. It was one thing to drape his jacket over her shoulders. But it wasn't right for her to wear his clothes. He-Seung was a man. She was just, just Myung-Ja. He-Seung would be furious. So would Dr. Lee. "What would your father—"

"He-Dong?" Ih-Duk came out into the hall. "Did you say something into the cone?" He stopped when he saw Myung-Ja. "Oh, hello. I'm He-Dong's best buddy—"

Myung-Ja laughed.

"It's you?" Ih-Duk took a step back. He looked at Myung-Ja, his eyes scanning up and down. "What—what are you doing?"

At that moment, I realized that Myung-Ja's idea worked. Better than the cone invention even. Myung-Ja looked like a funny animal to me. However, others would see her as a boy.

He-Seung wouldn't care about his uniform. He'd hated it anyway. More than anything, he'd want me to keep Myung-Ja safe. "We need to walk her home."

"You mean him." Ih-Duk spoke through his cone.

Myung-Ja picked up my end of the invention. "It's a phone?"

"Sort of," I said.

She smiled. "A cone phone."

"Of course. That's it." Ih-Duk agreed. "A Cone Phone."

I don't know what protected her more, He-Seung's clothes or Ih-Duk's muffled instructions through the cone that it was safe for us to come on. Ih-Duk was convinced his invention was the key. Whichever it was, we got Myung-Ja home safe. He-Seung would be pleased.

Thursday, April 26, 1945—same day

Mother (*Uhmony*)

Jae-Won sat next to me in the living room sucking on her small fists.
At the rate I was sewing, I'd be able to hem He-Seung's old uniform for
He-Dong. If I could just remember where it was. I thought I'd left it in this
pile.

Concentrate. That's what my dear had said. He had meant on the
church, I knew. He didn't appreciate Jae-Won *uhmony* and me spending so
much effort sewing clothes for non-Christians. Still, our church
membership had shrunk to just a handful of people. Even with their
generosity, we couldn't survive without extra help. Jae-Won *uhmony* sat at
the market and got customers. I watched her daughter and sewed up the
rips and holes.

Outside, Kwidong barked.

"Perhaps that's your mother now." I patted the child's toes, as I pulled
the thread through a tear in the knee of a girl's skirt.

I tied off the thread, and leaned forward to stand. It was then I heard
He-Dong talking to his dog. He would want to know if we'd had a letter
from He-Seung. That was always his first question. We hadn't.

He would want to know if I'd hemmed He-Seung's uniform. I hadn't.
I'd have to tell him I was having trouble concentrating.

Funny, I had told He-Dong to concentrate, as well. On his studies, his
future, our safety as a family. I had heard about his test, his answer, his
thoughts that Japan might not be winning the war anymore. Those were
dangerous thoughts to have, even if we all held them in our hearts.

He-Dong came inside, wiping sweat from his forehead. He looked at
me, his gaze pausing at baby Jae-Won. "What's she still doing here?"

Jae-Won *uhmony* always left her daughter with me while she worked at
the market. He knew this. "Jae-Won *uhmony* should be here soon."

He looked out the window at the darkening sky. "Why is she so late?"

These days there were more and more women at the market offering
sewing services, any kind of services, to put food on the table. Jae-Won
uhmony always tried to sell as much as possible, but no less than ten

mendings a day. Perhaps she'd stayed late to get one or two more customers. "I don't know."

He opened his mouth, then closed it. He latched onto Jae-Won's fingers. "Let's go find her."

"I'm sure she'll be here—"

"But we're hungry now." He-Dong picked Jae-Won up and plopped her in the cloth sling on my back. He handed me the pile of clothing. Then he raced out the door, walking so fast my side ached as I kept pace with him.

Jae-Won *uhmony* wasn't in her usual spot near the oil seller. Instead, two old women sat hunched over a sad pile of cabbage.

"Have you seen the Seamstress?" I paused next to the oil seller's cart. The sweet smell of the oil made my stomach tighten. I hoped my older boys were getting more food than we had.

"The pretty young woman?" she asked. She lifted the oil out of the bin and poured it back slowly.

"Where did you see her?" He-Dong asked.

"I don't remember." She dropped the spoon in her bin with a clank. "I got distracted watching the Army officers marching through. They take whatever they want. Fortunately none of them needed oil." She smiled, revealing a missing front tooth.

"Army officers?" He-Dong grabbed my arm and hurried me on as if we were in a race. There was an urgency to his search which seemed motivated by more than hunger.

Jae-Won *uhmony* wasn't near Mrs. Hong's *kimchee* jar stand. In her place, a woman sat on her haunches and mashed red beans with her giant stone grinder. Jae-Won *uhmony* wasn't by the tofu seller. Instead, a fish seller dumped water from her bucket. Another woman lingered on the street corner, her hair tied up, the smell of cheap perfume lingering in the air. We turned around and around. "Perhaps we missed her. Maybe she's already left and is on her way—"

"There she is," He-Dong pointed down the block to where Jae-Won *uhmony* sat on her piece of cardboard. An Army officer stood in front of her, his steel-toed boots glinting in the kerosene firelight. I saw those boots and still felt the ache in my shin where the policeman had kicked me years ago. We hurried closer.

"You say you're just a seamstress," the officer said to Jae-Won *uhmony*. "But I don't see any clothes you've mended."

"I just haven't had any customers today." Jae-Won *uhmony's* mouth trembled.

"I'm happy to oblige." The officer put both thumbs in his belt. He took a step closer.

I walked forward, setting down the pile of clothing. "I brought your mending."

The officer frowned at the sight of all of us. He smelled of rice wine and tobacco.

"Thank you." Jae-Won *uhmony's* face lit up. Sweat beaded her forehead. "Thank you for coming."

"It's late." He-Dong said. "We're hungry."

"I was just telling your dear *seamstress* that, myself." The officer wobbled back and forth, as he lit up a cigarette. Smoke curled through the air and into my empty stomach, making me feel sick. Or maybe it was the man's eyes lingering on Jae-Won *uhmony*'s chest. The way he did not walk away.

"Mother?" He-Dong stepped forward, putting one hand on Jae-Won *uhmony*. "Can we go home now?"

"You're a mother?" The officer gave Jae-Won *uhmony* a slithery glance. He kicked her cardboard, sending her abacus flying across the road. But he stumbled with his efforts. And, embarrassed, he hurried off.

While He-Dong retrieved the abacus, I helped her up. I held onto her trembling arm. "I'm sorry I didn't come sooner."

"No, no." Jae-Won *uhmony* said, taking her daughter from the sling on my back and holding her tight. "I shouldn't have stayed so late. But I haven't had any customers all day. Not even one. I kept hoping. It was foolish of me. Thank you for coming when you did."

It hadn't been my idea. I felt shaky, and not just from the encounter with the officer. Why had He-Dong thought to put his hands on Jae-Won *uhmony*, as if she were his mother? Why had he wanted to rush to the market in the first place?

As soon as we saw Jae-Won *uhmony* and her daughter to their door, I turned to him. Darkness had fallen, so I could not see his face. "You recently mentioned the Storybag...what do you know?"

He didn't answer. I didn't think he'd heard me. But he sucked in a deep breath. "Maybe you and Jae-Won *uhmony* should sell men's clothing."

"Oh?" I said. "But there aren't many men around anymore."

"They could be pretend wear." He-Dong swallowed. "For girls."

"Did the Storybag suggest this idea?" I hated to think he was listening to this Storybag. It was too dangerous. On the other hand, he had helped our dear friend.

"Actually it was Myung-Ja's idea. She borrowed He-Seung's uniform today as a test."

So that was where the missing uniform had disappeared to. I was relieved his actions had nothing to do with this Storybag. Still, my son was growing too fast in more ways than one. Perhaps I needed to concentrate on him, as well.

Do you know what this means?
Men like me are obsolete.
There will be no more wars. No more wars.
—General Douglas MacArthur on dropping of Atomic Bomb

Tuesday, August 14, 1945—about four months later

Baby He-Dong

Monsoon clouds covered the sky like a lid on Mother's pot of rice porridge. The heat of the morning stayed beneath the clouds, making the back of my knees sweat, my armpits itch, even though, according to Ih-Duk, we were sitting in the coolest spot in our yard.

Ih-Duk had just figured out that breezes ran through a spot behind Kwidong's pen. I had discovered that, by sitting back here, we could hide for a bit longer from Mother. And listen. Or try to. We each had our own Cone Phones now.

The Cone Phones didn't work as well as Ih-Duk had initially imagined. *What if we could talk from your house to mine?* In order to hear even a bit of something, you had to keep the string tight and straight. If we weren't hiding, I would have put the cone directly on the vent. That worked best.

I pulled out my map, which now had the various cities of Japan written out so I could keep track of where the bombs were being dropped in relation to Okinawa. I put my Phone Cone up to my right ear, pulling the string tight. The other cone was taped with Scotchman's tape onto the front of the Print Shop vent.

"Why aren't they saying anything?" I asked.

"Maybe nothing's happening." Ih-Duk untangled a knot in the string of his Cone Phone.

"Something's always happening." I swatted away a mosquito.

The man-to-man fighting in Okinawa had ended in June, but now the Americans were dropping strange bombs. Last week, they'd dropped this new bomb on Hiroshima, Japan, an island right across the water from us. Then the Russians had decided to join the war. A day later the Americans had dropped another big bomb on Nagasaki, which was further away from us, but closer to Okinawa. As Japan was still not surrendering, we waited to hear where the Americans' next target would be. We still had not heard from He-Seung.

I twisted the cone back and forth, as if I could fine tune the sound. It sounded like there was a radio playing in the print shop. "Do you hear static?"

"Yes." Ih-Duk nodded his head toward the house. "And more than one kind."

Most of Father's parish had gathered. This morning he was baptizing Jae-Won. She was already crying, whether it was because she was hungry, or hot in the white baggy dress Mother had sewn for her, or just whining. Probably the last.

I should have been inside helping Mother seat the guests, but each time the church group gathered, they spoke in hushed voices of war rumors. I couldn't listen to them without wanting to tell them what I knew. They would ask about He-Seung, and I hated to see the sad look in their eyes when Mother said that we hadn't heard anything lately. I felt a heavy weight on my heart, a smothering weight, and I just preferred to be with Ih-Duk, sitting near Kwidong.

Although the string attached to my Cone Phone was as tight and straight as could be, I couldn't hear anything but scuffling. I dropped to my belly, indicating Ih-Duk to follow. We scuttled across the backyard on our bellies to avoid detection from guests looking out the window. I bellied up to the vent and pushed my ear to the Cone Phone stuck in the grate.

"I thought you said there was going to be an announcement," the soft-spoken voice came through the vent. "This is just noise."

"No. Don't touch that," the other man said, sucking on his pipe. "I'm sure one is coming. I'm sure."

"About where the Japs will bomb next?" the soft-spoken one asked.

"Do you hear that?" I looked over at Ih-Duk who was listening through his Cone Phone. He nodded.

"He-Dong?" Mother called to me from the kitchen. "It's time—" She came outside, looking from me to the vent. Her eyes widened. "What in the world are you doing?"

"A radio announcement," I explained, pointing to the vent. "The Storybag."

"Your father is about to start the prayer."

I knew Father had suffered many long years, and was excited that he could finally do a baptism, even a small one secretly done at our house. He'd changed his suit three times this morning, lost his glasses. I knew this was important to him, and that it was disrespectful of me to sit out here instead. Not only to Father, but to God. But maybe God wanted us to hear whatever was on the radio. Otherwise He wouldn't have had the Storybag men talking about this now. Yes, surely God wanted us to hear. I didn't have time to tell Mother about the bombs, the ones just across the water, just a few hundred miles from Okinawa. "This is important, Mother."

From inside the house, Jae-Won screeched. Father called for me. Mother rubbed her hands together.

"A bad bomb might be coming our way," Ih-Duk said.

I nodded. I put my hands together in prayer. Praying she'd understand.

"Let me get your Father." Mother went back inside.

I listened. A squeaky voice sounded over the static of the radio, the person speaking in very formal Japanese. *War. Bomb. Thousands dead.* I picked out some of the words. I looked up at Ih-Duk, but he shrugged.

"What's going on out here?" Father came rushing outside. His temples were pulsing. His hands trembling.

Sweat rolled down my calves. I swallowed. "Please, Father." I handed him the Cone Phone. "Tell me what you hear."

"This is not the time or the place to be doing, doing inventions." Father dropped the Cone Phone on the ground.

"It doesn't sound like the regular radio announcer," Ih-Duk whispered.

"Please." I held the cone up to Father's ear. "Listen."

Father shook his head at us. He frowned. I thought he would crush the Cone and return to the living room. But some words caught his attention. He closed his eyes, listening.

One by one, the parishioners came out onto the back step. First the two men, Dr. Lee and Mr. Im, then the women—Jae-Won *uhmony* and her daughter in the white baptism dress which she'd already managed to rip, Mrs. Im, Myung-Ja *uhmony* and Myung-Ja in the farmer boy outfit Mother had made her, and finally Gong-Tae *uhmony*.

Gong-Tae *uhmony* made a clucking sound in her throat. "What are you doing out—"

"Shh," Father said. He motioned for Dr. Lee to kneel down next to the vent. He took Ih-Duk's Cone Phone and put it to Dr. Lee's ear.

"Dear?" Mother said, looking at Father.

Father closed his eyes. He whispered, translating what he heard into Korean. *"The war situation has developed not necessarily to Japan's advantage, while the general trends of the world have all turned against her interest. Moreover, the enemy has begun to employ a new and most cruel bomb, the power of which to do damage is, indeed, incalculable, taking the toll of many innocent lives."*

"A bomb is not such big news." Gong-Tae *uhmony* crossed her arms on her chest.

"It's a special bomb that the world has never seen before," Ih-Duk explained.

"Young man, how do you know—"

"Should we continue to fight," Father opened his eyes, which were now glistening. *"Not only would it result in an ultimate collapse and*

obliteration of the Japanese nation, but also it would lead to the total extinction of human civilization."

"*Aigo,*" Mother said. Oh dear.

"This sounds like nonsense," Gong-Tae *uhmony* said. "Who is saying these things?"

Father looked to Dr. Lee, raising his eyebrows.

"It must be the Emperor of Japan," Dr. Lee said.

"God himself," Ih-Duk whispered to me, clapping me on the back. "On the radio."

"*This is the reason,*" Father continued to translate, his voice trembling. "*Why we have ordered the acceptance of the provisions of the Joint Declaration of the Powers.*"

Dr. Lee let out a sound as if he were gasping for air. He closed his eyes. Tears streamed down his cheeks. Father reached over and grabbed onto him. His eyes were also full of sadness.

"What's the Joint Declaration of Powers?" Mother asked.

"Yes, what is it?" Had there been an agreement I didn't know about? Hadn't Japan agreed that they would fight until there was nothing left? Of Japan? Of Okinawa? Of Korea?

"Well, if God's talking on the radio," Ih-Duk said. "That must mean he's not God anymore."

"You're right." Father closed his eyes again, nodding, a tear streaking down his cheek. "The war is over."

"*Mansei.*" Ih-Duk jumped up, throwing his arms in the air. Long Live Korea.

This was unlike anything I'd ever felt. Not the throbbing sense of relief I'd felt when *Sensei* had ordered me to raise my hands in front of me for five minutes and then finally allowed me to let them drop to my sides. Not even that relief of safety I'd felt when He-Seung finally came to rescue me in the dark.

Now, He-Seung would come home. He would have to. There would be no more waiting for his letters. And He-Chul would come back. We would get our house back. We might even have beef again.

This was better than Christmas and New Year and Easter all put together. I grabbed onto Father's hands and shook them. I hugged Mother. I even picked up that whiny baby Jae-Won and twirled her in a circle. She giggled.

"Come," Father took quick breaths to control his crying. "Let us pray."

"*Mansei!*" Ih-Duk called again, probably thinking that was what Father intended by prayer.

Father stood above us. "Dear Lord, we come to you with such gratitude, our hearts are exploding. We have been praying so long for this day, and it has come at last." Father took a deep raggedy breath. "All through the war, we have looked for your blessing and guidance, always looking for your sign. Because of your grace, our children will soon be home. Because of your strength, we will be families at peace. We ask for your continued wisdom and guidance as we step toward the unknown. We will eternally rejoice in your name. Amen."

"Amen." Everyone chorused. Even Ih-Duk.

"Mansei!" Ih-Duk shouted again, so loud surely Heaven heard.

"You best keep quiet, young man." Gong-Tae *uhmony* waved her hand at him, shooshing him. "Do the Japanese know the war is over?"

The. War. Is. Over. Those words seemed not real. I felt a catch in my throat. "We'll just have to tell them."

"We can't do that." Dr. Lee smiled at me. "Besides, we have a baptism to participate in."

Ih-Duk sat down. He kept looking about him, raising his head as if expecting to hear celebration in the streets.

"It will become common knowledge soon enough." Gong-Tae *uhmony* said.

All these years I'd listened to the Storybag men, I thought the things I heard were confusing, interesting, even frightening. I'd never cared too much about sharing what I heard. Today, though, I thought I'd explode if I didn't. This was the day we had waited so long for.

I looked to Mother.

She reached in her pocket for a pair of scissors and cut off a small snippet of Jae-Won's already-ripped white baptism dress. She handed it to me. "Let's all go."

"Go where?" Gong-Tae *uhmony* frowned.

I knew where. Mrs. Hong's stall at the market place.

I was already walking over to Kwidong's pen to get him. We would all go and drop the white cloth in her jar. We would become like the servant in the fairytale, untying the master's storybag to help spread the best news in the whole world.

On the evening of August 10, 1945, with Tokyo suing for peace and Soviet troops on the move, an all-night meeting was convened in the Executive Office Building next to the White House to decide what to do about accepting the impending Japanese surrender in Korea and elsewhere in Asia...Working in haste and using a National Geographic map for reference, they (Dean Rusk and Charles Bonesteel) proposed that U.S. troops occupy the area south of the thirty-eighth parallel, which was approximately halfway up the peninsula and north of the capital city of Seoul, and that Soviet troops occupy the area north of the parallel.

—Historian Don Oberdorfer

Tuesday afternoon, August 20, 1945—six days later

Baby He-Dong

Partially thanks to our church members taking the white surrender cloth to Mrs. Hong, the whole city was wild with celebrating. It was like one big wedding party, with people hugging one another and smiling and exchanging news. Two days ago, school was supposed to start. But with the Japanese no longer in charge of Korea, no longer our teachers, nobody knew what would happen. Instead of school, crowds of people climbed Mt. Nam San to help tear down the stupid shrine. Mother forbade me from joining. She said that the temple had been a belief system for many innocent people, and it wasn't right to participate in tearing that away. Besides, we had plenty of our own work to accomplish.

The day after we helped spread the news of the end of the war, we were allowed to return to our home. I laughed as we tore down the Japanese flag hanging on our porch, the picture of the Emperor in the living room, and the Japanese scrolls covering every wall. We dragged their desks and chairs to the storage room of Father's church to be used in winter as firewood. I praised Kwidong when he grabbed at the strings to one of the scrolls and tore across the yard with the art in his mouth.

This morning, Father had walked to work in his church office for the first time in two and a half years. Mother and I had plans to go get He-Seung. I prayed that's what we would be able to do. We still had received no letter from him. But Min-Kook *uhmony* had told us that a train full of returning Korean soldiers would be coming.

I stood in the hallway and tapped on the bathroom door. "Are you ready?"

Mother had been fussing in the bathroom long enough for me to read through Ih-Duk's science reader on Mr. Thomas Edison another three times. Mr. Thomas Edison never said he failed. He always said he succeeded in finding a way that didn't work. It took him twenty thousand successful eliminations to invent the light bulb.

"Mother?"

"I'm coming." She hummed off-key.

I knelt down and peered through the tiny slat under the door. I saw a sliver of light, but nothing to give me a clue as to what was taking her such a long time. I put my ear to the door and was reminded of listening at the print-shop vent. Too bad I didn't have my Phone Cone.

Since we were home, and Min-Kook *uhmony* was back, we no longer listened at the vent. But, Min-Kook *uhmony* kept Mother informed of the latest news. She said that the U.S., instead of punishing the Japanese further, had forgiven them. The Americans had even gone to Japan to help them fix their country. That was amazing grace. More amazing than Mother not wanting me to tear down the shrine.

She had said that the Americans would be coming here, too, to watch over half of the country, the southern half. The Russians were going to watch over the northern half. Surely these big countries would soon tire of our tiny land, would soon see we didn't need all their watching.

"Mother!" I bellowed into the small crack under the door. I wished I could stick my fingers through there, making them grow longer, and pinch her leg, the same way I used to do when she prayed too long. "There's someone coming."

"Who?" The door to the bathroom opened. Mother cocked her perfectly combed head listening for the knock at our door. She ran her hands down her crisp *cheemar* to smooth out any wrinkles. Her eyes sparkled.

"He's waiting at the station." I scrambled to my feet.

"You silly boy." She took one last look in the small round mirror above the sink, patted her bun, then touched my elbow. "Let's go."

We hurried to the train station. The sun pierced through clouds, sending shafts of light in all directions. Sweat cloaked my body like an extra skin. I couldn't remember being so happy.

"Look there." Mother pointed down the road where an oxcart ambled by with a piece of cloth draped off its backside. On the cloth was printed a circle surrounded by four trigrams, representing Heaven, Earth, Water and Fire. Our Korean flag. "How lovely a sight is that?"

In the past couple of days, we'd seen our flag on people's windows, outside market stalls, on hats and clothes, and hanging from tree branches. Still, she pointed this out as if it were a rare sighting. In fact, for Mother, everything was wonderful.

As we walked, she talked non-stop, pointing out the balsam leaves she used to pick to paint her nails with, the white puffs of clouds, the way the earth crunched sweetly beneath our feet. I made noises like I was listening. I was really wondering if He-Seung would want to play a game of *bahduk*. I might even let him win this time.

The train station was more crowded than our market when there was a rumor of fresh fish. Everyone shoved forward toward the train tracks. Mother held tight to my wrist, as we pushed through the crowd. Surely she would lead us to a good spot so we'd be the first people He-Seung saw when he got off the train.

"Gong-Tae *uhmony* said to meet her at the entrance, but I don't see her." Mother pulled me through a tangle of people and thrust me down on something hard: a pile of wooden beams. Beside me an old man tapped his cane on the ground. Squished next to him an old woman smoothed her *cheemar* again and again. We were stuck at the back wall of the station.

"This is so far." I couldn't even see the tracks. "I want to get closer."

"There are too many people." She sat down next to me, wiping her face with a small towel.

"But Mother..."

The clickety-clack of an approaching train sounded. I looked at the crowd of people. I wouldn't make it through all those people in time, even if Mother allowed me. I jumped up and stood on the wood pile.

I couldn't wait to tell He-Seung about the Storybag men, the Phone Cone, how Kwidong was so happy to be back in his own yard. Tears pricked at my eyes. My nose burned.

Clickety-clack. Clickety-clack. Clickety-clack. The train didn't slow. A white tail hung out the vents of one car. A brown snout stuck out the vent of another. The sharp smell of fresh dung filled the air.

"Cattle car." I called to Mother and the old couple. I hoped the train wouldn't travel too far, that we would get some of that delicious beef. I could almost taste the tender salty barbecue on my tongue.

I stayed standing up on the bench, waiting, craning my neck. My legs ached from standing when, finally, the clickety-clack of another train sounded. I couldn't wait to hear of He-Seung's adventures. Would he show me how he hid in air-raid ditches? How he had fought off the enemy in the big battle of Okinawa? Had the Japanese given him a sword? I patted his pocketknife. I had kept it safe for him. The big black cars of the train roared by. Feathers floated through the air. I was careful to breathe through my mouth again.

"Chickens," I called out.

Perhaps He-Seung wouldn't care about my experiments or my adventures with the Storybag. He might only want to hear about Myung-Ja. He wouldn't be happy to hear how I let her wear his uniform. How Mother had made her some boy's clothes. I could hear him storming through the house, banging up the steps and slamming the door. Clickety-clack.

"Grain." I looked down to Mother and the old couple. The old man rested his head on his cane.

Perhaps Gong-Tae *uhmony* had given us the wrong information. Besides, I didn't even see her. Then again, why would all these other people be waiting? I rolled my head from side to side. I twisted my body back and forth. Two more trains passed through the station. None of them had passengers. My stomach growled.

"There you are!" Gong-Tae *uhmony* called, rushing over to where Mother sat. "This place is so crowded, I didn't think I'd be able to find you, much less my own son." She was dressed in her fancy Easter *cheemar*.

Clickety-clack. Clickety-clack. I held my breath, in case it was another animal train. Singing filled the air. Singing. Shouting. Weeping.

"They're here!" Mother stood up. "They're here!"

The train rolled into the station. A stream of arms waved military hats and white handkerchiefs out every window, making the black train cars look as if they flew on white wings. A lightness ran through my body, and I thought I could lift off and fly to the train. My brother was home. Finally.

"I want to be up there." I pointed to where the people on the platform crowded close to the track like one giant wave, rushing toward the doors of the train. "I want to be there when He-Seung steps down from the train."

"It's better to stay here." Mother craned her neck to see. "We don't know which car he'll come out of."

"Why don't you stay here and look?" I helped her stand up on the stack of wooden beams. "And I'll move closer. That way I might have the chance to be there as soon as he steps from the train." Already people were calling out, *You're home. You're home.* "I'm small and fast and—"

"Take care not to get hurt." She squeezed my hand.

I pushed my way past skirts and dresses, past babies strapped to their Mother's backs. I pushed my way all the way to the train steps and gripped tight to the metal railing. Young soldiers were already clambering off the train.

A young man in a tattered soldier's uniform hobbled down the steps, dragging his right foot behind him. Cries erupted to my left. "My dear, you've come home. You've come home."

Another man hopped off the train. He had no problem with his legs, but he had a dirty bandage across his eye. He wore a Japanese military hat, but he'd painted the sun rays of the Japanese flag over with the yin-yang symbol of the Korean flag. A group of women surrounded him, wailing louder than babies.

Another man stepped down, his shirt dirty and crumpled, his left sleeve empty of an arm. His face was dirty, unshaven. In my mind, I saw him lugging the church bench away, throwing the Emperor's red rubber ball across the yard, whittling a slingshot. I saw him with two arms.

"Gong-Tae?" I stepped forward. I tried not to stare. "You're home."

He looked up, his eyes angry. He turned the left side of his body away, as if to hide his missing arm.

"We've all been waiting so long." I led him to the pile of wood where Mother and Gong-Tae *uhmony* stood.

Gong-Tae *uhmony* rushed forward. She stopped when she noticed his missing arm. "My boy."

"Mother." Gong-Tae bowed, his eyes filling.

I wanted to stay with them and hear all of the news from Gong-Tae. I wanted to know what happened to his missing arm. But I needed to get back to the train. Would He-Seung be injured, too? Would he have lost his arm, his leg, his eye? No, surely he'd jump off the train just like he raced down the steps at our house.

I wedged myself in between an old man and a young woman with a small baby, and I waited. More and more soldiers came down, using crutches, wearing bandages, their faces tired and dirty. Where was He-Seung?

Thousands landed on the beaches of Okinawa, I remembered the Storybag. I held tight to the side of the train. My legs trembled. My throat ached.

No more soldiers came down the steps. The train huffed and puffed as though readying to leave. The platform cleared, as the crowd moved toward the exit.

He-Seung must have fallen asleep. I put my foot up on the first step and pulled myself onto the train. The sound of footsteps stopped me. Of course he was here. I looked up.

An old man walked toward me. He wore a blue uniform. He did not smile. "Where do you think you're going?"

"My brother's on this train." I looked around his wrinkled uniform to the seats. The ripped cushions. The grimy windows. "He must have fallen asleep."

"There's no one sleeping on this train." The man shoved me back toward the steps. "Go home."

"But I was told he'd be on this train." My voice shook. "He's a soldier."

"Kid, there are lots of soldiers. Hundreds of thousands, millions even." He picked me up by my shirt collar, as if I was a puppy dog, and he plopped me on the platform. "They can't all fit on this one train. Another one's coming next week."

I walked back to Mother, my brain buzzing. *Thousands landed on the beaches of Okinawa.* She sat alone on the wood pile, as rigid as a statue. She held tight to the wood, as if she couldn't let go or she would fall off the world.

"Where did Gong-Tae go?" I looked around, but the station had emptied, except for a beggar sitting on the ground, shaking his hand up and down.

"He was tired." Mother's eyes looked vacant. "Do you think He-Seung didn't see us and went on home?"

I could hear the fear in her words. Not that we had missed him, and he would bang around the house in anger. But that he wasn't coming home. She hadn't heard the Storybag, but there had been enough rumors the past week about the fighting that happened in Okinawa.

"Maybe." I said, thinking of what Mr. Edison would have said. "Or maybe we succeeded in coming for the wrong train." I forced a laugh as I helped her stand. "The ticket taker said another train's coming next week."

Mother's eyes widened. "Did he say He-Seung would be coming then?"

Father said lying was a sin. I imagined God's fiery pits of hell waiting for me upon death. But I felt Mother's hell right in front of me. Felt her dark eyes on me, begging me for a happy answer.

"Yes. He'll be here next week." I gripped Mother's trembling hand, leading her to the exit, mumbling to myself. "Surely."

My throat felt thick. The light feeling was gone. It didn't matter if I called our trip a success or a failure. If I lied or told the truth. Either way hurt just as bad.

When Japan surrendered to the Allies, (Governor General of Korea)
General Abe's responsibility had one focus:protecting 163,255 Japanese
servicemen and 378,714 civilians from the vengeance of Koreans.
—Historian Allan R. Millett

Tuesday, September 11, 1945—three weeks later

Mother (Uhmony)

He-Dong and I walked down the road away from the train station without He-Seung. For the twenty-first time. We had visited the station day after day, waiting for him. Some days a bunch of trains would come. Some days not even a cattle car would roar through.

When we weren't at the station, He-Dong sat out on the front step with Kwidong, his eyes trained on the path coming up to our house. I was reminded of the times they had waited for my dear. My dear had come home. I had to believe He-Seung would, too.

Our church had been open for three weeks, and while people hesitated at first to climb the steps to the door which had recently been used by the Japanese military, the last few days my dear had had at least a dozen people in the Morning Prayer service. Gong-Tae's family was not among them. I had tried many times to visit their home, but my knocks went unanswered.

This morning, on the way to the station, He-Dong and I had spotted a peanut seller on the road. That was a rare treat. We bought a small bag, He-Dong saying this was a good omen. He-Seung loved peanuts. But, yet again, we spent a long morning waiting for that train that would carry He-Seung back to us, and he did not come.

We continued down the road home, not discussing the trains or the possibilities. It's not as if I hadn't heard about the battles that had happened right on top of He-Seung. I knew He-Dong knew of them, too. It's that if either of us gave voice to our doubts, we might crumble.

An angry male voice came from around the corner. "What are you still doing here?"

"You're supposed to be back in your own country," shouted another. "Didn't you hear your bean-curd of an Emperor? You lost."

From the way they were yelling, I could only guess that the subject of their anger was a Japanese person. Neither of the voices sounded like He-Seung, but their angry words did. We weren't that far from the station. What if He-Dong and I had missed seeing him? I felt a surge of hope and raced forward. He-Dong must have felt it, too, for he hurried after me.

Around the corner, I spotted a group of boys, about He-Dong's age, standing in a circle. There was no He-Seung. I was about to turn away, when I spotted, in the middle of their circle, a young Japanese boy crouched, his face bloody, his arm hanging at an odd angle.

"Boys, boys!" I approached them as if they were children I knew.

One of them looked over. He nudged another one. The boys stared at me.

I held up the roasted peanuts we'd bought. "I've got a treat."

He-Dong sucked in his breath. "But, Mother. Those were for—"

"To celebrate that the war is finally over." I stepped forward. "That we all are finally at peace. Here. Enjoy these. Enjoy our new world of harmony."

The boys blushed, disappearing faster than the leaves in the wind. All except one reluctant fellow. He smiled at me. He took a handful of the peanuts from my bag, shook the treat back and forth in his palm. Then he threw the peanuts in my face. "Jap lover."

He-Dong stiffened. He stepped forward, a menacing look on his face.

I grabbed onto He-Dong's arm. "Peace."

"Yeah, peace." The boy smirked. Then he kicked the Japanese child one last time, before running off to join his friends.

The Japanese boy struggled to stand. He-Dong bent down, his face as blank as a stone, but his eyes full of anger. Certainly it was the same anger everyone held a bit of—anger over the war, his missing brother, even his gone peanuts. I patted his shoulder. "Peace…and Grace."

He-Dong took a deep breath. He grabbed onto the boy's good arm, pulling the injured child up.

The boy said nothing. But he bowed, as tears streamed down his face. Then he ran off, gripping his dangling arm.

"Joy is one thing, but revenge is evil," I said, insisting we follow him for a bit, to make sure he arrived home safe. When he disappeared into a courtyard, we turned back. We found ourselves at the base of Mt. Nam San. People stood in groups holding signs with funny characters. Had they come to revel in the destruction of the shrine even more?

I shook my head. What was becoming of our joyous country? "Like I said, 'Joy is one thing—'"

"These people aren't here for revenge, Mother." He-Dong pointed to the signs. "They're holding English signs which say, 'Welcome.'"

He-Dong was such a smart boy. Just like his elder brother He-Chul. "How do you know?"

"I saw those shapes in Father's book describing California." He-Dong looked around on the ground. He picked up a piece of the charred wood from the shrine, a small stick. He began copying the funny shapes onto his palm with the burnt edge of the wood. An upside-down mountain with two sharp peaks. The prongs of a pitchfork on its side. A corner of a room. I was tempted to stop him. His hands would get so dirty. But I hated to put a dent in his excitement.

"Welcome." He held up his hand. Then he looked up the road. "It must be for them."

A long line of giants in green military uniform marched up the road. Foreigners. Some of them had dark skin, the color of charcoal. Some of them had little dots on their skin like pox. Some of them were white as rice.

He-Dong pointed to a tomato-faced man with a big nose. "Isn't that Reverend Thomas?"

"I'm not sure." I squinted. He did look a bit like the Reverend, but surely he would have contacted my dear if he was in town. The man marched by with but a passing glance.

"Do you think these are the Americans Min-Kook *uhmony* said would be coming?" He-Dong asked.

"Maybe." I clutched tight to his arm.

"They sure are big." He-Dong wriggled loose. "I don't know why they couldn't win the war earlier."

"*Urser-oseyo.*" A group of men in suits bowed as the foreign soldiers passed. Welcome.

The soldiers smiled and waved. But following a noise from the tomato-faced man at the front, they kept moving. A rice-colored soldier pointed at the sign the welcoming group held, squinting his eyebrows and frowning. He-Dong held up his dirty hand with the strange writing on it and waved. The soldier looked over at us, took a rectangle from his pocket and threw it at He-Dong.

If the soldiers were throwing things, it was time to get out of here. I grabbed onto He-Dong. "Let's go."

He-Dong leaned down to where the rectangle lay on the dirt road. Min-Kook *uhmony* had told me those two horrible bombs that killed lots and lots of people in Hiroshima and Nagasaki were small things. I put my hand out. "Don't pick that up."

"But Mother." He-Dong looked down at the rectangle, his eyes as bright as if he'd been given a new red rubber ball. "The soldier threw it to me."

Did he throw it to He-Dong or at him? My heart raced. I closed my eyes and nudged the rectangle with my toe.

"I've got it." He-Dong scooped up the mini-bomb. He peeled back part of the wrapping. I held my breath.

"Maybe you should wait until we get home." I put my hand on his arm. "You could let your father look at it."

"But Father's at work." He lifted the strange object up. Underneath the dark wrapping was beautiful silver paper.

"Can you just hold it like that til we get home?" I asked.

I assumed his silence meant agreement. We hurried on. When I looked over at him, though, he had peeled back the silver paper. Underneath was what looked like a piece of dirty lard.

"Why would someone give you that?" We were in need of lots of necessities, but I had enough rancid grease.

"It smells sweet." He-Dong sniffed at the contents.

What would we do with sweet lard? Then I remembered that Reverend Thomas had enjoyed sweet foods more than spicy. Perhaps all Americans liked sweet foods, and this special lard ensured a tasty meal.

"Mr. Benjamin Franklin was experimenting with things to eat after a big meal." He-Dong turned the lard over in his hand, sniffing at it. "Things that would, well, keep the air fresh after a big meal." He looked up at me. "I wonder if this is something like that." He licked his finger and rubbed it across the surface of the black piece. He brought his finger to his mouth.

"He-Dong." I grabbed his hand. "You can't just stick anything in your mouth. You'll make yourself sick." I sniffed his strong fingers. I put my tongue out and licked a small bit of the dark smudge. "Mmm. It's sweet."

"I bet it's candy." He-Dong looked back, as if trying to spot the soldier. "Maybe that soldier was the candy uncle for the group."

"Maybe." What a strange-looking candy.

He-Dong broke off a small square. He smiled at me, that devilish smile that He-Seung always had. Then he put it to his lips. "Mmmm. This is the best candy I've ever tasted. Here, you try."

I couldn't get past the dirty look of it. "I did already."

We went back and forth like this all the way home, with him insisting and me refusing. I realized that the soldier had done us a favor by keeping our minds off of He-Seung.

When we reached our front path, Kwidong was already barking. On the porch, I spotted a rucksack. I felt bubbles of joy exploding in my heart. Finally. Finally. "Someone's here."

He-Dong looked up from his candy. He saw the bag, and ran around to the back. I hurried to keep up.

A tall man in a wrinkled suit stood next to the tomato plants. He had one hand on He-Dong's shoulder, measuring the height against his body. His face was sharp and proud. He looked so much like my dear once had, I caught my breath. My eldest son, He-Chul.

He came close. He smelled of tobacco and sweat. "I wondered when you'd get home."

"Have you been waiting long?" I grabbed his hands. They were strong and smooth.

"My boat got in a while ago." He led me back toward the front of the house. "Where were you? The market? School?"

"School hasn't started yet." He-Dong ran in front of his brother. "We were welcoming American soldiers."

"So they're really here." He-Chul snorted. "I imagine He-Seung is shouting at them to go home and let us be."

He-Dong and I exchanged a look.

"His train hasn't come yet." He-Dong mumbled.

He-Chul crossed his arms over his chest, putting one hand to his chin. He tapped one long finger against his lips, frowning. "You're not surprised, are you?"

"Well, his last letter—"He-Dong looked at the ground, scuffing his shoe in the dirt. "It was so long ago."

"The trains—the whole country—is a mess." He-Chul patted He-Dong's arm, but he looked over at me. "He'll be home."

This was my son, strong and faithful. His jaw was sharper, as if someone had taken a knife and carved off all the baby fat. A few black whiskers protruded from his chin. "You must be thirsty and tired."

"Affirmative to both of those." He-Chul smiled. "I saw the dog out back. Looks delicious."

"That's not dinner." He-Dong's mouth dropped open. "That's Kwidong."

"So that's the Precious one?" He-Chul's eyes danced with merriment as we walked to the front door. "Not the delicious one?"

He-Dong made a fierce face. He crossed his arms. "That's not funny."

He-Chul smiled at his brother. "I guess we'll have to have a menu change then."

He-Dong let out a deep sigh, as if he really thought his elder brother would dictate that I barbecue his dog.

"Here. Try this." He-Dong held up the long black rectangular piece of sweet. "An American soldier gave me this."

"That's disgusting." He-Chul wrinkled his nose, frowning. "It looks like compacted mud. Or worse."

We had reached the front door. He-Dong leaned down to pick up He-Chul's rucksack, but He-Chul put out an arm to stop him.

"I've got it." He-Chul smiled as he hefted his own bag.

He-Dong opened the door for his big brother. He-Chul walked in, and I followed. His eyelashes were long and dark. His face so handsome, I couldn't stop looking at him.

He-Dong automatically leaned down to untie He-Chul's shoes.

"I can do that." Again He-Chul stopped his brother.

He-Dong looked up at me with confusion. Wasn't it his job to serve his elder brother? I just smiled. I had assumed Manchuria followed the same customs as us, but maybe not. Maybe he had become used to carrying his own bags, taking off his own shoes. His long, thin fingers were fast.

"Where's Father?" He-Chul looked up toward the staircase.

"He's at the church." I reached out and held onto his hand again.

"Despite everything he's been through?" He-Chul wrinkled his nose.

"Because of everything he's been through," I said.

He-Chul wrinkled his nose again, patting my hand. "Karl Marx grew up as a Jew. In fact he came from a long line of rabbis. But he discovered a more important calling."

"Who?" He-Dong asked. "Was this one of your professors?"

"You could say that." He-Chul laughed a deep laugh.

What a wonderful sound. I hadn't heard that sound in years. He-Dong and I automatically laughed with him.

"I missed this room the most." He stepped up into the living room and turned around and around. "Where we ate. Where we read. Where we talked. It looks just like I remembered except—wasn't the grandfather clock in the other corner?"

"It was." He-Dong joined his brother and pointed to the shadow on the wall where the clock used to be. "But the Japanese got a soy sauce stain on that part of the wall. So Mother said we should put the clock there."

"A soy sauce stain?" He-Chul raised his eyebrows.

"Or something," He-Dong said. "Mother likes to think of it as soy sauce."

"I understand there are a lot of Japs still in the country." He-Chul sat down on the floor, stretching out his long legs. "Hopefully those US soldiers you saw have come to shoo them back home."

I frowned. That was no way to talk. "He-Chul."

"Actually we saw a boy this morning," He-Dong started.

"Well, the sooner they get out." He smiled. "The sooner we can build our own perfect country from the ground up."

This was my son. He was back and he would make our life, our country wonderful again. I felt a surge of pride which brought tears to my eyes.

"What are all these clothes?" He-Chul pointed to the pile of clothing which Jae-Won *uhmony* had dropped off days ago. With all the celebrating and confusion of packing and unpacking, I hadn't gotten around to finishing even one piece.

"Oh, Mother was doing some sewing at the market for a while," He-Dong explained. "Although now that Father's church is open again she shouldn't have to."

"Like the new leader of China, Mao Tse-Tung, says, 'women should hold up half the sky.'"

"I thought God held up the sky," He-Dong said.

"Let me get you something to drink." I hurried off to the kitchen to get some honey water, listening to the two boys make various starts and stops. I found I wasn't even listening to their words but the sound of their voices. I still worried about He-Seung, but the cadence of He-Chul and He-Dong trading stories soothed my heart.

On September 11 he (MacArthur) ordered Hodge to terminate the Japanese civil government and replace it with a military governor, General Arnold, who took office the following day. In an act of more than symbolic importance, Arnold announced that English was now the official language of the government of Korea.
—**Historian Allan R. Millett**

Sunday, September 16, 1945—five days later

Baby He-Dong

The tomato-faced soldier guided He-Seung to the door, both of their packs filled with black sweet bars for all of us. My heart sang. My mouth watered so much, drool ran down my chin.

"Wake up, wake up." He-Chul's strong voice sounded nearby.

I opened my heavy lids. The room was dark. The soldier and He-Seung had disappeared. Had the voice been part of my dream, as well?

"Hurry up." He-Chul touched my shoulder.

Negative to that being part of the dream.

The morning air was cold. I burrowed beneath my covers and turned on my *eebul,* feeling every muscle in my legs cry out. Ever since He-Chul had been home, he had me exercising like a soldier. I had thought I would be safe today on the Lord's day. "Isn't it Sunday?"

"Not yet." He-Chul nudged me.

For more than the first time, I wished I still slept in Mother's room. He-Chul wouldn't have risked disturbing her. Now I slept in my own room, Father's old office.

"Hurry up." He-Chul nudged me again.

I sighed, pulled my comforter back, and stood up. I stumbled after He-Chul downstairs into the living room. A small lamp brought some light.

He-Chul was dressed in a pair of shorts and a thin undershirt. He made big circles with his arms. He had dressed like this every morning. I shivered just looking at him.

"It's not summer anymore." I hopped from foot to foot.

"This is nothing." He put his hands on his hips and leaned back as far as he could. "In Manchuria, I often woke with frost on my eyelashes, my limbs so cold I couldn't move."

He had told me this every morning. I imagined frost on his long lashes. I rubbed my arms. I really wanted to go back under the covers and sleep some more. At least until the sun came up, until Mother woke up and made us some hot rice porridge to eat. But I loved my brother being home. I loved that he was doing what He-Seung would, by making me strong. I loved that he was trying to fill in for my still-not-home brother.

"Cold is a state of mind." He did deep knee bends.

"I thought that's what pain was." I stared at him, not wanting to move. My thighs still burned from yesterday.

"Pain is, too."

State of Mind. That was another of those He-Chul expressions. Affirmative, Negative, Efficient use of time. Self-Discipline. Class struggle. I had started keeping a list, asking him each time I didn't understand one of his expressions. I thought of them as his expressions, because nobody else I knew talked like this. I looked over at the clock. Four-oh-two. "How did you manage to wake up so early?"

"Self-discipline, Brother. Self-discipline." Using the flat of his palm, he gave the back of my legs a chop.

I crumpled, almost falling to the floor. Pain shot through my calves and my thighs. Every muscle in my body burned.

"Now, hold your stance for three minutes," he instructed. "Watch the grandfather clock."

"I don't think Father would like us to exercise on God's holy day." I thought of how I used to tiptoe around the house to make sure God didn't get irritated with me making noise. I wasn't so worried about making noise anymore, but this was definitely not observing the Holy Day. Would God know and punish us by not letting He-Seung come home?

"You're right." He-Chul put his hands on my shoulders. "But the day hasn't officially started. The rooster hasn't even crowed." He put his hand up as though ready to give me another karate chop. "Now, get going. When you have a strong mind and body, you'll have no fears."

I remembered He-Seung training me, leaving me in the dark or making me sit next to beetles so I would have no fears. But now I didn't think it was possible to have no fears. I didn't think there was any exercise that would keep me from being afraid that brother would not come home. Still, if this bending and hopping made He-Chul happy, I would do so. I bent my legs halfway, holding the position although my legs burned so bad that I thought I'd look down and see flames.

A pop sounded. The room descended into darkness.

"Don't be afraid." He-Chul said. "It's only the bulb."

"I'm not afraid." I felt injured by the suggestion. "I used to stand in the woods by myself in the dark."

"Don't move." He fumbled around toward the staircase. "I don't want you stepping on glass."

I was happy to be able to stand up straight, but the dark made the room feel colder. The sweat on the back of my neck felt like drops of ice water. I was tempted to sneak back to bed. Just as soon as I had that thought, I heard He-Chul bounding down the stairs.

"I got another bulb." The sudden burst of light hurt my eyes. I blinked. Glass had shattered all over the floor. Certainly this would put an end to our exercise session, and He-Chul would tell me to get Mother. She would be unhappy to wake up to this mess.

"Go get me the broom." He-Chul ordered, surprising me. He had never been one to clean up after himself. This He-Chul had learned a lot of strange things in Manchuria.

I sat in the church pew next to He-Chul, my calves burning, my head buzzing. The last time we'd come to church together I was crowded in the women's section next to Mother. Now, I was not only here in the men's section, but my feet even touched the ground. I aligned my feet next to He-Chul's.

Every week more followers arrived, but this week I was sure many had come as much to see He-Chul as to hear Father. I spotted Mr. Im, Dr. Lee, Deacon Mah and several other men. I could sense them looking at us. My smart, handsome brother was home. At least one of them.

Since He-Chul had been home, Mother and I had only been to the train station twice. He-Chul refused to go, saying the train station was just one more reminder of our broken country. That our presence at the station would not make the trains run any more efficiently. He had been right. Both times we waited all afternoon and only two soldiers returned. Instead of cries of happiness, the station was filled with the sobbing of people like us who still waited. I told Mother we should take it as a good sign, the soldiers were still returning.

Now I turned around to look at the women's section. Mother sat between Min-Kook *uhmony* and Jae-Won *uhmony*. They all smiled in our direction.

"Please turn to Isaiah chapter 61, verse one." Father looked at us, his gaze lingering on He-Chul. His voice was as strong and loud as I'd heard since he came home from prison.

I reached into the pew for the Bible. I turned the rice-thin pages as fast as I dared, sweat prickling at my forehead. Surely He-Chul would become impatient with my slowness.

"Here. I've got it." I held the Bible out to him. He nodded, but instead of taking the book, he closed his eyes. Mother normally did that, too. In fact a lot of the ladies did. Most of them couldn't read—except Min-Kook *uhmony*. I felt embarrassed that He-Chul acted like one of the ladies. Still, maybe he knew better. I, too, closed my eyes.

"The Spirit of the Lord God is upon me said Isaiah." Father's voice boomed. *"Because the Lord has anointed me to bring good news to the poor; he has sent me to bind up the brokenhearted."*

I opened one eye to see if He-Chul still had his eyes closed. He didn't. In fact, he was scribbling notes on a piece of scrap paper. I leaned over to look, but his writing was all jumbled.

"They shall repair the ruined cities, the devastations of many generations." Father looked over at He-Chul, his face filled with joy.

"Amen," I called out, sitting up straight looking to He-Chul and hoping he had heard my voice. He scribbled more notes.

I looked over again. "Opiate." I think that's what one of the words said. But I didn't really know what that meant. I wished I could ask, but I didn't want to be disrespectful. I looked on the ground, hoping to spot a piece of charcoal or mud I could copy the letters with on my hand. I knew I would forget the word.

The sermon dragged on and on with me repeating the word to myself over and over and not really hearing anything else Father said. When Father said the final "amen," I turned to He-Chul, "What is an opiate?"

He gave me a surprised look. Then he lifted his arms to encompass everyone in the church before pushing off the bench and toward the door. I thought maybe this was a secret word not to be mentioned in church, that he would tell me when we got outside.

We joined Father by the door as he greeted parishioners. "My son has returned," Father said over and over.

He-Chul greeted people as well as Father ever had, talking and telling jokes. He was so confident, calm, intelligent. All of the parishioners seemed boring, dull grey in comparison. Mr. Im with his limp. Deacon Mah with his complaints about life in the countryside. Dr. Lee with his concerns that Myung-Ja still enjoyed wearing farmer clothes.

I thought of the dark living room this morning. The lamp sending beams out, lighting up the surroundings. That's what He-Chul did. I stood there by this beacon of light. I forgot about the latest new He-Chul word as I enjoyed a warmth and happiness I hadn't felt in a long time.

Disposing of Japanese textbooks proved no problem.
Koreans burned them for warmth.
—**Historian David Halberstam**

Saturday, October 6, 1945—twenty days later

Baby He-Dong

Outside it was already dark. The autumn wind seeped through the cracks in the living room windows. I sat next to Mother on the warm ondol floor while she mended a hole in He-Chul's shirt. I was already so bored with my writing exercises I was watching her needle go in and out, in and out.

School had started again. We now had Korean teachers, which should have been a good change. But my teacher had us repeat the same exercises over and over, as if we'd all suffered a head injury. I never looked forward to school.

Besides, the real excitement was in the streets. The Soviets had occupied the northern half of our country. Americans had taken charge of the south. We Koreans just wanted everybody to please go home and let us have our country, our whole country, back. There were angry people in the street, and they were doing more than throwing clumps of dirt on furniture.

Houses and stores were broken into, people beaten and robbed. He-Chul said it was because people were angry with Americans who didn't understand our language or culture, and didn't know how to advise us in building our country. On that subject, he and Father agreed and could discuss for hours. On that subject alone.

Mother must have felt me staring at her. She paused, looking up from her lapful of white cloth. "Are you taking care with your letters?"

"Oh, Mother." I put my pencil down and let my hands rest on the heat of the floor. "We've spent all week on this exercise. I don't think it's an efficient use of my time."

"You sound like your brother." Mother frowned. She and Father didn't always appreciate the way He-Chul talked. Especially Father.

"Seriously." I rubbed the side of my head with my now-warm fingers. "I feel like my brain is turning to sludge."

"Oh, dear." She patted me on the hand. "I'm sure your teacher just wants to be certain you understand your Korean letters."

Her hands were like icicles, and I shrugged them away. "How long do you think that will take?"

"Don't be too critical." Mother put her head to the side. "Be grateful you have a teacher. Not only that, the war is over, we're in our own home, your father's back in his church and He-Chul's been given a respectable position at the university."

She paused, and I knew she was thinking of He-Seung. We had never said we would stop going to the station. But with He-Chul constantly talking about the chaos of the country, the corrupt leaders, the horrible structure of the system, Mother and I came to some strange, silent agreement. One day we stopped going to sit on the cold wood beams at the station, waiting as our hearts turned to stone.

"Just be patient." Mother nodded at my paper, but I knew she was also talking about He-Seung. "With that which is tedious, try to find something new."

I looked at the letters. The Korean alphabet, unlike the hen scratchings of Japanese characters, had many circles, circles with straight lines above or below or beside. I looked at those circles, letting my mind wander. I wanted our family to be a circle again. Peaceful. Whole.

It was nice to have He-Chul back, as he helped out a lot bringing in the wood and bringing home extra money from his job at the university, and sometimes even telling a funny story. But I hated all the noisy discussion with Father.

Mr. Benjamin Franklin had listed thirteen good things he hoped to achieve to become a perfect person. Good things I knew both Father and He-Chul admired—like order, avoiding extremes, peace, fairness, helping oneself and others. Instead of practicing more characters, I wrote down his list. Around this perfect list I drew a careful circle—our family. It wasn't a Korean character, but it felt good to draw.

"That's better," Mother rubbed her head. "One day you'll have to show me how to write."

A creaking sounded on the front porch. That would be Father. Or perhaps, He-Chul. Before either of them had a chance to struggle with their keys after such a long day at work, I dropped my pencil and rushed to the entryway. Mother hurried off to the kitchen to warm some tea.

Father and He-Chul both stood on the porch. I looked from one unhappy face to another. My heart bounced up and down, like a tiny bedbug hopping around, hoping for a place to rest. "You're both home at the same time. What a coincidence."

"Yes, well I spotted Father being harangued by a beggar." He-Chul shook his head. "I had to come to his rescue."

"We're all God's children." Father stepped inside. I leaned down to untie his shoes.

"Yes, Father kept offering solace." He-Chul laughed. "The beggar just wanted money."

"You don't know that." Electricity already filled the entryway so full, the hair on my arms stood up.

"Come, come inside." I pulled Father up into the hall. "The *ondol* is warm."

I automatically turned and leaned over to help He-Chul. Too late, I remembered he didn't like to be helped. *Self-sufficiency* he called it.

"I can do this." He-Chul patted me on the head, slipped off his leather shoes, and placed them side by side facing the door.

"It's not a matter of what you can or cannot do." Father gave a grunt of disapproval. "It's a matter of accepting the honor that is accorded your station in life."

He-Chul jumped up into the hallway, next to Father. He stood as tall. "Father, you sound so bourgeoisie."

I wasn't sure what that was, and hoped it was a compliment as in *Father, you sound so healthy and strong.* I opened my mouth to ask He-Chul. But then I caught sight of Father's pulsing temple. Now was not the time to improve my vocabulary. "Did I ever tell you about Mr. Franklin's list?" I hurried into the living room, went over to my homework and grabbed my list to show He-Chul.

"In fact that's the basic problem with our whole society." He-Chul pushed the list away, pacing back and forth on the *ondol*, as if he were delivering a lecture in class. "What we need now is for everyone to do his and her utmost. Not wait for others to clean up after us or take care of us. The only way our country is going to recover is if everyone works hard together."

"Everyone is working hard." Father did not sit in his rocker, but also paced back and forth. "You can't expect people to change the rules of society—to create a new country—overnight."

"When a rule no longer serves a purpose." He-Chul turned on his heel. "Except to delineate class and status—it's time to expunge it from the system."

I half-wanted to write down more He-Chul words—expunge, delineate. I half-wanted to wave the paper in between the two of them, beg for their attention. My brain was spinning.

"Well, I think we can only ask for the Lord's guidance when it comes to tradition." Father tapped the back of one hand onto the palm of his other. "For now we should focus on getting trains to run and rice to the market."

"But don't you see? It's all linked, Father. My colleagues and I agree on this. In fact we're holding a special study session tomorrow morning to discuss this problem. You might want to join us."

I held the paper up in front of He-Chul's face, as if I could stop the words from travelling to Father's ears. How could He-Chul even think to ask such a thing?

"I appreciate the offer, but I'll be busy." Father's jaw was clenched. "So will you."

He-Chul looked at me, and I gave a slight nod. My brother worked so hard, reading and writing day and night, I could understand him losing track of days. I mouthed, "church."

"Oh, that's right." He-Chul tapped his finger to his mouth. "Well, I'll let you know how the session goes."

"What do you mean?" Father's voice was a low rumble.

He didn't mean anything. I looked to He-Chul, begging him to smile and laugh and say it was all a stupid joke. Of course he'd be at church. I wished Mother would hurry up with the tea.

"Nothing is more important than the Lord," He-Chul said, and I breathed a sigh of relief. "At least not for some people."

I had once worried that Father's snoring would raise the roof from our house. Now, looking at Father's face, I wondered if his anger would do the job instead. Outside, Kwidong barked. I stood between them. "I hear the dog."

"Some people need that balm in their lives," He-Chul continued.

Slow, heavy steps sounded on the porch. A slight tapping sounded on the door.

"Perhaps He-Chul's colleagues have decided to come tonight instead." I turned to Father. Maybe they all realized tomorrow is Sunday—"

"My colleagues don't care if it's Sunday or—"

"Go see who it is." Father's back was rigid.

I looked to He-Chul, hoping he would want to go greet the visitor. Hoping that as soon as he left the room, the miserable tension would disappear. That I could show my chart to Father, and he would try to understand He-Chul's strange words, strange ways.

"Well, go on." He-Chul waved me away.

I hurried to the door, straining to listen to Father and He-Chul, hoping that Father would sit in his rocker with his Bible, and He-Chul would go up to his room to read. But their voices tumbled over each other. I swung open the door, ready to untie the shoes of whomever stood there and push them into the living room in hopes of breaking the tension. An odor like the sewage drain on a hot summer day wafted inside. The porch light illuminated a soldier in a ragged brown outfit. A backpack hung from his shoulders.

Was this the beggar Father had talked to? Had he followed He-Chul and Father home? The man slouched against the door frame, sending another wave of his sewage odor into the house. My throat filled with salt, and I swallowed the thick liquid.

"Father," I called, grabbing the door to close it.

"Do I have the wrong house?" He smiled, stepping forward to put his hand out to grab onto my biceps. Despite my long shirt, his fingers felt colder than Mother's, and as rough as the bark of the oak tree. I tried not to flinch. "Isn't this the house with a bean-curd boy and a mother who feeds every beggar?"

A warm bolt of electricity ran through my body, melting a cold layer around my heart, a shield I hadn't known was there. Tears burned my eyes as I stepped forward and grabbed onto his swollen, rough hand.

"Soldier." Father's voice sounded behind me. "What can we do for you?"

This same hand had helped me shoot a slingshot.

"Go on home now." He-Chul had come to join forces. "It's late."

This same hand had patted my shoulder and told me I could do anything.

Perhaps you'd like to visit the church tomorrow." Father pulled me back to close the door. "But my son is correct. It's time for you to go home."

"He is home." I found my voice. Tears streamed down my face. "Mother!" I called. "Our train has arrived."

"That's you under all that dirt?" He-Chul jumped forward, clapping He-Seung on the back. "You made it!"

Father held onto the door for support. Then he did something I'd never seen any Korean elder do, especially not someone as important as Father. He bowed. He bowed as one does to a great man, an elder, a wise one.

"Thank you," he said, his head down, his hands folded together. "Thank you, my son, for your sacrifice."

"He-Seung?" Mother came rushing to the door, wiping her hands on her *cheemar*. She dropped to her knees, crawling towards him, her tears falling on the porch like rain. "Thank God. You're home."

I smelled a stench worse than ever. Down the road I heard people shouting at one another. I felt a bitter wind blowing against my chest. But in my head I saw the Korean alphabet, the circles. We were one of those circles—finally—a family together again, standing on the porch for that one moment in perfect harmony.

No division of a nation in the present world is so astonishing in origin as the division of Korea; none is so unrelated to conditions or sentiment within the nation itself at the time the division was effected...in none does blunder and planning oversight appear to have played so large a role.
—**Gregory Henderson, former U.S. Foreign Service Officer.**

Sunday, October 7, 1945—next day

He-Seung

I stood in my room, fumbling with the buttons on my shirt. The Army nurse had warned me to keep the area around my abdomen clean. I could still see the dimples on her cheeks when she smiled. Could smell the feint touch of roses behind the chemical scent. For a moment I heard the whoosh of air, felt the sensation of falling, falling, falling. Shocked voices surrounded me, calling to me as if I were in a deep, dark well. I pushed the thoughts back down, grasping at the sides of my clean shirt, feeling the wooden desk beside me, breathing the air still scented with rice and a broiled mackerel Mother had fought for at the market early this morning.

He-Dong tapped on the door and came in my room. "Want me to come with you?"

"I don't think so, Little Brother." I pulled my shirt closed, standing in front of the small bottle of mercurochrome on my desk. Mother had mentioned Gong-Tae was home. Except for Myung-Ja, he was the one friend I had waited years to see.

He-Dong watched my trembling fingers as I re-buttoned my shirt. "You might not remember the way."

"I haven't been gone THAT long." I smiled at him.

"It felt like forever," He-Dong mumbled. "We could take Kwidong. I'll show you how well he fetches. Oh, and you have to see Mt. Nam San. There's no shrine now. Also, someone painted a huge Korean flag on the wall of the school. And—"

"You can show me all those things." I led him out of my room. "Some other time."

"The soldiers live on the way to Gong-Tae's house, though." He-Dong's eyes grew large. "Sometimes, if you get lucky, they'll throw you a piece of chocolate."

"A piece of what?" I wondered if he was still mispronouncing words like he did as a child.

"It's a sweet."

"I'll keep an eye out for that." I laughed, holding onto my stomach. Life was good when your kid brother's biggest worry was about sweets rather than a soupy bowl of rice, bedbugs, lice, surviving til the next day.

We passed the bathroom. Mother and He-Dong had prepared a bath for me last night, He-Dong insisting on carrying the boiling hot water to the bath to show me how strong he was. All I'd wanted to do was sink beneath the welcoming warm water and soak. But I knew I couldn't sit down. So I stood in that bath, half of my body freezing.

"They only toss the chocolates to kids." He-Dong gave me a doubtful look. "And, well, you don't really look like a kid anymore."

"Neither do you, Little Brother. At least, not the one I remember." He seemed concerned about letting me out of his sight, as if I might disappear. "They might offer me one as a fellow soldier."

"You don't look like a soldier either." He looked at the new pair of pants Mother had given me to wear, the new white shirt. "You might have to show them a karate chop."

"I don't think that's a way to start winning friends." I leaned forward as though laughing, but I really wanted him to go downstairs first. As soon as he had started down, I held my stomach as I made my way down the steps. Down. Down. Down. I took a deep breath, resting at the bottom.

He-Chul sat in the living room with a pile of papers before him, a black book under his arm. "Glad to see you're finally up."

"I'm sorry I missed out on your morning call to exercise. But I'll be getting my share this morning. I'm going over to Gong-Tae's before church."

He-Chul nodded. "Yes, well don't expect him to sit in the back row with you and kick a soccer ball down the pew."

"You did that?" He-Dong frowned.

My older brother was angry with me for throwing my pillow at him and telling him to get lost this morning. He was out to rile me. "That only happened once, Brother."

"And you're lucky you lived to be a day older." He-Chul's eyes scanned the page he was reading. "I've never seen Father angrier."

"You mean he was angrier than he got last night?" He-Dong was incredulous.

"What happened last night?" I raised an eyebrow.

He-Chul made a big show of straightening his papers into one big pile. "A schedule conflict is all."

He-Dong sucked in his breath, looking up at the ceiling as if expecting the roof to cave in. He whispered, "He-Chul's not going to church."

Surely I had misheard. "What?"

"I have a conflicting meeting." He-Chul took the pencil from behind his ear and made a quick notation on one of his papers.

He'd always been so much smarter than all of us, going through books so fast, I thought he was faking it until he spouted back the contents in summary and criticized the logic of the author. Father and Mother sat enraptured. I never thought there'd be something too hard for him, and it had made me want to throw up all over his clean shoes, his perfect papers, his glowing reports. Perhaps my brother had finally met his match. "I guess working at the university's not easy."

"It's not the university, He-Seung." He made a tsk-tsk sound, as if I'd given the wrong answer. "You're just getting back. You've no idea the troubles we face as a nation." He rolled his papers up and patted them on his palm. He paced back and forth across the floor. "Why do you think it took you forever to get home?"

Surely he was talking about the inefficient train system—bombed-out sections of track that took forever to repair, conductors who thought their train should go first, never mind what the schedule said, workers who decided to show up late or not at all. That wasn't what kept me from getting home, though. I felt a whoosh, falling, falling, falling.

"On top of that, there's little food coming from the countryside." He-Chul was still talking. Lecturing, really. "Prices are through the sky. There's looting in the streets."

So many times I had not wanted to go to church. I hated sitting there, Father's words hammering like a mallet on my head. The only thing I ever prayed for in church was that Father would say the final *Amen*, so Gong-Tae and and I could sneak outside and play. But Father went to prison for his belief in the church. He spent months suffering through horrible conditions. He came home a tired old man. Whether or not He-Chul believed in what Father had to say wasn't the issue. "These troubles of ours can't wait for a couple of hours while you go to church?"

"They can't wait a couple of minutes." He gave a disgusted snort. The one which always made me feel like an idiot. "Father will understand. Eventually. He's an intelligent man."

I had the old urge to grab He-Chul's papers and whack him across the face. He was a head taller, had obviously been exercising a lot, but I might be able to take him on. Pain seared across my stomach.

You always like to kick the stone, don't you? I imagined my buddy Dae-Hyung's face, his hand holding his cap down as we drove off in the jeep to help fix the airplane hangar.

I closed my eyes and took a deep breath. I put my hands over my stomach to try to stop the pain, waiting for the moment of anger to pass.

"Is your stomach bothering you?" Mother was in front of me. She put the back of her hand up to my cheek. "You feel warm. Do you have a fever?"

"I'm fine." I took a step back, pushing the memories aside. "I was just about to go get Gong-Tae for church."

"An inefficient use of time." He-Chul had already returned to the table and was scribbling notes. "He'll never come."

"Shall we make a bet?" My stomach burned again.

"Would hate for you to be disappointed on your first day home." He-Chul raised his eyebrows.

"How will you know whether he comes or not if you're not there?" He-Dong asked.

"I've already explained the paramount nature of this meeting." He-Chul's face reddened with anger.

I needed fresh air. The voice of an old friend. For my stomach to stop burning. I turned for the front door, leaving them to argue about what was more important.

It took me longer than I remembered to get to Gong-Tae's house. The leaves on the maple trees had turned blood red, a flock of crows cried out, and I felt the earth below me, each step a blessing. I was actually walking in my own neighborhood, breathing cool air, seeing the blue sky, hearing the birds.

I recalled racing down these streets with Gong-Tae, kicking the soccer ball back and forth, jumping over rocks and carving our names in tree trunks along the way. I paused, turning around and around.

The whole place seemed different, smaller somehow. I felt like I was looking at familiar things through a windowpane, the same way I used to watch Myung-Ja's shadow in her bedroom window.

"Can I help you, buddy?" A man called out. I turned. A soldier stood at the base of Mt. Nam San. His English words were a trip back to my childhood when Reverend Thomas' son, Jim, and I used to play stones or catch.

It was strange to see soldiers who yesterday had pointed guns to our heads and thrown bombs in our barracks, now guarding us, protecting us, asking if I needed help. Had this soldier been in Okinawa? A flash of Dae-Hyung's chipped-tooth smile filled my mind. I saw blood. The fear in his eyes as I stood by his stretcher.

My stomach throbbed. I paused, trying to breathe. Cool air in. Cool air out.

"You looking for something?" The soldier asked. He did not stand in front of a candy cart, as He-Dong had described.

I pushed aside the thought of missing legs, of blood dripping all over the infirmary making the place smell of an iron pipe. "No." I pulled the words Jim had taught me from my childhood memory. "No looking."

"Then, move along." The soldier nodded for me to go.

Move along. This was my city, and a foreigner was asking me to move along? I put my hands over my stomach. I took a deep breath. Then I put one leg in front of the other until I reached Gong-Tae's small house.

"He-Seung?" Gong-Tae *uhmony* opened the front door. The smell of old soy sauce, burnt rice, and body odor accosted me. I took a step back. For a moment, I felt as if I'd fallen onto the hospital cot. *Hold him down, boys.* I heard the voices in my memory. *Now.*

"You're home." She smiled wide. The top portion of her hair had turned grey as if she'd stood outside during a snowstorm. She looked me up and down. "Your parents must be very happy to see you. All in one piece. They were—we were all so worried."

"Thank you." I reached up to pull myself back to the present. I grabbed onto my stomach. The entryway was a hodge-podge of shoes. The wooden floor was scuffed with dust. The soy sauce smell made my nose itch. "Is Gong-Tae here?"

"He's asleep." She whispered as if he were a baby lying on her shoulder.

"Oh." I could see my brother's mocking smile. *An inefficient use of time.* "I see. Well, then, I'll come again—"

A loud crashing sounded. Gong-Tae *uhmony* hurried toward the back room. I slipped off my shoes and followed.

Gong-Tae, my dear buddy, stood next to his desk with his right shoulder facing me, the left one hidden. A brass bowl lay on the floor by his feet, the soup splattered every which way. The stench of his room made my throat close.

"Oh, dear." Gong-Tae *uhmony* raced to clean the spill. She wiped the soup with her *cheemar,* and took the mess from the room.

"You know, I had a bunkmate who reminded me of you—played soccer, good with his feet." I shook my head, moving forward to grab onto him. "But fumble fingers with his hands."

"You mean hand." He stepped back, his eyes flashing. "Just hand."

I nodded. He used to be the one to tell me that I looked like a bullfrog when I got angry. Now I knew what that looked like.

"Did your bunkmate lose his arm, too?" He lifted his empty sleeve.

"No." I shook my head, closing my eyes. If I breathed slowly through my mouth, I might be able to keep a smile on my face.

"Lucky for him." Perhaps Gong-Tae was seeing the world through a window, too. Although maybe his window was even smaller than mine.

"Lucky for me." I felt my mind drifting back. *Just hold on. Hold on.* "He and I did everything together. Shoveling air-raid ditches, stealing extra food from the mess hall, cleaning out the latrines."

With his right hand, Gong-Tae picked at the scab on the end of his stump. "You had a regular old vacation. Did you get to play soccer?"

I leaned on the edge of his desk. I let out a slow breath. "Dae-Hyun always suggested we kick around a rock or something. But that was usually after we'd been digging ditches in the hot sun for twelve hours and we could barely make our legs move back to our cots."

"Funny guy." Gong-Tae didn't smile.

"What happened?" I indicated his missing arm.

"Oh, weren't you there?" Gong-Tae lifted his chin. "Some Jap tricked me into going to Siam where I was supposed to meet my girlfriend."

I felt my eyebrows furrow. "It was a fellow Korean—our good old *friend*, the guard—who tricked us."

"Oh, that's right." His eyes flashed anger. "The Japs were too busy jumpin' my girl's bones. Again and again and again."

I didn't want to think about poor Myung-Hae right now. One thing at a time. I indicated his missing arm. "What happened?"

"Did I say I wanted to tell you?" Gong-Tae put his hand up over his empty sleeve.

"I know you do." I stepped forward. "I'm your friend. You missed me."

He cocked his head to the side. "Like malaria."

I grabbed onto his one arm. "Let's get some air."

"Your parents have already been by numerous times to drag me back into the fold. Like some lost sheep. But God's never listened to me. If He had, Myung-Hae would be home and I'd have my arm."

"I'm not talking about Church, idiot." I pulled him towards the door. "You're alive. It's a beautiful day. The leaves are bursting with color. The birds are singing."

He cocked his head again, as if hearing a strange noise. I'd seen that look in He-Dong's eyes, as well. "Why would you want to be seen with me?"

"Actually, I don't care about being seen with you. It's the being smelled with you that worries me." I wrinkled my nose. "But the fresh air might get rid of some the—"

"Aren't you full of jokes?" Gong-Tae pulled away, but he shuffled toward the door.

We walked around his block. Water had trickled down the side of his neighbor's wall. A huge leaf sailed to the ground, red and orange with just a faint tint of gold. In Okinawa, there were no such leaves. I stopped, slowly bending to the ground. "Look at this."

"Yeah, winter's coming." Gong-Tae used his one hand to pull his jacket around him. "I can feel it already. The cold air's hurting my skin."

"Oh, stop being such a bean-curd boy." I put my hand on the wall to help myself up. "Your skin is screaming with pleasure that you're finally outside.

He stopped walking. "Leaves bursting with color? Birds singing? Skin screaming with pleasure? Are you on medication?"

I pushed him forward. "They don't have medicine for the likes of me."

"I'll bet they don't." He looked me up and down, examining. "What's your problem?"

He was my good buddy. I should talk to him. I remembered the whoosh sensation, the falling, falling, falling. I could see the sharp metal pipe, feel the warm blood oozing over my fingers. I opened my mouth. "It's just good to see you." I put my hand on his shoulder. "As He-Dong said, it felt like forever."

"Right." Gong-Tae looked back towards his house. "You've gotten weird." But he stayed by my side, hiding behind my shoulder each time we passed someone.

"Isn't the fresh air wonderful?" I took a deep breath.

He made a show of taking a look around. "No gun smoke. No blood. No rotting bodies—This must be heaven."

"It is," I nodded, pointing out a small yellow bird landing on the tree branch.

"Siam was miserable." He did not follow my gaze. "Flying cockroaches, leeches the size of your thumb, all that sun. My feet were always swollen, and I felt as if someone had tied a hot, wet towel over my nose."

"Okinawa was the same." I remembered my feet swollen to the size of squash, rotting in my boots. "And mosquitos with better dive-bombing accuracy than even the Allies."

He stopped so abruptly that my arm was yanked back. A red-hot sliver of pain shot through my stomach. "What?"

"If you already knew, why'd you ask?" His eyes burned with anger.

"What are you talking about?" I held my stomach, gently massaging.

"What are we doing out here, anyway?" He looked back toward his house.

He-Dong asked me to get him some kind of sweet from the soldiers." I mentioned the first thing I could think of. "But he didn't go into excruciating detail like he used to, making you think his lips would never stop moving. Didn't even mention the important detail, like where the hell are the soldiers with the candy carts?"

The fire left his eyes. He actually smiled. "They carry the sweets in their pockets."

I imagined the pieces of caramel sticking inside some soldier's pocket, picking up lint and fur. "That's disgusting."

"The sweets, you fool." He let out a bark of laughter. "They come in a wrapper. You would probably say a 'beautiful wrapper.'"

I smiled. "Well, where do we find this sweets man?"

"Any soldier is a sweets man." He lifted his good arm and pointed to the soldier I'd passed earlier. "There's one now."

We walked over to where the soldier stomped from foot to foot, blowing on his hands.

"He's not very well trained," Gong-Tae whispered, walking as close to me as possible. "All that hopping and blowing would have gotten me a railroad tie on the back of my shins."

"Can I help you fellas?" The soldier stood ramrod straight, as if he might have heard Gong-Tae, although surely he didn't understand us speaking Korean.

"Is lovely day," I said. Gong-Tae stood half-hidden behind me.

"Where I come from this is cold." The soldier blew on his fists.

"You from where?" I asked.

"I'm from San—" He paused. "California. I'm from California."

I thought of Jim. I wondered what he was doing now. Maybe he'd joined the army, too. "My friend from California."

The soldier cocked his head, raising an eyebrow. "Really?"

"Maybe you know him." I stepped forward. "His name Jim."

The soldier's stern scowl broke into a wide grin. "Of course I know Jim."

I couldn't believe the coincidence. "You do?"

"There's Jim Miller. Jim De Silva. Jim Hardwick. Jim Applegate." The soldier laughed until his whole face was red. "Oh, and Jim Fancy Pants from across the Bay. He tried to steal my girl."

"Jim Thomas." I smiled at the soldier, pleased he was enjoying himself so much. He even had stopped blowing on his fists. All that laughter was warming him up. "His family name Thomas."

"Lordy, lordy." He patted his chest, coughed. "Do I know Jim?" He shook his head. "That's a good one. I'll have to write that down."

I remembered taking mental notes like that. I could see the words in my head as I went through the day. Especially that day. Falling, falling, falling. I turned to Gong-Tae and translated.

"Buddy." The soldier's voice was now sharp. "I don't know your Jim. Is there something else?"

From up the road, I spotted another soldier, perhaps the man's superior, marching toward us. I was reminded of Scumbag Tanaka. He jumped each time Officer Nakamura walked by, and he usually jumped at me. Making me lug his bags from spot to spot, insisting I clean the latrines, getting me assigned to work on the airplane hangar that day.

"Do you have—" I looked to Gong-Tae, nudging him for the word.

"Chocolate?" Gong-Tae said the word as slow as if he were making it up.

But the soldier seemed to understand. He patted the sides of his uniform. He searched his back pocket. He shook his head.

"All out." He put his hand up, shooing us away. "Come back tomorrow, Jim's friend. I'll have some for you then."

"Well, that was a waste of time." Gong-Tae turned back towards his house.

"You sound like He-Chul." I walked next to him. "But we got a good laugh."

"You mean he got a good laugh." Gong-Tae paused.

"I saw you smile," I said.

Gong-Tae looked off over my shoulder. "A mosquito bite."

I automatically swiped at the air, ready to kill the nasty pests which had carried malaria through the base. Then I remembered we were home now. I felt silly, letting my arm drop. "It's too cold for—"

He let out a grunt of disgust, lifting his empty sleeve. "And to think I always told you to stop itching your rash."

His arm. He was confiding in me. He'd lost his arm from a mosquito bite. "An infection?"

"How stupid is that?" He swatted at his arm as if it was still there.

I stepped forward and grabbed onto his shoulders. "God, man, you're lucky to be alive."

"That's what people keep telling me." He looked away. "But most days I can still hear the scraping of the dull saw across my bone, the pain ripping through my body, the stench of iodine and rotting flesh. Lucky doesn't describe it."

"You fool." I hugged him, ignoring his stiff shoulders, ignoring the pain spiking across my stomach. "Come. Let's go sit in on Father's service. It will be like old times."

"Naw." He pulled away. He held onto his empty sleeve as if in pain.

"We won't have to carry any benches. I promise." I put my hands up, palms out. "In fact, according to Mother, the place is flooded with people. Migrants from the north. The women from the north have the smoothest skin, you know."

"What about Purple Face?" He jutted his chin up at me.

"You mean Myung-Ja?" I raised my eyebrows. "There's no harm in looking at beauty, is there?"

He ground his foot in the dirt. I could imagine his strong calf muscles. I could see him bouncing a ball back and forth. That seemed a lifetime ago.

"Hey look at that." The stark peak of the mountain reached towards a perfect blue sky, perfect except for one small white cloud. I pointed up at the shapely cloud. "One of the women is beckoning us towards the church now."

"Go." Gong-Tae pushed me away. "Please. I've had enough of your weird self."

I watched as he slunk back toward his home. He-Dong would be disappointed I had failed to get him chocolate, Mother that I had failed to bring Gong-Tae to church. He-Chul would say I had wasted my time. But despite Gong-Tae's coldness, I felt a warmth in my heart, a small flame which spread across my body, making me smile. Like Gong-Tae had said, I was in heaven. I was home.

The northern Koreans greeted the Russians with joy, until they learned that the Soviet soldiers, many of them Muslim Asians, regarded the Koreans as a conquered people, not liberated victims of Japanese oppression. Although the Soviet troops' behavior did not reach the scale of violence that it did in Manchuria, the Twenty-fifth Army conducted its share of rapes, beatings, murders, and looting that marked the advance of all Soviet armies into enemy territory.
—Historian Allan R. Millett

Friday, October 19, 1945—twelve days later

Baby He-Dong

I yawned as I hurried downstairs toward the kitchen. I paused when I spotted He-Seung's school rucksack all ready by the front door. This was another clue to add to the He-Seung page of my notebook.

I was happy my brothers were home, but they both felt like splinters in my finger, the small kind I got from bringing in kindling, the kind I could feel but couldn't see. There was something not quite right with either of them.

My big brother had always used big words and had big theories. I remembered that. But the real He-Chul would have had time to attend Father's sermons. The real He-Chul thought exercise was for idiots.

This new He-Chul was busy every free moment—and Sunday was now considered a free moment—in some kind of study session. Every morning he was up early doing physical training, and insisting I join. My thighs always ached.

And then there was He-Seung. The real He-Seung hated school. The real He-Seung would be up at 4am with He-Chul and I doing exercises before racing out the door to play soccer until the school bell rang. He would get scolded for sleeping during class.

This He-Seung locked the bathroom door. He spent hours by himself in his room. He never raised his voice. And yesterday, he had gone to visit Gong-Tae again for the purpose of studying—yes, studying. Once again he had his school rucksack all ready by the front door.

Ih-Duk had told me a story about a group of Martians who landed on the earth in a round ship with flashing green lights. Inside their spaceship the Martians were tiny and green, but they stepped out into the world as regular people. He was the one who suggested I give my brothers a quiz, starting with He-Seung. We'd made a list of questions. *Were you always so enthusiastic about school? What kind of training did you have me do before I got a puppy? When did you bring me the puppy? From where? I* particularly wanted him to hear that last question. I wanted him to remember Myung-Ja.

The past two Sundays when I saw Myung-Ja sitting in the church pew, her eyes following us to the front row, my heart felt funny. He-Seung never even looked her way.

I walked into the warm kitchen. He-Seung stood at the kitchen counter, dressed in his school uniform. Mother hummed off-key. She was always humming now that He-Seung and He-Chul were back. I didn't want her to stop humming. At the same time, I didn't want to live with a couple of Martian brothers. I fumbled in my pocket for the list of questions.

The sound of slurping made me look up. He-Chul paced back and forth as he scooped down his porridge. He-Chul always left earlier than us.

"Don't you need to be going?" I asked him.

"Good observation." He-Chul tapped his bowl with his chopsticks. "I'm going to be late today. It's part of my lesson plan."

"What kind of lesson is that?" I asked.

"Well, nobody's really hearing me." He-Chul took another slurp of porridge.

"Do you have disabled veterans in your class?" He-Seung blew on his broth.

"Hearing can mean more than the physical act, brother." He-Chul set his bowl down. "The students have decided who I am based on campus rumor. The revolutionary, the rabble rouser—"

"The troublemaker, the Commie," He-Seung finished.

I spotted a familiar glint in He-Seung's eyes. I could already predict He-Chul grabbing Brother by the ears and pulling him outside for a fight. I imagined He-Seung, the strong soldier that he was, would fight hard. I felt a strange sense of relief. What had I been worrying about? Green people in spaceships?

But when He-Chul stepped forward, He-Seung chuckled. And winked.

He-Chul paused, a look of confusion on his face. "Yes. Well. They've decided who I am before I even open my mouth. So I thought I would change their expectations by doing the unexpected. By being late."

He-Seung glanced at me. I thought he would roll his eyes. The real He-Seung would have.

Instead he smiled and gave a sympathetic nod. "Then again, if you're too late, they might just think you overslept."

"It's brave of you to try new approaches." Mother ladled more porridge into He-Chul's bowl.

"Yes, it's good of you to be so concerned," He-Seung said, without any hint of sarcasm.

"I'm not concerned." He-Chul put his bowl down. "I just need them to listen to what I'm teaching. And right now, they're not."

"What was the purpose of all that question and answer stuff you tried last week?" He-Seung asked. "If it wasn't concern."

"That's a teaching method, too." He-Chul shook his head, as if how could anyone not know. "The dialectic approach. Through question and answer, I can show students the faultiness of their logic."

He-Seung didn't even raise his eyebrows. He didn't even respond to He-Chul's know-it-all voice. He took another slurp of porridge.

"Sometimes it's good to listen, too." Mother rubbed her hands together.

He-Chul slapped one hand against the other. "I'd be listening to fools."

Mother dropped her soup ladle. It fell to the floor with a loud clatter. She leaned down to retrieve it, her hands shaking. Surely she was nervous around these strange people that were supposed to be my brothers.

"As long as we're here together." I pulled the list from my back pocket. "I have some questions."

"He-Chul might be able to choose the time of his entrance." He-Seung put his bowl down on the counter. "But we don't have that luxury, do we, He-Dong? We need to get going or we'll be late."

"And so?" I asked, looking at one of my first questions. "Were you always on time to class before?"

"Don't forget this." Mother handed He-Seung his *bento* box, not waiting for him to answer my question, perhaps not having heard me. Now that my brothers were home, she didn't hear me much.

"I'll be back down in a moment." He headed down the hall toward the steps, walking funny.

He said he didn't want to be late for school, yet he was sneaking back upstairs. Of my two brothers he felt like the biggest splinter. I swallowed down my breakfast in one long slurp, grabbed my list and went to find him.

The Russians also showed no inclination to provide any economic resources to the south: the only immediate export from the Soviet zone was thousands of refugees, who crossed into the American zone at the rate of 4-6,000 a week for twelve weeks...September-November, 1945
—Historian Allan R. Millett

Friday, October 19, 1945—same day

He-Seung

I hurried to the bathroom to take a final leak. It was difficult to do so at school. There was never a moment when the bathroom wasn't crowded.

I gave the door a quick shove and rushed over to the toilet. If I didn't hurry, I'd be tardy. Our teacher had us do push-ups as a punishment for lateness. I knew I couldn't even do one.

I lifted my shirt. I still hated to look down. Even though I'd been using the mercurochrome like a daily prayer, the area around the wound was getting worse. Redder, puffier. Like the small red balls the Emperor used to hand out when Japan conquered a country. Here Japan had finally been defeated, but every day I got to see a celebratory red ball protruding from my lower stomach. I smiled at the irony.

I knew I should say something to someone. But who? I was a grown man. Besides, Father had all he could take right now with He-Chul. He-Chul was so busy building New Korea he couldn't see straight. Being late to class to teach his students a lesson? That was the dumbest thing I'd ever heard. He-Dong said Father had gotten better since his fall in prison, but I saw the way his hands shook, the way his steps faltered, the way his shoulders stooped each time he and He-Chul argued.

Besides, my wound would get better. I might not ever be able to be a husband to Myung-Ja, but I would live somehow. I let the last of the urine drip down and wiped off the end of the red rubber tube sticking from my belly.

The door creaked open. He-Dong stood at the door, staring at my stomach. "Ehhh?"

I yanked my shirt closed. "I didn't hear you coming."

"What was that?" His eyes were wide, wider than the time I told him he had to wait half an hour in the dark by himself. Wider even than the time I told him I'd be leaving for the army and he was in charge until Father returned.

"Go ahead." I indicated the toilet.

"I saw something." He gulped, staring at my shirt.

"Hurry or you'll be late." I patted his shoulder.

He flinched, pointing at my stomach. "I saw something."

I chuckled. How much had he seen? I moved back to the sink to wash my hands.

"Boys?" Mother called from the bottom of the steps. "Are you still up there? You're going to be late."

"You first." I motioned my arm in a swooping gesture toward the door.

He-Dong backed his way out the door. Suddenly, he stopped. I ran into him, instinctively putting my hands out to protect my stomach.

"What are you?" he asked.

"I'm a man...who needs to get to school." I turned him around and pushed him forward. "And so do you. Mother's calling."

He nodded, probably calculating how much of the trip to school he'd have to run. But when he looked back once more at my mid-section, he was still nodding. "So Mother knows. I'll just ask her later."

If he asked Mother, she would immediately go see Dr. Lee. Within minutes, Myung-Ja, and the entire community would know of my failing as a man. I would be one more worry to Mother, one more disappointment to Father. I grabbed onto his arm, pulling him back into the bathroom.

He-Dong's jaw dropped. "You're hurting my arm."

I let him go. "This is our secret."

"You mean Mother doesn't know?" He backed away. "That you've got some red thing sticking out of your stomach?"

His voice was loud. I wanted to drag him inside and lock the door. Mother's footsteps sounded on the staircase. She was coming up to check on us.

"No." I pulled at the hem of my shirt. "They have enough worries right now." I reminded my body to slow down, to breathe, to be calm. I whispered, "I'll tell you another time."

"Boys?" Mother had reached the top of the steps.

"Coming." He-Dong sounded too eager. I could see him racing down the hall, shouting, *Brother's hurt. Look at his stomach. Announce it from the pulpit. Tell the whole world.*

"This is our story." I grabbed onto his arm again. "Right? No telling Mother or Father. Or even He-Chul. Understood? No telling anyone."

His eyes blinked faster than a dragonfly's wings. "Does it hurt?"

"No more than the time Mr. Yee farted in our home service and I tried so hard not to laugh I thought I'd explode." I took a deep breath, smiling.

He-Dong's eyes widened, as if surprised I remembered such a thing. His face broke into a huge grin. He grabbed my arm. "Yeah, and you pulled me out of the room."

"Exactly." I tried to sound as if I too were lost in this old moment. At the same time, I put out my hand to shake his. "No telling. Promise?"

"Boys?" Mother stood a few feet from us, her face lined with concern. A lock of hair fell onto her forehead. "Why are you still up here? You'll be late."

The hallway felt so small, I couldn't breathe. I grabbed He-Dong's hand, my eyes burning into his. I gave his hand a squeeze. He dropped his head, giving me a small nod. Despite my relief, my stomach throbbed.

...The division of Korea evolved around them (the Koreans) without being fully understood by them. The joy of emancipation and the will for independence blinded them from fully comprehending the rapid political developments that ensued.
—Historian Dae-Suk Suh

Friday, October 19, 1945—same day

Baby He-Dong

I don't know how I sat through class. Ih-Duk kept trying to make eye contact. I knew he wanted to know about the Martian quiz. If I'd picked up on any other signs. Part of me wanted to return to that fun story. A Martian. The idea seemed stupid now.

All morning I thought of the Storybag tale Mother had told me years ago. How the man shoved the tales in his pouch and those tales eventually turned around to kill him. I had shoved He-Seung's story down only a few hours and already I felt like a thousand snakes were biting me.

During lunch I stayed in the classroom pretending to read. Really I was counting the minutes left til school ended. Perhaps I could convince Father to hold a prayer session at the house. We hadn't done that in a long time, not since the church was officially opened. If Dr. Lee came to the house, I would find a way for him to examine He-Seung.

At the end of the day, Ih-Duk hurried to catch up with me to walk home together. It wasn't that that bully Kee-Wok bothered us anymore. In fact, he had stopped coming to school, having discovered he could make lots of money selling stolen beer and canned meat on the black market. But Ih-Duk and I always were together.

"Finally." Ih-Duk sighed as we walked past the Korean flag and out of the school gates. "I thought the day would never end."

"Me, too." I wanted to tell him. Then I remembered He-Seung looking at me, shaking my hand. *Promise?*

"Look what I traded for during lunch." He opened his palm to show me a dirty metal object. "That fool Bon-Hwa didn't even know what it was. But I could tell. It's obviously from space. You could ask He-Seung—"

"He's not an alien." My throat hurt just saying the words.

"How do you know?" His eyes got wide. "Did you do the quiz?" He looked hard at me. "You didn't, did you?"

I shrugged. I wished I had a piece of string to tie around my neck to keep the stories inside. I did not trust my voice to talk.

"I know it's hard to do to your own brother. But, really," Ih-Duk looked around, lowering his voice. "I heard from my friend's brother that

He-Seung's been helping his teacher after class. That he stayed back for extra lessons. Perhaps he's been trying to get secret information to give the Russians."

I wondered if He-Seung hid in the classroom just as I had, hoping no one would ask him to play soccer or baseball, waiting for the chance to walk home in peace. It was painful to walk beside noisy Ih-Duk, listening to him talk about He-Seung like he was some space monster. All I wanted to do was turn and beg Ih-Duk for help.

"Here." He thrust the metal piece at me. "Take a closer look."

I turned the metal this way and that as if I cared. A clump of dirt fell from the back. "I think you had it upside down."

"You know this secret code?" He stepped back as if I too might be some alien.

My ears hurt, listening to his foolishness. "It's English, you fathead. And if you weren't so busy trying to see a code, you would have noticed it yourself." My voice was getting louder and louder. "Remember the chocolate bars? Remember? There's some of the same letters on this. U.S. AR-MY. It's a belt buckle, moron."

"What did you call me?" He clenched his fists.

"Just stop trying to make something out of nothing." I pushed him away hard, racing home, my heart banging up against my throat.

Mother stood in the front yard with a broom and basket, collecting leaves for use as kindling. I hesitated, taking deep breaths. All I wanted to do was rush over and spill all my worries. But I kept seeing He-Seung's eyes. *Promise?*

"He-Dong?" Mother smiled, leaning down to add more leaves to the basket. "You're home. Come help me."

I put my rucksack on the ground and went over to where she stood. I felt pressure in the back of my throat. I leaned down and picked up a handful of leaves, the oranges and reds burning my eyes.

"Get the brown ones first." She came beside me and leaned down. "These colorful ones will need more time to dry out."

Her cotton skirt brushed against my arm. I had a sudden urge to hide there, as if I were a small child.

"Mother." I grabbed a handful of dead leaves, reminded of how Ih-Duk and I had used leaves as battle markings. The battles were over, but He-Seung was hurt. "Why don't we have morning worship at our house anymore?"

"There's no need now that the war is over." She smiled looking off in the direction of the church. "Praise the Lord."

"Still we should do it one day." I made my voice as nonchalant as possible. "For old time's sake."

"Old time's sake?" She stood up, a small leaf attached to her hair.

"Besides, maybe some people can't make it to church on Sunday." Gong-Tae and his parents hadn't been to the church at all. "Maybe if we offered a home service, more people could come."

"Your father's always at the church, from early morning to late at night. Anyone who can't make Sunday mass comes to see him then. Besides, I'm not sure having a service here at the house would draw more people, especially with He-Chul holding his study sessions here..." She shook her head at the thought, and the leaf floated to the ground.

My one and only idea was sailing away like that leaf. "Well, Father may get to see these other parishioners... but we don't."

Mother looked at me. "Who is it that you're so eager to see?"

"I don't know." I put my foot in her basket to tamp down the leaves. *Dr. Lee. Dr. Lee. Dr. Lee.* "Gong-Tae might come."

She sighed, indicating a pile of leaves near me. "There are some behind you."

I understood this was the end of Mother talking about my grand idea. I felt a pressure in my heart so strong, my throat hurt. I bent to pick up more leaves, but couldn't bring myself to do this mundane, meaningless, not-helping-He-Seung act for one more minute without spilling the story. I dropped the few leaves I held. "I need to check on Kwidong."

"He-Dong?" Mother called after me.

I hurried to the back. Kwidong rushed to greet me, making my throat hurt even more. He nudged my side with his wet nose. I knew he wanted to play, but each time I looked at his red rubber ball in the dirt, I remembered He-Seung standing in the bathroom, the strange tube sticking from what must have been a red swelling on his stomach.

I grabbed onto Kwidong's fur. He licked my hand, over and over. As if I was a bone. Then he stopped to scratch himself.

I reached down and rubbed his neck. "Stop all that scratching."

Kwidong pushed my hand out of the way with his paws. He scratched his neck hard. Mother had said he'd had a scratching problem before, not to worry. Now, watching him, I had a great idea.

I would visit Dr. Lee. I wouldn't have to mention He-Seung's name. I would tell Dr. Lee I was worried that "our precious" was sick. That I'd noticed it recently, when He-Seung came home. Perhaps He-Seung had brought home some strange Okinawan bug. I would point to Kwidong as evidence, and suggest that we all might need to be examined.

"You're a genius, you are." I hugged Kwidong's neck, tying the leash to his collar.

As we got closer to Dr. Lee's house, Kwidong barked. I rounded the corner. Kwidong barked again. A silver wrapper fluttered in the wind, blowing across the road.

"Don't be silly," I scolded Kwidong. "It's just a wrapper."

There was always litter now along the roads. Nobody cleaned the streets anymore like when the Japanese were in charge. Nobody emptied the toilets either. People dumped buckets of smelliness in the drainage ditches.

Poor planning, He-Chul always said. *From a country with no strong leader.*

Kwidong sniffed and ran about the closer we got to Myung-Ja's. As if he recognized her house. He barked so much that she opened the door before I even knocked.

She leaned down to pet Kwidong. "Hello."

"Is Dr. Lee home?" I asked.

"He's probably in his office." She looked up at me. "Why?"

"I think our Kwidong..." I let the words—*our Precious*—hang in the air.

"Yes?" she asked.

"Is sick." I looked at her meaningfully.

"My father isn't a dog doctor." She looked down at Kwidong. "Besides he looks fine to me."

What had seemed like the perfect idea in the safety of my backyard now seemed as dumb as Ih-Duk thinking an army belt buckle was from a spaceship. I'd spent the entire walk over here planning the phrase about *our precious* and she didn't get it. I didn't know what I'd expected from her. I guess I'd thought she would rush in, grab Dr. Lee and follow me to the house. Not stare at Kwidong and pretend to be an animal doctor. Still, if this idea didn't work, who would help He-Seung?

"But he scratches all the time." I said, my voice pleading. "I just noticed it after He-Seung came home."

"You're joking, right?" She cocked her head at me.

"Maybe he's got some kind of infection." I kept seeing the tube sticking from He-Seung's swollen belly.

"They're fleas, silly." She shook her head, smiling.

"How do you know?"

"I just do." She put her hand on the doorknob as if to put an end to our discussion. "Just don't play too close to him, or you might soon be scratching like that."

Fleas were common. A doctor wouldn't make a house call for them. She was retreating into the house. I stepped close to the door, so she wouldn't close it. "Do you think that's what He-Seung had all those years? Fleas?"

"Come to think of it, I haven't noticed He-Seung's rash since he's been home." Her eyes turned flat. She reached to push the door closed. "Then again I haven't seen much of him. Is he all cured?"

Yes, I almost said. *Yes, his rash is gone, thanks to your father's skill which we need now.*

"No, no, no." I clasped my hands together. I felt my insides warming as if I'd been stuck on a cold rock and suddenly the sun appeared. "In fact, I'm glad you mentioned that. Dr. Lee hasn't checked his rash in so long. Too long. He-Seung needs another check." I nodded so vigorously my neck hurt. "Yes, I think that's what he needs."

"Why doesn't your Mother talk to mine, and they can arrange—"

"Mother doesn't—" I stopped. I couldn't say she didn't know about He-Seung's rash. All she'd done for years was mix the urine paste Dr. Lee recommended. "Mother's so busy now with all of us home. With all the visitors from the north. I think she can't worry about He-Seung now."

Myung-Ja let out a small sigh. "I'll talk to Father."

"How soon?" My voice was loud, urgent. "When can Dr. Lee come?"

She opened the door wider, cocking her head, pursing her lips. Her eyes were now creased in concern as if she was trying to decipher my meaning. "Do you think his—uh, this rash—needs immediate attention?"

It was all I could do not to reach out and grab onto her, beg her to get her father now. I stared at her, and nodded once.

"I'll ask Father to go as soon as possible."

"Thank you." I bowed again and again. Then I thought of something. "But wait. He-Seung—he—please don't mention I suggested his rash needed checking."

She raised her eyebrows. "It will be between you and me." She pushed against the door.

As soon as the door shut behind me, I jumped up and down on her front step. Then, despite her caution that I might get fleas, I leaned down and hugged Kwidong close. "We did it, my precious. Dr. Lee is coming."

...Through the years of Japanese oppression we remained unconquered
and undivided. We intend to remain so even at the cost of our lives.
The Allied Powers might as well know that now.
—Syngman Rhee speaking for countrymen at public appearance,
October 1945

Saturday October 20, 1945—next day

He-Seung

I sat out on the front porch, the fall breeze humming in my ear. The
teacher had dismissed us early this morning. While my classmates had
complained that the teacher was slow, unprepared, I was happy to get
home. It felt good to just sit, waiting for Mother or He-Dong, hoping that
Gong-Tae would show up.

He still walked sideways half the time hoping people wouldn't notice
his empty sleeve, still didn't go to school, refused to even talk about
church. Still, Gong-Tae was starting to come out of his shell, he was
starting to be like the old friend I remembered. Miracle of miracles, he had
even offered to come to my house today. He would probably wait until the
cover of darkness. Silly fool.

"He-Seung," a familiar sweet voice called.

I'd dreamed so often of that voice, of being alone with her. But not
now. Not like this.

Myung-Ja climbed the steps, filling the porch with her talcum powder
scent. Two butterflies flew nearby, dancing above her. I pointed to them.
"It's like one won't let the other fall too far."

She looked at my arms and neck and face, as if searching for
something. When I smiled, she looked away, her cheeks turning red. The
butterflies so caught up in their dance bumped against her arm.

"Did they have butterflies in Okinawa?" she asked.

Okinawa. The place felt so far away from the daily bustle of school,
homework, Mother's home cooking. Like some strange dream. I could
remember our barracks, the brown wool cloth always hopping with bed
bugs. I could remember my shovel piercing the airplane hangar. The
strange dream felt so close, my stomach ached. I didn't want to think
more.

"I remember shovels," I offered. I could remember Dae-Hyun's
chipped-tooth smile despite the blood dripping from his legs after the
Allies attacked. "And shit."

She frowned at my words. I didn't know how to talk to her. I looked
down the path, again hoping to see Gong-Tae sidling his way toward us.

"Mother's not here." I sat up, pulling my shirt further down. "She mentioned something about a new group of northerners arriving, helping to do something. Sew probably. Was she supposed to have something ready for you?"

Her eyes turned cold and angry. "No."

"Father's still at—"

"I didn't come to see your mother or your father." She looked at me with such venom, I thought she'd spit. "It looks as though I've been made a fool of. Again. Listening to that runt He-Dong and his foolish hints."

"You're speaking in code." I closed my eyes, taking a deep breath, closing off her angry eyes. "We used to do that."

"We did not."

"In the army," I explained. "I had a good buddy Dae-Hyun. When the Japs were switching this battle plan or that, he would sniff the air and say, "The winds are blowing.""

"Why did he sniff the air?"

I opened my eyes, smiling at the curiosity in her voice. I remembered how she used to ask about why things happened. She knew all kinds of interesting fairytales and strange facts. Golden rays from the sun shone on her, and I was reminded of an angel. I didn't want to talk about Dae-Hyun. He filled my head day and night, and I wanted to push him away for just one moment. But Myung-Ja stood there, head tilted to the side, eyebrows raised. Waiting.

"Dae-Hyun was funny like that." I looked off, as if I could see him in the distance, his eyes begging me not to goad the Commanding Officer. "He swore he could smell the winds of desperation."

"You—" Her eyes filled with tears. "You jerk."

"What?" I sat forward, reaching out to her.

She leapt back. "You think I'm desperate to chase you down at your house? You think you can do better than me, an ugly cow with a scar on her face, the sister of a Japanese comfort woman? You think you're so special 'cause you saved your father from the Japanese prison, and now he's back to being some big minister? Well, let me just tell you. You're nothing but a five-star jerk."

She turned away so abruptly, she lost her balance. She tumbled forward, pitching straight for the steps. I jumped up and grabbed onto her. Pain seared through my abdomen.

"Don't touch me." She regained her balance and pushed against my stomach. "Keep your hero hands to yourself."

I crumpled back into my seat. I saw stars. I closed my eyes, listening to her race down the path, a sob hiccupping from her chest. None of what she'd shouted was true. She was intelligent and humorous and beautiful to me, and I cared about her sister being a comfort woman only because of the pain Myung-Hae must have endured. I wanted to say all of that. But a violent sea churned in my stomach, salt filled my throat.

I took deep breaths, the kind that had seen me through months of laying on the corner of the hospital floor with no anesthesia. With only the daily visits from Dae-Hyun to keep me from going insane with agony.

Today, like Dae-Hyun had always coached, I hadn't worried about my feelings. I hadn't risen to meet Myung-Ja's anger. I hadn't *kicked the stone*. Dae-Hyun had always accused me of doing that. Still the pain in my stomach was so unbearable it was all I could do not to cry out.

I took in another slow breath. As soon as I was sure she was gone, I would go upstairs to my room and lie down. The wound wasn't healing despite what the nurse had promised. I exhaled slowly.

I could still hear Dae-Hyun's voice, as we were driven out to fix the airplane hangar, another punishment job from scumbag Tanaka. *He-Seung? He-Seung? Why do you always kick the stone? It's only you that ends up being hurt.* It was only that day up on the hangar that I'd finally understood his words.

I had been up on the roof with that Jap soldier yelling at me to hurry up, to not throw gravel down near him. I had let myself get so angry I rammed my shovel through a bombed-out portion of the roof which was no thicker than paper. I could still see the world flying by, the grey and the brown and the black. I'd fallen flat on a sharp drainage pipe which stuck up from the ground. I had really *kicked the stone* that day. Now, I put my hand gently over my wound.

"He-Seung?"

I opened my eyes. Myung-Ja stood frozen at the end of the path. Her delicate hands covered her button nose, her sweet lips. Her eyes were wide with confusion.

I'd thought she'd left. I swallowed. "Goodbye." I attempted a wave, my stomach still throbbing. "Hope—hope to see you. In church." I contorted my face into what felt like a smile. My lips trembled.

She came closer, kneeling beside me. She grabbed onto my arm, pulling my hand away from my stomach. "Something's wrong."

"No, no." I patted her hand.

"Don't you say that to me. I'm a doctor's daughter." She reached up and pulled up my shirt. "Oh, dear God."

"It's nothing." I pushed her hand away with more force than I intended. "It looks worse than—"

"I've never seen anything like—" She reached out to grab my shirt again. "Let me get Father."

"No." I wrapped my fingers around her wrist, stopping her investigation. Her skin was tender and warm, and I wished we could just stop this moment. I wished I could hold on like this forever. At the same time, my insides burned, not just with pain, but with the shame of my beautiful Myung-Ja seeing the rubber tube. "It'll be okay."

"Why didn't you say anything?" She pulled away. "You who is always telling Gong-Tae to move on with life, that his wound is not fatal, that there's no shame in relying on friends."

"How do you know all that?" I smiled at her.

"Like I said I'm the doctor's daughter."

I took a long slow breath.

She shook her head. "Dear God. What happened?"

I forced a smile again. "I got lucky."

She frowned. "That doesn't look lucky to me."

"Dae-Hyung and I got—well—punished for my big mouth. We got assigned to work on an airplane hangar. My shovel went through the roof of the hanger and I fell to the ground, landing on a metal pipe."

"You call that lucky?" She crossed her arms tightly around her chest.

I leaned forward, my stomach throbbing. I could still hear Officer Bulldog shouting for the men to move me to the debris pile, to get working, to hurry up. I could feel the warm, sticky liquid oozing from my stomach. I could smell the fear in Dae-Hyung, as his arms trembled beneath me, his voice telling me to *Hold on.*

"It's lucky because Dae-Hyung wouldn't let this bastard—sorry—this cruel bulldog-of-a-soldier haul me to a corner of the field to bleed to death." I closed my eyes. "It's lucky because a doctor stitched me up."

"Isn't that what a doctor's supposed to do?" Her voice was as gentle as the sweet, cool breeze.

"One would think." I could still feel the hands of the medical staff clamped on my legs and arms. The plunge of the needle in my stomach. There was no anesthesia for Korean grunts. I saw pain in red and brown. I felt a rag being stuffed in my mouth before I even had a chance to scream. "Most of the time the doctors only took care of their own."

"Their own?" she asked.

"The Imperial sons. The Japanese." I took a deep breath. "So, I'm lucky because there was no medicine for me, and I was still recovering on the floor of the clinic the following month when the Allies invaded. Most of my squad was killed, including my buddy Dae-Hyung."

"I'm sorry." She rubbed her arms, as if suddenly cold. She stared down at her long fingers. Fingers that had brushed against mine so many times in her backyard. Fingers that could fill me with electricity like I'd never known.

"Father always teaches us about signs from God." I leaned forward. "I figured this was a big sign that I was supposed to come home. To see Mother, Father, He-Chul, He-Dong." I looked up. "And you."

She took a ragged breath. "I'm sorry I doubted you. I'm sorry you're hurt. I'm sorry you went away to the army in the first place. It's all my fault."

She sounded like a worried little He-Dong, the raw pain in her eyes so endearing my heart skipped. I reached up and pushed the hair from her face. "Don't talk nonsense."

"If I had told your mother of your visits to the prison, instead of worrying what she'd think of the two of us talking alone together." Tears streamed down her face. "Maybe she could have stopped you from joining the army."

"Shhh." I grabbed her wrist. "Nobody could have stopped me. I was on fire." I pulled her delicate hand to my lips, kissing her palm. "I'm just glad you're safe. Alive. Sitting here with me this minute." I looked to the railing. "Enjoying the golden butterflies."

"Oh, He-Seung." She grabbed both my hands. Tears rolled down her cheeks. "In my mind, I'm always here with you. I always will be."

I felt the sensation of falling, falling, falling. I let my head fall against her. I breathed in her scent of talcum powder and soap. I was lucky all right. At that moment, there was no luckier man on earth.

There are three things American troops in Japan are afraid of:
diarrhea, gonorrhea, and Ko-rea.
—General John R. Hodge, 1945

Saturday, October 20, 1945—same day

Mother (*Uhmony*)

I pumped the hearth, stoking the fire beneath the stove. The small crackling flames warmed my fingers, sore from a day of sewing dress after dress after dress. Since the end of the war, Jae-Won *uhmony* and I not only sewed for customers at the market, but we had our hands full making dresses for visitors from the north.

He-Dong was in the living room studying and hungry. He-Seung was up in his room, also probably hungry. I put the pot of water on the stove.

At least He-Chul and my dear were still off working. Although He-Chul worked as a philosophy professor at the university, I didn't really understand what he did or why he had to have so many meetings and study sessions. My dear was back to his old self, most of the time. He had been working late every night recently on preparations for next month's All Soul's Day. Our congregation, with the influx of northerners, was so large we'd taken to borrowing Mr. Kang's bench again.

"Those northerners will keep us busy, " Min-Kook *uhmony* had said, giving me a meaningful look as we parted ways this morning.

Our streets overflowed with visitors fleeing from the north, most of them with no place to go. It did keep us busy. But her look had said more.

Recently I found myself trembling at random moments. As if my heart knew something my brain didn't yet understand. I set a pot of water onto the stove. We'd prayed for so many years. At least we had our family, our congregation, our small corner of peace.

What peace? Min-Kook *uhmony*'s doubting voice filled my head.

She'd started walking all the way to my house each morning to pick me up to go to the market. Every day she filled my ears with stories of oxcarts rolling over small children and not stopping to help, of men robbing shoppers at knife-point, of fights breaking out in the government buildings. Every morning, we watched beggars shaking their hands up and down as they went from food seller to food seller asking for a handout, garbage being left to pile up and rot, prices rising by the minute. This morning we had spent half an hour bartering for the last small piece of tofu in the market, and ended up splitting it between us. A two-inch square of tofu to feed my whole family.

"The Lord will provide," I had reminded her.

"I certainly hope so," she said. "Because our own farmers aren't doing the job."

Now I chopped up the small block of tofu, setting the pieces aside to add when the water boiled. I reached over and opened the jar of bean-paste flavoring. We would have a delicious soup to accompany our rice and cabbage.

Out back, Kwidong barked. His chain rattled as he raced across the yard, certainly craning towards the front. I involuntarily tensed. Would it be He-Chul? My dear?

I had a memory of when my dear and I lived with his parents. Every time my dear or my Father-in-Law uttered a word, a disagreement began. Now, our house had become like that.

A gentle knock sounded at the door. Surely just a visitor. I let out a small sigh.

I dropped the tofu into the pot. I heard voices in the front hall. He-Dong, and what sounded like Dr. Lee.

What prompted his visit at this hour? Had he heard news from Myung-Hae? Many of the girls who'd worked in Japanese factories had already returned. With horrible stories. His daughter had not.

Then again, maybe He-Chul's constant absence from church concerned him. People were often asking my dear about He-Chul's whereabouts, his beliefs. I wiped my damp hands on my *cheemar* and went out to greet Dr. Lee.

He stood by the door, his black leather satchel on his arm. He pushed off one dusty shoe, then the other. He-Dong retrieved the shoes and put them on the rack by the door. His eyes followed the doctor's bag. As a child, He-Dong had investigated the contents of that satchel, playing with the metal tongue depressor, scattering the cotton balls, shaking the mercurochrome. It looked as if Dr. Lee had come immediately from another house call. Did he need my dear to pray with a sick parishioner?

"Come in. Come in." I ushered Dr. Lee into the living room. "I'm sorry, but my husband is still at the church."

He gave me an odd look. "I'm here to see He-Seung."

I had watched the way He-Seung acted towards Myung-Ja. He was not inappropriate. Perhaps a bit cold. But surely that wasn't urgent business. "Oh?"

Dr. Lee looked down at his leather bag. "I understand he's unwell."

He-Seung's eyes sometimes wandered off, as if he was seeing something other than what was in the room. I'd heard him cry in the night. I knew he was quieter, more private, as if talking might be too painful. But lots of returning men acted like this. Some were worse. Besides, while Dr.

Lee was good at fixing rashes, I didn't see what he could do about memories. I felt myself blush. "I think he's just a tired soldier."

"Is that all?" Dr. Lee looked back for his shoes. "Well, then—"

A sound erupted from He-Dong, a strangled noise. I felt a funny feeling in my limbs. That trembling sensation. I reached out to steady myself against the door. "Is that all, He Dong?"

"The doctor—" He-Dong stammered. He stuffed his hands in his pockets. "He's come all this way."

"Tell your brother to come down then," I said, gripping tight to the door.

He-Seung made his way down the steps. He-Dong walked in front. Rather than pushing his little brother down the steps, He-Seung seemed to be leaning on him. It struck me that I hadn't seen him bounding down steps like he used to. Hadn't seen him running around at all.

"He-Dong said you needed me." He-Seung said to me as he rested at the bottom. Then he spotted Dr. Lee.

"Dr. Lee stopped by. He seemed to think that you..." I went up close and put my hand out to touch his forehead.

He backed away. He forced a laugh, putting his hands over his stomach. "I'm fine."

"Mother, Can you get Dr. Lee a cup of water?" He-Dong asked.

My little He-Dong. Why was he suddenly acting like the man of the family again? His eyes blinked fast. He looked from Dr. Lee's bag to He-Seung.

"Of course." I hurried into the hall and paused to listen.

"Sit in your father's rocker," Dr. Lee instructed. He didn't offer any of his usual pleasantries. No questions about schoolwork or soccer. "Let's see this thing."

What thing? What did everyone know but me? Had He-Seung gotten himself into man trouble in Japan like many soldiers? Is that why Dr. Lee was so short with him? Is that why they had all seemed eager for me to leave the room?

"It's really nothing." He-Seung said. "I don't understand the fuss."

"Neither do I, but I'll continue not to understand if you don't let me see what we're fussing about. Unbutton your shirt."

I held my breath, stepping close enough to the room that I, too, could see. The sound of the grandfather clock ticked loudly in my ears. He-Seung's fingers shook as he fumbled with his buttons. His chest looked stronger than I'd ever seen it. There wasn't even any sign of his childhood rash. He was fine. Then I spotted the left side of his stomach. I hurried back into the living room.

"Mother." He-Seung grasped at the sides of his shirt, attempting to hide his stomach.

I stared at the volcano that was my son's stomach. A red angry eruption with a tube sticking out. Had I been so absorbed in the church and sewing and keeping peace between He-Chul and my dear that I'd neglected my own child? I held onto the side of my dear's rocker. "What happened?"

"A doctor did this?" Dr. Lee's jaw tightened. His brow furrowed.

He-Seung shrugged his shoulders. His eyes wandered off to that world I couldn't imagine. "I think so."

When? Why didn't he tell me? I leaned forward to ask. He-Dong put pressure on my arm.

"Does that hurt?" Dr. Lee pushed on the redness.

He-Seung took a quick breath. "It's a bit sensitive."

"How about that?" Dr. Lee pushed harder, peering over his glasses at He-Seung.

He-Seung flinched. He pushed back further in the chair. He looked as if he were going to vomit.

"Yes," I said for my son, putting my hand up to stop Dr. Lee's probing fingers.

"Well, I'm glad we found out about this now." Dr. Lee fished in his bag. He removed a small clear vial which he handed to me. He pulled out a cotton ball, dabbed some brown liquid on it and rubbed He-Seung's arm. Then he pulled out a needle.

"What's that for?" He-Dong asked.

Dr. Lee took the vial of liquid from me, sticking the needle into the end of the bottle, sucking out the clear fluid. "Penicillin."

"Ih-Duk told me about that." He-Dong's eyes got wide. "It's the new miracle drug."

"He's right," Dr. Lee said, tapping the needle and flicking a few drops of liquid on the floor. "Smart boy."

Dr. Lee plunged the needle into He-Seung's right arm. He-Seung didn't even flinch. He-Dong however sucked in a big breath.

"He-Dong feels my pain." He-Seung smiled. "He's my voice."

"Well, we all want to hear your voice." Dr. Lee coughed. I assumed Myung-Ja was included in the *we*. "So next time, don't wait so long to get help."

"Yes, sir." He-Seung buttoned his shirt, his fingers trembling.

Dr. Lee took a small brown bottle from his bag. "Rub this on the wound three times a day, and of course each time you use the toilet."

"I have some of that." He-Seung said.

"Whatever you've got wasn't working." Dr. Lee put the brown bottle in He-Seung's hands. "Maybe it was just a knock-off from the black market. Try this."

"Thank you." He-Seung put his feet forward to stand.

"Stay seated, my son." Dr. Lee put his hand on He-Seung's shoulder. "It's been a long couple of years."

He-Dong clapped his brother on the shoulder. "I told him that too."

Dr. Lee nodded to me. I led him into the hallway.

"It appears that when he fell, his urinary tract was severed," Dr. Lee whispered.

When he Fell? Was the tube the place from which my son urinated? What about the rest of his parts down there? I clasped my hands together, blinking fast. *Will he be all right?* I wanted to ask.

How could I have not known there was something wrong with my son? In hindsight, I could see the signs, the shallow laughter, the lack of any desire to run around and play, the careful way he sat down on the floor and got up. Why hadn't I ever asked? *Will he be all right?*

I wanted to run to the church and get my dear. Why wasn't he home, standing nearby so I could lean on him, so he could listen to Dr. Lee's words and make sense of them? *Will he be all right?*

"...cases like this, so perhaps—"

"Pardon me?" I forced myself to hear Dr. Lee's words, to try to understand.

"I said it appears this *doctor* was nothing more than a butcher. But I have a colleague who performed many surgeries during the war. He may have some new techniques which he could use to help He-Seung once this infection clears."

The words echoed through my body. The hall felt unnaturally warm. My mind flashed to the tofu Min-Kook *uhmony* and I had found at the market, now surely burning at the bottom of the soup pot. I dabbed a drop of perspiration from my forehead. "So he will be all right?"

"Don't worry." Dr. Lee nodded. "Nine times out of ten a shot of antibiotics is all it takes. But keep him home for now."

"Yes. Of course. Thank you." I closed my eyes. *Thank you, God.*

"And we can worry about the other—the other issues later."

Other issues. I bowed with deep gratitude to Dr. Lee, a tear rolling down my cheek. I inhaled the scorching scent of bean-paste and tofu. There weren't any other issues as long as my boy was all right.

The difficulty of applying right and left to Korean politics in 1945-1950
is that virtually all factions represented some elements of both positions.
American officers and diplomats observed that all Koreans were
Communists, by which they meant that all Koreans, wanted
revolutionary changes to occur in all or most aspects of Korean political
and economic life.
—Allan R. Millett, Historian

Sunday, October 28, 1945—six days later

He-Seung

I stood in the entrance while He-Dong tied my shoes. I could hear my elder brother's voice inside my head. *Self-sufficiency is the highest class one can achieve. Tie your own damn shoes.* Fortunately he and father were engaged in a whispered debate.

"Where are you two going?" Mother came into the hall, holding a tray full of goodies. Ever since Dr. Lee's visit, she had been watching me as if I were a toddler just learning to walk. "I was bringing you some honey water."

He-Dong saw the treat and frowned. "He-Seung promised to go to the park with me."

"Dear," Mother called out. "Dear? Did you know this? They're—He-Seung is going to the park."

Father came into the hallway, He-Chul on his heels. I felt a strange thrill. To think they were so concerned about me that they'd interrupted their debate about the future of Korea.

"That park has turned into a garbage heap." He-Chul gave a disgusted grunt. "Another gift from our incompetent leadership."

Father nodded his head in false agreement. "Your brother's right."

He-Dong and I exchanged a look. In the last few days, Father had forced himself to find common ground with He-Chul, to keep peace in the house until I recovered.

He-Chul shook his head. "You'd think after months—"

"The Americans haven't been here for months." Father hissed, despite himself. "The war has just barely ended."

I bit my cheek to keep from smiling. Their peace never lasted long, despite Father's efforts.

"Well, it seems they've been here long enough to fix things, if they were planning on it." He-Chul put his hand out to count the problems. "But the sewage is still a mess, the mail never arrives, the black market's eating us alive, the electricity turns on and off at random times." He looked at He-Dong and I. "And that park? The homeless northerners have ruined it. It's not a place you want to wander, comrades."

Father flinched at that word. *Comrades.* He hated when He-Chul insisted we were all equal even if, as of course He-Chul pointed out, the Bible said the same thing.

I let my gaze fall on the cups of honey water Mother held up as a peace offering. A drop of liquid ran down the side of one of the metal cups. I could taste the sweetness.

He-Dong cleared his throat. I knew what he was thinking. He'd been asking me for days, ever since I'd gotten that shot of miracle medicine, to go somewhere with him. I was sure he wanted proof that I was going to be okay now. I kind of did, too.

"I haven't been to the park in years." I put my hand on He-Dong's shoulder, pushing him out the door. "Soon it will be too cold to go."

The autumn air felt welcoming, caressing my skin. I stopped every few steps to appreciate the cold smell. To catch my breath. Perhaps I'd been resting too much.

"Is the pond too far?" He-Dong looked back toward the house. "We could just get Kwidong and take him for a short walk in front of our house."

"No, no." I took a deep breath. "This is wonderful."

Those words echoed in my head, wrapping around me like an old friend. *This moment is wonderful.* I heard Dae-Hyung saying the same thing on a scorching day in Okinawa when we escaped to the beach. We lay there in the shallow waters, feeling the sand scrape our backs, letting the cool water hold us up like a pair of invisible hands.

"Are we going then?" He-Dong nudged my arm.

I shook the memories away. "And when we get home, there will be honey water waiting for us."

"He-Chul might drink it all." He-Dong looked back over his shoulder.

"That wouldn't be the fair thing to do." I imitated He-Chul's stern voice, rubbing my hand thoughtfully on my chin.

"Yeah, well he might forget about all that." He-Dong frowned.

"Not our dear brother," I protested. But I could see He-Dong wondering if He-Chul would really be fair and selfless when two extra cups of honey water sat right before him. "Think of it as an experiment. Fairness versus desire. Which will win?" I leaned on him. "This could be interesting."

He nodded. "Ih-Duk would certainly think so."

"Where is that nerd?" I found myself counting steps. Four. Five. I would take a rest at ten. "I haven't seen him—"

"He's an idiot." He-Dong's face got dark.

I thought of Gong-Tae. How he still refused to go outside unless it was dark because he was so concerned what people thought. How he sat at home and brooded over the Japanese, convincing himself they were more and more evil.

"Most friends are." I paused catching my breath. "But that doesn't mean he's not your friend."

He-Dong lowered his head, rubbing his arms as if suddenly chilled. A gnat flew near his neck, and he swatted so hard I was sure he'd put a hole in his flesh. He gave me a triumphant smile, pulling his hand back. A flattened bug decorated his skin. He flicked at the crumpled bug.

Wasn't that what we all were? Bugs crumpled by one enemy after another? I remembered the day the Allies came through Okinawa. The ocean was so full of our blood it looked like melted red-bean ice cream. I paused, grabbing onto my head, as if I could push the images away. I thought time would make the memories disappear. But these days, every breath took me back to Okinawa.

"Did you want to go there instead?" He-Dong asked, a note of hope in his voice that all my stopping and starting was just shyness.

I realized we stood at the crossroads to Myung-Ja's home. Of course I wanted to stop and visit. I glanced down the path, doing a mental calculation of the steps to her place. Ten steps, then a pause. Another ten steps, a memory. At least three more rest stops worth. I remembered a time when I thought nothing of racing to the park, leaving He-Dong to do laps while I hurried back to visit Myung-Ja.

"No." I pretended I'd just changed my mind. "Let's go to the park."

Myung-Ja had been by every day. She brought me *kimchee* and soup and a small pillow with two embroidered butterflies. Each time she was with me felt like just a second passing on the clock. A moment that went by so fast I couldn't hold onto the happiness before being covered in a blanket of pain and darkness.

"When is she going to come live at our house?" He-Dong blushed.

It was all so simple in He-Dong's little head. No concern that I hadn't even graduated high school, that I had no job, that I had a rubber tube sticking out of my stomach and a head full of bad memories. He saw our happiness and thought we should be together under one roof. "Well, there's always the matter of He-Chul. He should marry first."

He-Dong stared ahead. "He's always going to this meeting or that meeting. When does he have time to worry about girls? Or us?"

"He's just busy, is all." I remarked, thinking not of He-Chul, but of Father. Of the times I'd come home with a new story from school, a new idea. I would be talking so fast the words jammed together and I'd look up to see Father turning a page in his bible, not listening to a word. "He's kind of like Father."

"At least Father is busy doing important work." He-Dong's voice was filled with adult-like disdain.

I pulled on his arm, acting as if I were trying to emphasize the point, but really needing to rest again. "Isn't organizing New Korea important?"

"Why can't someone else do that?" He-Dong gestured to the world in front of us. "Besides if he ends up in hell, what difference will all his New Korea ideas make?"

He was worried that He-Chul never made time for church. My bright little brother still thought sitting in a building made a difference. "Do you know what hell is?"

"Of course." He stood straighter. "It's a mile-long track paved with red hot coals where sinners are condemned to walk, back and forth. They scream and cry, but nobody stops to save them."

I paused. We were almost at the park. Almost.

"Isn't it?" He-Dong looked up at me.

"Maybe." I sighed. "But sometimes when Father and Brother are arguing so fiercely and the spittle is flying, the tea cups are rattling—"

"The roof is trembling," He Dong added.

"Those times, I think what difference does it make who, what or where God is? I'm in hell already."

He-Dong laughed. An eruption. The first laugh I'd heard from him in days. Then he quickly put his hand over his mouth, as if his feelings were sinful.

I grabbed that hand. I wanted him to step firmly on the earth, to laugh out loud, to shout at the top of his lungs, to not be so afraid of his every move. "Go on, bean-curd. Laugh."

"I'm not a bean-curd."

We walked further. Three steps, four, five. I could hear Dae-Hyung's voice calling me from the bottom bunk, telling me to stop tossing and turning, that all that rustling around wouldn't make it any cooler, wouldn't shoo the bed bugs away. "Dae-Hyung always called me bean-curd."

"Did you pop him one?" He-Dong had his fists clenched.

"No." In fact I'd give anything to hear him say those words. "I decided it's not such a bad thing."

He-Dong pointed out the park to me, as if to tell me we'd made it, and please not to pause again. "What do you mean?"

"Think of it like this. You're tough on the outside, but you're sensitive and understanding on the inside."

He-Dong rolled his eyes at me. Then he stopped walking, staring at the park entrance. "Oh, geez."

"I guess dear old Brother was right again." I followed his gaze. The park was littered with broken dishes, burnt wood, fish bones, dirty rags, torn newspapers. "A garbage pit."

"Even the pond is ruined." He-Dong brushed his hands on his pants, as if he could get rid of the dirtiness. We stared at the pond. Several naked children laughed and splashed, shivering from their cold bath. Their mothers sat on the rocks, washing clothes. Visitors from the north.

"I think we should go back home." He-Dong sighed, looking back the way we'd come.

"This place is home, too." I pointed out a tiny purple flower, poking its six perfect petals out in defiance. "You slipped on that rock there. Gong-Tae and I had a mud-pie fight over there. You shot the sling—"

"I know. I know." He-Dong heaved another sigh. "But I'm talking about the place with four walls and a dog. I mean that home."

"There's magic in that word, you know." I headed for the pond, ignoring He-Dong's frown. "The sound of Mother humming off-key. The smell of *kimchee* and barbecued beef." I licked my lips. "I can't count the times I lay on my cot dreaming of home."

He-Dong frowned as a mother hung her laundry to dry on the branches of one of the Rose of Sharon bushes. "Maybe we should check on our honey water experiment."

I looked away, considering the long journey back. I don't know why I'd insisted we come so far. I felt like I needed a day's rest before making the trek home.

"Let's just sit a while," I patted his shoulder, leading him to a large rock and holding onto his arm as I lowered myself to the ground. "You know." I indicated for him to take off one of my shoes, then the other. "Gong-Tae and I found a garter snake beneath this rock once. Then we argued over who spotted it first. Who got to keep it. While we were yelling, the snake slithered away."

"What did you do?" He-Dong remained standing.

"I gave him a fat lip." I nodded. "He deserved it." I rolled up my pant legs. "That was my snake, and he knew it."

"Then how—" He-Dong hunched down next to me and peeled off my socks. "How did you become friends again?"

"Father gave a sermon about how all creatures belong to God. That nothing is ours. I realized what a fool I was."

He-Dong's mouth hung open so wide, I could have tossed a pebble inside. I let my hand drag across the ground, scooping up a handful. It was tempting.

"I'm kidding." I dropped the pebbles. "When winter time rolled around and you started crying that I had stolen your snow—*your snow*—that made me realize how dumb the snake thing was. Besides, I missed playing with him."

"So what did you do?" He held his breath.

I realized we weren't talking about my friend anymore. Perhaps that's why I hadn't seen Ih-Duk around all week.

"You just apologize." I looked over and smiled. I dipped my toes in the water. "Ahh, delicious." The cool water caressed my feet. "We should bring Father and He-Chul next time. This is heaven right here."

He-Dong looked at the water. His lips were curled in disgust. "You're different."

"Oh, yeah?" I smiled. "So are you, Bean-curd. So are you."

He stiffened at his nickname. "Should we go now?"

I heard Dae-Hyung's voice asking me the same thing the day we had snuck to the beach. We would get in trouble, he said. We'd end up doing latrine duty til we died. We wouldn't get dinner. We'd have to stand up all night long. *Soldier* we heard a voice calling. *Soldier.* It was a Korean woman, searching the shore, looking out to the ocean. We hadn't seen women for so long, we stared. And we had never once been called soldiers.

She was looking for her friend, she had gulped. Her friend was missing. Had we seen her? She bombarded us with so many questions we didn't get to ask any. What part of Korea was she from? Why was she here? Could she call us that name again? *Soldier?*

"He-Seung?' He-Dong tapped my shoulder. His eyes were wide with alarm. "I can't hear you. What are you saying? Something about a soldier?"

If I could just sit a moment without my mind wandering. Dr. Lee said he could make my stomach better, but who would mend my head? I put my hands to my head, trying to clear it.

"I was giving a whispered order." I looked around, pretending I knew what I was doing. "Didn't you get it? Your target is situated at two o'clock."

He raised his head and looked to the right. There was nothing there except a Rose of Sharon bush, its branches dripping with laundry.

"You brought your slingshot?" He leaned forward, his eyes already aiming rocks at the pants and shirts hanging there. Not stopping his barrage of fire until the branches were bare and our Rose of Sharon bush was lovely again.

"Something better." I took my pocketknife from my pants. "We just need a small branch." I opened the blade for him. "Then we can start our own Rose of Sharon bush for Mother."

He-Dong looked over at the bathers and then up at the bush. He stabbed the knife in the dirt beside him, again and again. "I shouldn't have to do that, scrambling among the bushes, and pushing through dirty socks and undies for what used to be naturally part of our home."

"What are you rambling on about?" I rubbed my forehead with the tips of my fingers.

"Maybe if we'd obeyed God more, He might have let us keep our own country….our own flowers." He stabbed the ground again. "And He would have kept you safe, too."

Surely my intelligent little brother didn't think that the war and all our miseries were God's punishment for us not being good people. Then again, he thought He-Chul was in danger of hell for not attending church. I leaned toward him, stilling the knife in his hand. "Some things you can't stop, even by being good."

"I hate them." He said the words so softly I thought I'd imagined it. "I've never felt this kind of burning feeling." He looked at me. "Well, I did once—when you were gone and the Japs—the Japanese took our house. I wanted more than anything to ruin all of their things. But that was nothing compared to now. I feel like the hate seeps out of my pores. Can you see it?"

"You sound as bad as Gong Tae." I poked him. "I just see a skinny boy whose all brains. You shouldn't waste that."

"My skinny body?"

"No, fool." I sighed. "Your brains. Like Dae-Hyung always told me 'Don't waste your energy kicking the stone.'"

He-Dong stabbed at the earth again. "What's going to happen?"

"Who knows?" I said. "As long as the two sides of our country are negotiating, we'll be fine. It's when they build armies that we need to—

"I mean with you." He-Dong looked up at me. "You're not getting better, are you?"

"Are you planning to tell Myung-Ja?"

"I don't need to," He-Dong shot back. "Mother's watching."

I looked from left to right, as if she might be coming to find us. I smiled at him. "You know, I never thought to confide in you about this…this issue. I thought you were too young. You surprised me. You're more intelligent than most men—"

"Aren't you afraid?" His voice was small.

"Not with you by my side." I nudged him. I put my hand on his arm. "It doesn't matter…that fear stuff. What matters is being full of fear and still moving forward."

"So you're scared, too?" He looked down at the ground fast, but not before I saw his eyes filling with tears.

I wished I could stop his sadness. That I could hold out a bright future with both of us standing in it. But I was nervous that the miracle medicine wasn't working, and that the last thing I wanted to do was stand up to make the long walk home. I let my feet sink back into the delicious water.

"Actually, my biggest fear is that you're not going to cut the branch right." I gave him a shove. "Now get your skinny little butt over to the bush before the sun sets."

Southern Korea can best be described as a powder keg
ready to explode at the application of a spark.
—**General Hodges, Military Commander of South Korea**

Thursday, November 1, 1945—four days later

He-Dong

"Hello?" I used my key to open the front door. Standing in the entry, I listened for Mother. She should have heard Kwidong barking at me. She should have come running from the kitchen to tell me how He-Seung was doing. She should have sensed I was bursting with news.

Yesterday, she'd walked with He-Seung to the hospital. This morning she had gone again to bring him food, to care for him after the operation which Dr. Lee's friend had done. I'd wanted to come, too, but He-Seung had insisted we go about our business.

He-Chul had gone off to his university and a study session. Father had gone to church to finish his All Soul's Day sermon for tonight's special service. I'd gone to school.

"Mother?" I looked down to the shoe rack. Her shoes were gone. Where was she?

I sat down in the living room to work on my writing lesson, the extra lesson the teacher had given me as a punishment for daydreaming. I had wanted to tell her I'd only been praying. Praying He-Seung would get better fast and hurry home. Praying that even after He-Seung got better, Father and He-Chul would still not argue. Praying that the rumors that the Republic of Korea's Army was recruiting 6th year high school students was a mistake.

I took out the book and stared at it, thinking of how He-Seung had said *As long as the two sides of our country are negotiating, we'll be fine. It's when they build armies that we need to worry.* I wondered if his operation had hurt, if they snipped off the red tube, if he'd be able to take a wee like the rest of us now. I wondered if he would join the army again.

Kwidong barked, alerting me that Mother was home. I raced to open the door as footsteps sounded on the porch. Myung-Ja stood at the door in her Sunday dress.

"He-Dong." Myung-Ja smiled. But her eyes looked worried. "I thought we should go visit the hospital."

"He-Seung said—"

"I know." She held up her hands. "But today this is our usual business."

I liked Myung-Ja. She made me feel capable and strong.

"Wait a minute." I went upstairs to He-Seung's room and grabbed the small pillow she'd embroidered for him.

We climbed the steps to the hospital and went through the glass doors. The lobby was crowded and dark. People stood around talking, laughing, smoking, eating. I was reminded of the train station, except over the smell of rice and chili was the smell of that medicine He-Seung had been rubbing on his wound. In the corner, a lady with a white cap on her head studied her clipboard.

I turned to Myung-Ja. "How will we ever find him?"

"You wait here." She put her hand on my arm before going off to talk to the lady in white.

I stood next to the door, hugging the pillow. A man limped up the steps. I held the door for him. His feet had dirty bandages. Blood seeped through near the toes. I felt my lips curl.

"Thank you." The man spoke with a northern accent. He rested against the door. "Where do I find the nurse?"

I pointed in the direction I'd seen the lady with the white cap. Myung-Ja was no longer with her. "I saw one over there."

I watched him limp away. Had he walked all the way from the north, and that was why his feet got like that? Was the north really such a bad place to be?

I thought again of the army men I'd seen walking on the street to the high school. How many students had volunteered? Was the north making an army, too? Would the two sides of our country really fight each other?

I felt the door bang against me again. A man came through the entrance holding onto his arm, an empty sleeve. I lifted my hand to point out the nurse and stopped, incredulous. It was Gong-Tae. He never came outside during the day—not to school, not to market, not even to church.

"How is he?" Gong-Tae asked. "You know, I had no idea there was anything wrong with him—"

"Dr. Lee says he'll be fine." My voice sounded loud.

Gong-Tae patted me on the arm before walking down the hall. His talking made me nervous. I wished Myung-Ja would hurry back.

"He-Dong?" Ih-Duk came through the door, his rucksack on his back. "I heard people talking about He-Seung on the way home from school." He stared at his scuffed shoes. "But I figured you'd tell me if he was sick."

I would have told him, if he hadn't been so convinced He-Seung was an alien. If he hadn't been such an idiot. *All friends are idiots. That doesn't mean he's not your friend.*

"Power must be out." Ih-Duk glanced up at the ceiling, at the dark bulbs dangling. "Either that or all their light bulbs went dead at the same time."

"Or they don't use the lights in the daytime." I heard the argument in my voice.

"Who knows?" Ih-Duk looked around at the old man smoking a pipe in the corner, the family hovering over a child with a gash on his face, the desk where the nurse sat. "I've never been here before."

I never had either. Mother had told me we were blessed to have such a dear friend in Dr. Lee, as most people didn't get to come to the hospital. I was going to say this, but it seemed a little too friendly for someone like Ih-Duk who'd insisted I give my brothers an alien test. I felt an invisible wall between Ih-Duk and me. Part of me wanted to reach past that wall, for things to be the same between us. *All you do is apologize,* I remembered He-Seung saying. "There sure are a lot of injured—"

"These people aren't injured." He shook his head.

"Oh, yeah?" I crossed my arms. Here I'd almost made the mistake of apologizing. "Why else would they be here?"

He pointed to the man with the bloody feet, now seated and smoking a cigarette as a nurse spoke to him. "Well, maybe some of them are." Then, he pointed out Gong-Tae and a group of guys. "But, those are your brother's friends. Look at their school uniforms. The short one, he's the one I heard talking on the road near the high school about He-Seung. They're probably here to help your brother go home."

Help your brother go home. My insides felt funny. Myung-Ja had been gone too long.

"Maybe we should find him." Ih-Duk said what I was thinking.

"I'm sorry," I put my hand out, thinking to grab onto his arm.

Ih-Duk stepped back, as if I'd burned him. "I don't have to come. I just thought—"

"I mean—" I took a deep breath. I stuck my hand in my pocket. "I'm sorry. About, you know—that day."

"Oh, that. I know, I know." With one hand, he pointed me in the direction of the nurse. With the other, he held up a chocolate bar. "I brought you something."

I raised my eyebrows. "Another souvenir from the U.S. Army?"

"Yeah." He laughed. "I can read those words now."

"My eldest brother says it's a waste of valuable resources for the U.S. army to airlift sweets." I already imagined the smooth sweet taste of the treat on my tongue. Perhaps I'd even convince He-Seung to try some.

"Well I'm glad they waste their resources on us." He pushed the bar into my hands.

We walked by a lady holding a baby, an old man trying to walk with two sticks under his arms, two boys fighting over who got the bigger portion of a rice cake. "Speaking of armies..."

"Can you believe it? Asking for volunteers from the high school?" Ih-Duk said. "It's just like the war."

"He-Seung said that building armies is a bad sign."

Ih-Duk frowned. "I wonder what the Storybag men are saying."

"Min-Kook *uhmony* told Mother that both sides want the same thing: for us to be a whole country again. They just can't agree on what kind of government will rule the whole country. The Russians want the northerners to have a Communist government. The Americans want us to have a Democratic government."

"What's the difference?" Ih-Duk asked.

I shrugged. "Big enough to fight over."

I felt tiny pin-pricks around my heart. Ih-Duk and I were talking. As if the last thirteen days of ignoring one another had never happened. I couldn't wait to tell He-Seung.

The nurse directed us to the second floor. Ih-Duk and I grabbed Gong-Tae on our way up the steps. Just as in the lobby, upstairs there were lots of people milling around the hallways, smoking and eating, lots of children playing on the floor. One boy played fetch with his dog.

There were lots of rooms on the second floor. A man with his foot propped on pillows. An old lady with half her face burned. A man with a bandage on his head. We hurried from room to room.

"Maybe the nurse told us the wrong directions." Ih-Duk looked back.

"He's got to be here somewhere." I kept moving forward.

At the end of the hallway, I heard Mother. She wasn't humming. We followed her voice.

He-Seung's room was small and dark. Mother and Myung-Ja stood next to his bed, their heads bowed. He lay flat, sleeping.

"Please keep my child from suffering." Mother prayed. "He gave everything so that his Father would rejoin us and the community, so that Your word would spread."

"Hey, buddy." Gong-Tae moved forward, patting He-Seung's covered legs. "Finally figured out a way to drag me outside."

"I thought Dr. Lee's friend was going to make He-Seung better." I clutched tight to the embroidered pillow. "He looks—he looks worse."

Myung-Ja came over and put her arm on my shoulder. Her body trembled. "The electricity went off during the operation. The doctor couldn't finish everything. He-Seung just needs to hold on until the power comes back."

Mother put her head down and continued praying. "He is but a small candle lighting the path so that Your glory will remain forever and ever. Please keep his flame burning."

"Stop this." I went to the window and pulled the drapes open. "You're all just confusing him. Making him think that he's a tired weakling."

Outside stood a cherry blossom tree, one which hadn't been chopped down yet to make way for Korea's national Rose of Sharon. It was dead. Its branches bare.

"Mother?" He-Seung's deep voice hugged us all.

"Oh, He-Seung." Mother sobbed. "Thank God."

"I knew we just needed some light in here." I turned to my brother, expecting him to sit up and stretch, ask for his shoes, say he was ready to go home and would come back another day for this operation.

His eyes were still closed. He lifted his arm. His pale fingers reached over and touched Mother's cheek. Mother grabbed onto his hand, her tears dripping all over him.

"I'm here, too, Brother." I patted his covers. I put the embroidered pillow under his arm. Next to his grey skin, the colorful butterflies looked too bright. "So are Gong-Tae and Myung-Ja. And Ih-Duk brought us chocolate." I leaned close to his ear, whispering. "I did what you said and we're friends again."

A faint smile filled his features. He lay silent for so long I thought he'd gone back to sleep. "My bean-curd."

I didn't mind him calling me that. It was a cool nickname. I'd ask him to call me that from now on.

"Does the light hurt your eyes?" Myung-Ja turned to close the curtains.

"No." He put his hand out. His eyes fluttered open. "Stay."

"I'm not leaving." Myung-Ja stepped closer.

He turned his head, slowly, as slowly as Father had when he was sick. "Father? He-Chul?"

"They should be here soon." Mother patted his arm. "But you know them."

How could Father and He-Chul be too busy to be here? I swallowed a burning sensation in my throat. "Lots of your friends are downstairs waiting for you."

He looked at each one of us, slowly, as though memorizing our features. "Precious."

Of course. Kwidong—our precious. He-Seung wanted to rub Kwidong's soft fur. "I'm sorry I forgot him. You'll get to see him when you come home, though."

He-Seung waved his hand at us. "This is."

Myung-Ja let out a sob. "Yes. This is precious."

They weren't talking about my dog.

Mother reached out and grabbed Myung-Ja's hand. She put her long thin fingers on top of He-Seung's hand. Then she pulled Gong-Tae forward and placed his hand on the bottom of He-Seung's. Ih-Duk stepped closer and added his hand to the pile. I wriggled my fingers inside what was now a ball of hands—Mother's cold one, Myung-Ja's small one, Ih-Duk's sticky one, Gong-Tae's only one, He-Seung's hot one. I envisioned Kwidong's paw on top of our pile.

"Dear Lord, please protect our boy." Mother prayed.

"Amen," Myung-Ja and I said.

Gong-Tae and Ih-Duk remained silent.

"Faith…" He-Seung stared at Gong-Tae. "is precious, too."

Gong-Tae shook his head. He glanced down at his empty sleeve.

"Amen?" Ih-Duk tried.

"Amen," Gong-Tae mumbled. His eyes were wet.

He-Seung squeezed our fingers. Then he sighed again, this time so loud the noise would have lifted the roof off of our house. I laughed, ready to tease him. But his hand went limp.

"Dear Lord, please no." Mother put her hand on his cheek.

"He-Seung?" Myung-Ja tapped his shoulder. She doubled forward as if she'd been punched in the stomach.

Gong-Tae grabbed He-Dong's arm, shaking it up and down. "You can't tell me to have faith and then check out."

He-Seung didn't react, his face as peaceful as if he'd just fallen asleep again. Where was God? Why had he abandoned us?

Outside, a wind picked up. The branches of the dead cherry blossom tree slapped against the window. *A flower blooms alone, destined to die alone.* I remembered my second-grade teacher lecturing to us in front of the Shinto Shrine. Telling us that when a soldier died, his family would get a card saying, *The cherry blossom has fallen.*

But those Japs had it wrong. He-Seung wouldn't be like a single blossom, dying alone. Mother would die. Myung-Ja would die. Gong-Tae, Ih-Duk and all of his good friends waiting for him would die. And me.

It's about being full of fear and still moving forward.

"No, Brother, please." I lay my head on his chest, already feeling a giant gash in my heart, feeling a bitter wind whipping up inside me. "Don't leave."

Down the hall, two men argued with one another. Father and He-Chul. They pushed their way into the room, getting stuck in the small doorway as they both tried to enter first. They were too late anyway.

Our perfect circle of a family had shattered.

Our perfect country had split in two.

How would I ever manage to sweep up these precious pieces?

TIMELINE OF WWII

Aug 22, 1910:	Japan seizes Korea
1931:	Japan seizes Manchuria, China, and converts it into the Japanese state *Manchukuo*
1932-1945:	Japan conscripts 200,000 Asian women and European POWS to serve as sex slaves.

1937

July 7:	Japan invades Beijing, China. Start of second Sino-Japanese war
July 28:	Japan seizes Beijing, China
July 30:	Japan seizes Tianjin, China
Aug 8- Nov 9:	Japan seizes Shanghai, China
August 25:	Japan uses navy to block the southern Chinese coast
Sept-Nov:	Japan invades northern China, gaining control of 5 cities
Sept 5:	Japan sets up a naval blockade of all of China with exception of Tsingtao, Hong Kong, Macau & Guangzhou
Nov:	Japan invades Yangtze region, seizes Suzhou, China
Dec 13:	Japan seizes Nanking, China. Over 300,000 Chinese killed in *Rape of Nanking*.
Dec 24-27:	Japan seizes Hangzhou and Jihan, China

1938

Jan 10:	Japan seizes port of Tsingtao, China
Mar 6:	Japan launches Yellow River Campaign
May-June 12:	Japan seizes port of Xiamen and number of key Chinese cities
July-Aug 10:	Japan and Soviet forces clash.
Sept 27:	League of Nations declares Japan an *Aggressor Nation*
Oct 21:	Japan seizes Canton, China
Oct 25:	Japan seizes Wuhan, China
Nov:	Japan announces *New Order* in Asia.

1939

Feb 10:	Japan occupies Hainan, China, gaining control over southern Chinese coast

| June 14 | Japan sets up blockade at Port of Tianjin |
| Nov: | Japan advances into south China, cutting off Chinese communication with French Indo-China |

1940

| Sept 22: | Japan invades Vietnam (a French Commonwealth country) |
| Sept 27: | Japan signs Tripartite Pact with Germany & Italy, entering military alliance known as the *Axis* |

1941

June 25:	Japan invades French Indo-China
Dec 7:	Japan attacks Pearl Harbor (Hawaii), Wake Island, Midway Island
Dec 8:	US Declares War against Japan; Japan invades British Malay Peninsula and Siam (Thailand)
Dec 10:	Japan invades Philippines
Dec 11:	Japan invades Burma
Dec 13:	Japan seizes Guam
Dec 15:	Japan invades British Borneo
Dec 20:	British declare war against Japan
Dec 25:	Japan seizes British Hong Kong

1942

Jan 1-26:	UN signs Declaration against *Axis*
Jan2-May 6:	Japan invades Philippines, seizes Manila
Jan 11-Mar 9:	Japan seizes Dutch E. Indies (Indonesia)
Feb 8-May 2:	Japan invades Burma (Myanmar)
February 15:	Japan seizes British Singapore
March 8:	Japan seizes Rangoon, Burma (Myanmar)
March 8:	Japan invades New Guinea with the goal of establishing a base of operations in Australia
April 9:	Japan seizes Bataan Peninsula, Philippines
April 12-24:	Japanese force 75,000 American and Filipino POWs to march 60 miles to prison camps.
April 18:	*Doolittle Raid*, the first US air raid on Tokyo
May 4-8:	*Battle of the Coral Sea*—Allied forces sink 100,000 tons of Japanese ships between New Guinea and the Solomon islands. Considered major turning point.

May 5:	Chinese General Chiang Kai-Shek leads troops in offensive against Japan, striking 7 cities
May 6:	Japan seizes Corregidor Island, gaining control of the Philippine Islands
June 4-7:	Japan attempts to seize strategic island of Midway in the central Pacific. Allies are victorious.
June 12:	Japan seizes Attu Island, beginning of Aleutians offensive
Aug 7:	US lands on Tulagi and seizes control of Japanese airfields at Guadalcanal
Aug 9:	Battle of Savo Island
Aug 13:	Roosevelt starts *Manhattan Project*, the development of atomic bomb
Aug 24:	Battle of East Solomons
Sep 29-Oct 10:	Australians operating from Port Moresby launch successful counter-offensive against Japanese
Oct-Oct '43:	Japanese Army constructs a military railway across the Burma-Siam border to get supplies to the army. To build the railway (an estimated 5-year project honed to 8 months) the Japanese use the forced labor of an estimated 60,000 Allied POWS and 180,000 conscripted Asian laborers. Known as *The Death Railway,* an estimated 16,000 Allies and 49,000 forced laborers die.

1943

Jan 16:	Iraq declares war on *Axis*
Jan 20:	Chili severs ties with Japan
Jan 23-Oct 3:	Allies capture airfield Salamua, N. G.
Mar 24-Aug 15	Allies defect Japanese at Komandorski islands in W.A. Alieutians, recapture Attu, recapture Kiska
June 30:	Allies land on Rendova Island, gain control of central Solomon Islands
Aug 7:	Allies capture Munda base
Nov 2:	Allies defeat Japanese at Bougainville
July 5:	Japan gives Thailand 6 Malay states
Aug-Dec:	Allies launch offensive from India to Burma (Myanmar)
Nov 21-24:	Allies secure Tarawa island

| Dec 1: | CAIRO DECLARATION: President Roosevelt, President Chiang Kai-Shek and Prime Minister Churchill announce their joint determination to force Japan to surrender unconditionally. Japan would be deprived of all land seized since 1914 and Korea would become a free and independent nation. |

1944

Jan 31:	Allies launch amphibious assaults on Marshall Islands. US gains control of Central Pacific.
Mar 1-Apr 24	Allied New Guinea offensive
Mar 15-Aug 22	Japan invades India, then retreats
May 17-Aug 3	Allied Burma offensive, Allies capture Myitkina
July:	First use of Napalm , Mariana islands
Aug 11:	Allies recapture Guam, liberate India
Oct 5:	Japan seizes last Chinese port of Fuzhou
Oct-Jun '45:	US offensive in Philippines. Allies destroy Imperial Navy.
Sept-Nov:	Japan loses Battle of Peleliu
Nov-Aug '45:	Allied firebombing of Tokyo, hundreds of thousands of casualties, destruction of 50% of the city

1945

Jan 9-July 5:	Allied Philippine offensive
Feb 5-23:	Allies regain Manila, Philippines
Feb 4-11:	YALTA Conference. President Roosevelt, Prime Minister Churchill and Premier Stalin agree on post-war terms. If the Soviets declare war against Japan, they will receive an *occupation zone* in Korea
Feb -Mar 17	Allies invade Iwo Jima, 750 miles south of Tokyo
March 21:	Allies invade Japan home waters, destroy Japanese Imperial Navy and 450 aircraft
Apr 1-Jun 21	Battle of Okinawa. Allies victorious.
July 5:	American seizes control of most of Philippines, except Palawan
July 26:	Potsdam Declaration: President Truman, Prime Minister Churchill, and President Chiang Kai-Shek

	issue statement demanding Japan surrender unconditionally or face *prompt and utter destruction.*
July 29:	Japanese reject demands for surrender
Aug 6:	US drops atomic bomb on Hiroshima, Japan
Aug 8:	Soviets declare war on Japan
Aug 9:	US drops atomic bomb on Nagasaki, Japan
Aug 14:	Japan surrenders
Aug 15:	End of World War II in the Pacific
Aug 28:	US occupies Japan
Sept:	Japanese government and military destroy documents relating to their wartime crimes. Japanese Education Ministry issues ban on wartime textbook material.
Sept 2:	Formal Japanese surrender. Korea placed under American and Soviet occupation, pending the establishment of Korean government.
Sept 9:	Japan surrenders southern half of Korea to the US and northern half to the Soviet Union

Fate of countries or major cities Japan occupied during war:

Burma:	Returned to British rule, gained independence by 1948.
Hong Kong:	Returned to British rule, gained independence in 1997.
India:	England relinquished rule and divided the country between India and Pakistan.
Indonesia:	Returned to Dutch rule, fought and gained independence by 1948.
Malaysia:	Returned to British rule, gained independence by 1946.
Philippines:	Gained independence in 1946 with agreement US could keep military bases there.
Singapore:	Returned to British rule, gained independence in 1965.
Chinese cities:	Returned to Chinese. Taiwan split off to become independent nation, October 1949.
Korea:	Japan surrendered rule to the Allies who divided the country between the Soviets and the United States. The country remains divided.

Chapter Openings

Japan has done... Tolischus, Otto D., *Through Japanese Eyes*, Otto D Tolischus, Cornwall, New York: Cornwall Press, 1945, page 146.

As the 1930s ... Ambrose, Hugh. *The Pacific.* New York, NY: Penguin Books, 2012, page 1.

Japan is expanding... Bradley, James. *Flyboys,* New York, New York: Little, Brown &Company, 2003, page 52.

Brothers-in arms!... Connaughton, Richard. *MacArthur and Defeat in the Philippines,* New York, New York: Overlook Press, 2001, page 206.

If we fight... Costello, John. *The Pacific War: 1941-1945.* Harper-Collins, 1982, page 193.

Japan is the foundation... Tolischus, *Through Japanese Eyes*, page 3.

There is a necessity ... Ibid, page 6.

If it is the boast... Ibid, page 34.

The divine mission... Ibid, page 15.

There is virtually... Ibid, page 42.

All the prisoners (of war)... Ibid, page 166.

This (Japanese-led) Asiatic... Ibid, page 20.

Japan is firmly... Ibid, page 7.

Japan's war aims... Ibid, page 6.

Men went mad... Hoyt, Austin, 1999, *American Experience:* MacArthur. PBS, WGBH Educational Foundation.

That the majesty... Tolischus, *Through Japanese Eyes*, page 34.

The dynasties created... Ibid, page 32.

The Greater East... Ibid, page 62.

The position of the United... Ibid, page 112.

The fruits of victory... http://www.worldwar-2.net/famous-quotes/famous-quotes-index.htm

Dear friends! Folks... Flaherty, Thomas, Jr (Editor). *The Aftermath Asia: WWII,* Chicago, Illinois: Time-Life Books, 1983, page 12.

Our citizens can... www.worldwar2.net/famous-quotes/famous-quotes-index.htm.

I believe that... www.whiskeyandgunpowder.com/the-importance-of-alaska-part-ii.

I feel sure... Tolischus, *Through Japanese Eyes*, page 148.

Devote yourself to your... Ohnuki-Tierney, Emiko. *Kamikaze Diaries,* Chicago, Illinois: University of Chicago Press, 2006, page 6.

A mother, at least ... Sheftall, M. Blossoms in the Wind: Human Legacies of the Kamikaze, New York, New York: New American Library, 2005, page xi.

To die for the Emperor.... www.worldwar2tributes.com/view_quotes.php

We nation of 90 million... Austin, American Experience: MacArthur

A victory of the democracies... www.2worldwar2.com/quotes

What kind of people... Bradley, James. *Flags of Our Fathers,* Broadway, N.Y: Bantam Books, 2000, page 57.

Before we're through... http://www.historynet.com/william-bull-halseylegendary-world-war-ii-admiral.htm

The leaders of America... Tolischus, *Through Japanese Eyes*, page 113.

And when he gets to Heaven... www.military-quotes.com/forum/Guadalcanal-epitapht1197.htm

Japanese floatplanes... http://www.historyplace.com/unitedstates/pacificwar/timeline.htm

The British-Americans... Tolischus, *Through Japanese Eyes*, page 155.

The end is near... Austin, *American Experience: MacArthur*.

Guadalcanal is no longer... http://en.wikipedia.org/wiki/Guadalcanal_Campaign

The decisive moment... Simons, Gerald (Editor). *Japan At War, WWII,* Chic, Ill: Time-Life Books, 1980, page. 124.

We must express... Simons, Gerald (Editor). *The Road to Tokyo, World War II,* Ill.Time-Life Books, 1979, page 106.

If we are prepared... Bradley, *Flyboys,* page 278.

We believed our Spiritual... Reilly, Robin. *Kamikaze Attacks of World War II,* Jefferson, N. Carolina: McFarland and Company, 2010, page 69.

Do you know what this ... http://www.pbs.org/wgbh/amex/macarthur

On the evening... Oberdorfer, Don. *The Two Koreas: A Contemporary History,* U.S: Perseus Books, 1997, page 6.

When Japan surrendered... Millet, Allan R. *The War for Korea 1945-1950: A House Burning,* Kansas: Univ. Press of Kansas, 2005, page 43.

On September 11 he (MacArthur) ordered... Ibid, page 59.

Disposing of Japanese... Halberstam, David. *The Coldest Winter,* Hyperion, 2008, page 67.

No division of a nation... Oberdorfer, D. *The Two Koreas: A Contemporary History*, page 7.

The northern Koreans... Millet, Allan R. *The War for Korea 1945-1950*, page 49.

The Russians also showed... Ibid, page 49.

The division of Korea... Sue, Dae-Sook, *The Korean Communist Movement 1918-1948,* New Jersey: Princeton Univ. Press, 1967, page 325.
Through the years... Flaherty, Thomas, Jr (Editor). *The Aftermath Asia: WWII,* Chicago, Illinois: Time-Life Books.
There are three things... http://www.Military.com\Koreanwar\mediavault
The difficulty of applying... Millet, *The War for Korea 1945-1950,* page 11.
Southern Korea can... http://www.militarymuseum.org.

Bibliography

Ambrose, Hugh. *The Pacific.* New York, New York: Penguin Books, 2012.

Bradley, James. *Flags of Our Fathers,* Broadway, New York: Bantam Books, 2000.

Bradley, James *Flyboys,* New York, New York: Little, Brown & Company, 2003.

Costello, John. *The Pacific War: 1941-1945.* HarperCollins, 1982.

Cumings, Bruce. *The Korean War: A History,* New York: Random House Publishing, 2010.

Chang, Iris. *The Rape of Nanking: The Forgotten Holocaust of WWII.* New York: Basic Books, 1997.

Connaughton, Richard. *MacArthur and Defeat in the Philippines,* New York, New York: Overlook Press, 2001.

Flaherty, Thomas, Jr (Editor). *The Aftermath Asia: WWII,* Chicago, Illinois: Time-Life Books, 1983.

Flaherty, Thomas, Jr (Editor) *Japan at War, WWII,* Chicago, Illinois: Time-Life Books, 1983.

Halberstam, David. *The Coldest Winter,* Hyperion, 2008.

Hastings, Max. *The Korean War,* London, England: Pan MacMillan, Ltd, 2000.

Hoyt, Austin, 1999, *American Experience: MacArthur.* PBS, WGBH Educational Foundation.

Hoyt, Austin, 1999, *American Experience, MacArthur, Part II: The Politics of War.* PBS, WGBH Educational Foundation.

http://www.historynet.com/william-bull-halsey-legendary-world-war-ii-admiral.htm

http://www.worldwar-2net/famousquotes/famous-quotes-index.htm

http://whiskeyandgunpowder.com/the-importance-of-alaska-part-ii/

http://www.worldwar2tributes.com/view_quotes.php

http://www.2worldwar2.com/quotes

http://www.military-quotes.com/forum/quadalcanal-epitaph-t1197.html

http://en.wikipedia.org/wiki/Guadalcanal_Campaign

http://www.pbs.org/wgbh/amex/macarthur

http://www.Military.com\Koreanwar\mediavault

http://www.militarymuseum.org

http://www.historyplace.com/unitedstates/pacificwar/timeline.htm

McEnery, Jim and Sloan, Bill. *Hell in the Pacific,* New York, New York: Simon & Schuster, 2012.

Millet, Allan R. *The War for Korea 1945-1950: A House Burning,* Kansas: University Press of Kansas, 2005.

Oberdorfer, Don. *The Two Koreas: A Contemporary History,* U.S.A: Perseus Books, 1997.

Ohnuki-Tierney, Emiko. *Kamikaze Diaries,* Chicago, Illinois: University of Chicago Press, 2006.

Reilly, Robin. *Kamikaze Attacks of World War II,* Jefferson, North Carolina: McFarland and Company, 2010.

Sheftall, M. G. *Blossoms in the Wind: Human Legacies of the Kamikaze,* New York, New York: New American Library—a division of Penguin Group, 2005.

Simons, Gerald (Editor). *Japan at War, World War II,* Chicago, Illinois: Time-Life Books, 1980.

Simons, Gerald (Editor). *The Road to Tokyo, World War II,* Illinois: Time-Life Books, 1979.

Tolischus, Otto D., *Through Japanese Eyes*, Otto D Tolischus, Cornwall, New York: Cornwall Press, 1945.

U.S. Department of State, *Korea 1945 to 1948,* New York: Greenwood Press Publishers, 1969.

Wheeler, Keith and the Editors of Time-Life Books. *The Road to Tokyo, WWII*, Chicago, Illinois: Time-Life Books, Inc., 1979.

Wright, Pattie. *The Men of the Line: Stories of the Thai-Burma Railway Survivors,* Victoria, Australia: Miegunyah Press, 2008.

Interview with Hi-Dong Chai

***Blossoms and Bayonets* is a fictionalized memoir. Are the characters based on real people?**
Some are—He-Dong, He-Seung, He-Chul, Father, Mother, Dr. and Mrs. Lee are real people. Others are fictional, but I can identify them with as real people.

Why did you decide to fictionalize the story?
Jana suggested we do that, because it gave us more freedom to express our thoughts.

Are you happy with the way the story turned out?
Yes, Jana has turned my original story into a moving, beautifully-crafted work of fiction where my brother and best friend, He-Seung, comes out as a hero. He even has a girlfriend.

When did you come to the U.S?
I left Pusan on February 3, 1953 on the freighter, Sea Serpent. I was sixteen.

What do you remember most?
As we approached California on the ship, I remember how the morning light shone on the Golden Gate Bridge as we passed under it. I remember green hillsides dotted with white stucco houses. Everything was so beautiful and different. At that time, Korea was very undeveloped compared to America, and I was amazed to see concrete floors, high rise buildings, and machines that you could put a nickel into and have a Coke fall out. There were cars everywhere—we had very few in Korea then— and six-foot-tall giants with long noses, blue eyes, and blond hair.

What did you do when you got here?
The first summer, I worked as a maintenance boy at Lakeside Bible Conference. There, I washed dishes for over a hundred campers and staff members, mopped the dining hall, cleaned toilets, took garbage to the dump, dug ditches, mixed cement, and painted cabins. These were all things that the lower class people did in Korea, so I felt humiliated. But I was proud of America, because Americans did not look down on me. Instead they were proud of me.

Have you been back to Korea?
Many times. It took me a long time to get back to Korea...the first time I was able to visit my mother was in 1962, nine years after I had left. The only communication I'd had with my mother was through letters, the only photo she had of me was one taken when I was a young boy. When my

new bride and I arrived at the airport, many of my old friends and classmates gathered to pick us up and take us home. I hurried up to my front door and knocked. When my mother answered, however, I was overcome with such emotion I could not speak. She looked at me, at the crowd of friends, then back at me. She asked, "Do you know where Hi-Dong is?"

Did your mother ever come to the U.S.?

Yes. She passed away at the age of 92 in San Jose.

What do you think He-Seung would say about our world today?

I think he would be happy to see the development of South Korea and the peacefulness of Japan.

This book is about Korea. How can Americans – and those of other cultures – relate?

Though this story is set in Korea, it's all about the universal experiences of human suffering, and triumph over adversity. No matter where you live or what your background is, these are things that we can all relate to, understand, and be inspired by. Americans will also be reminded to be grateful to live in a country which is beautiful, powerful, and free.

CPSIA information can be obtained at www.ICGtesting.com
Printed in the USA
LVOW08s0759030913

350646LV00004B/5/P